Honey & Spice

Honey & Spice

A NUTRITIONAL GUIDE TO
NATURAL DESSERT COOKERY

Written and Illustrated by

LORENA LAFOREST BASS

Coriander Press
Ashland, Oregon

ISBN: 0-912837-00-4
Printed in the United States of America

Library of Congress Cataloging in Publication Data

Bass, Lorena Laforest, 1945–
  Honey & Spice.

  Bibliography: p.
  Includes index.
  1. Desserts.   2. Cookery (Honey)   I. Title.
II. Title: Honey and spice.
TX773.B37   1984   641.8'6   83-15221
ISBN 0-912837-00-4

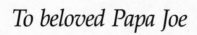

To beloved Papa Joe

~ Contents ~

PART III / RECIPES 193

Dessert Cheeses, Fruits & Nuts 195

Fruit Desserts 210

❧❧❧❧❧

Parfaits & Puddings   227

❧❧❧❧❧

❧❧❧❧❧

Frozen Desserts   238

❧❧❧❧❧

❧❧❧❧❧

Cookies and Candies   247

❧❧❧❧❧

Toppings & Fillings (continued)

Pies & Pastries 305

Desserts
❧ *Without Guilt* ❧

HOW TO CREATE A POSITIVE, HEALTHY
ATTITUDE TOWARD DESSERTS

How MANY TIMES have you heard people lament about all the calories they just consumed in their favorite dessert and how much weight they're going to gain? If you are one of these people, read on!

The purpose of this chapter is to provide a bridge from your old negative thoughts to a more positive, healthy attitude toward desserts and food in general. The bridge I offer comes from the experiences generated during my own struggle with fat; it is built of three simple guidelines, which really work if you seriously want to enjoy food again.

As these guidelines began working for me, my self-image improved greatly. I started to like myself again, and as a result, I noticed I wanted to treat myself to the very best foods I could get. I desired desserts with substance; fresh, natural, unadulterated ingredients were at the top of my list! Because it was difficult to buy such "natural" desserts that also tasted moist and delicious, I began experimenting with old recipes, changing to healthier and more nourishing ingredients. I also created new desserts using as many of the fresh and dried fruits and nuts I could, so as fruits came into season, I made desserts that used them.

1

This recipe collection grew over a few years, and *Honey & Spice* was born. I feel very good about including my experience of overcoming fat along with the recipe collection. The one provides the key to enjoying the other. I must add that this introduction is really only a brief look into this subject; space does not permit a complete treatment. However, if you are interested in pursuing this subject further, I have included at the end of the chapter some books that will provide more information on this subject.

my own experience ✍

All my life I have been concerned about my body. I was an active girl, busy playing ball, riding my bike, swimming laps, and skiing, yet I remember being only eight years old, looking down at my thighs, and hating them because they seemed to bulge. And so began a long history of self-hatred and negation.

When I was a senior in high school, a traumatic move brought on a big weight gain. My normal weight of 125 pounds ballooned to a very chubby 140 pounds, but I was able to force it down again, with the usual diet of grapefruit, lean meats and fish, and no sweets whatsoever.

At the end of college, another traumatic event brought my weight up to a new high of 148 pounds. At the time I was in the process of becoming vegetarian, and my emotional trauma was further aggravated by my body's confusion over its deprivation of meat and white flour products. I could no longer control my desires for junk food and began madly stuffing white bread and packaged sweets (which, ironically, I had never eaten up to that time).

I was able to again bring my weight down to 130 pounds, but I always had a fat consciousness. I was constantly worrying about my weight getting out of control, and I could never relax about eating food. After all, food had caused me a lot of problems, and I regarded it as an enemy. I envied the people who could eat anything they wanted, enjoy it, and still look trim and fit. I wanted to be like them, but I never believed I would.

During a particularly aggressive battle in my fight against fat, I was jogging a mile a day, counting every calorie eaten, and fasting on juice one day a week. During this six-month campaign, I embarked on a three-day fast, which brought my weight down to 118 pounds. I remember feeling very smug and deliciously thin. I reveled in this new feeling of thinness. Fortunately my husband took a photo of me in my bathing suit, because when I saw it, the hard objective truth was right there for me to see. I was *not* thin. Instead, I had become just a smaller version of an overweight person. My muscle had been consumed as food by my body, my large bones stuck out in the wrong places, and my skin hung loosely on my legs.

The disappointment I felt made me realize that all my life I had been comparing myself to the fashion models in magazines. This was how a woman should look, I had thought. Now I realized I would never be like that. I had a large frame, and I looked best when my muscle and strength were developed.

At some point during these struggles, a rebellious thought began to nag at me: "Dieting seems all wrong. Food was put here on the planet for us to enjoy, so all food, whatever I wanted to eat, is O.K." So I began eating what I wanted. This meant all the desserts and fattening foods I had been told to avoid in order to lose weight. But now I didn't care. I ate what I wanted, and without guilt. Although I didn't lose weight, I felt free, and I was enjoying food again! It was during this time I began to write *Honey & Spice*. I was happily making my own desserts and enjoying them tremendously.

After I finished writing the recipes for the book, another thought worked its way into my mind and wouldn't let go: "I can eat what I want and also have a nice body. I can have my cake and eat it too!" Because I didn't quite know how to go about achieving this result, I attended various weight-consciousness workshops.

These workshops were very helpful. I learned to eat with awareness, so that food became an exciting, fun experience for me. I was able finally to get down to the deep-rooted causes of my weight problem, and to see how this affected me on a day-to-day level. And I learned how to use affirmations to clear out old negative thoughts that were preventing me from making the changes I wanted.

Now *you* too can have a positive, healthy attitude toward

desserts, plus a slim body, if you wish. The following techniques I want to share with you have worked for me and many of my friends. I will outline them briefly and then go into each one of them in greater detail.

1. *Eat with awareness.* You can start doing this right away. It is very simple and basic, and with this technique you will immediately begin to experience new freedom toward food.

2. *Understand the true cause of fat.* Fat is not caused by overeating, or by eating the "wrong" foods! In fact, fat is not related to food at all. When you discover the reason you are using fat, and take responsibility for the function your fat is serving, permanent weight loss will begin.

3. *Use affirmations.* Affirmations reprogram old negative thought patterns about our bodies, weight, and food, even the way we feel about ourselves and others. This easy-to-use tool is very powerful, and will get you the desired results.

Let's begin first with the technique of eating with awareness.

eating with awareness ❧

Counting calories takes the responsibility of weight control away from us and puts it on our food. It is impossible to have a positive, healthy attitude toward food, and particularly toward desserts, if we continue to count calories. There is a point when deprivation of the foods we truly want becomes counterproductive. Eventually so much desire builds up that we can't control it; we become compulsive and binge. Then we feel guilty, and with renewed resolution and fervor we get back to calorie-counting, followed by more feelings of deprivation.

Why not give up this vicious cycle? If you are a reasonably healthy person whose extra weight is not caused by a medical problem, you can begin to change yourself through greater food awareness. Here are a few simple guidelines to follow.

EAT WHAT YOU WANT. Put all guilt out of your mind and eat what you want, but eat it slowly and appreciate every bite. Then stop when your hunger is satisfied. Here's a little story of how I learned the importance of this guideline.

I was at a shopping center where I knew the most fantastic chocolate chip cookies were sold. I struggled with myself for a while, then finally decided to buy a cookie. I felt weak and defeated by temptation, and instead of one, I bought two large cookies. I sat down and thoroughly enjoyed the first cookie. I noticed that the last couple of bites didn't have as much flavor, but I went right ahead and finished the second cookie, all the while just staring blankly ahead, not even noticing the taste.

Afterwards I got a tremendously uncomfortable sugar rush, and my face broke out later that night. Had I bought the cookie right away without going through a mind struggle first, I probably would have only bought one, and enjoyed it with no negative effects.

BE AWARE OF YOUR FEELINGS. When you are desiring a sweet or your favorite binge food, notice what you are feeling at that time. Are you angry, resentful, unhappy, needing love or approval? What is going on in your life during the times you really want to eat that whole bag of cookies or chocolates? Keep a journal and write down your feelings when you want to binge.

I love rich cakes and chocolate goodies. I noticed that I most often desired these foods when I wanted to reward myself. Perhaps I felt depressed, and wanted to make myself feel better. Occasionally I found myself eating sweets when I was angry, and instead of expressing my negative feelings, I would stuff myself with desserts. Perhaps I hoped they would make my disposition a little sweeter!

This eventually got out of hand. I was soon consuming sweets for breakfast and lunch and after dinner. Regular food had even begun to look much less appetizing than dessert. I looked at my life and saw that several long-standing projects of mine had been on the back-burner for some time, and I was feeling frustrated, thinking they would never be finished. My frustration was temporarily soothed by indulging in sweets. I began to find other ways to express the creativity that needed to come through. I also found other ways to reward myself, such as taking a sauna, going for a walk, getting out of the house, or going to a movie.

EAT ONLY WHEN HUNGRY. This seems so simple, and it really is. But you must be honest with yourself: are you eating because everyone else is, because it is "time to eat," or because it is more convenient to eat now rather than later?

Eating becomes a real adventure when you break through the chains of old habits. I have found that by following my inner voice (in this case, my hunger signs), the right food is usually available to me. If I am in a situation where I must sit with people who are eating, some tea, juice, or mineral water or a light snack help me enjoy the company of friends without stuffing when I'm not hungry.

The main thing is to eat for physical nourishment, when *you* need it. Allow your intuitive inner voice to direct you, and you will be able to give up the tedious job of figuring out when and what you should eat. Eat *when* you are hungry, and *what* you wish.

Should you become filled with the urge to eat when you aren't hungry, I have found a good way to prevent giving in. Instead of eating, write down what you are feeling. Explore everything that pops into your mind, jot it down, and then look it over. Chances are you won't be hungry anymore, and if you still want to stuff, at least you'll know why.

EXERCISE. I can't let it go without saying a little about exercise. Exercise is a lot like food. We have guilt feelings about what kind of exercise to do, how much, and how often. Usually we feel forced to do it because "it is good for us," "we'll live longer," "we might avoid heart trouble."

Follow the same guidelines for exercise as for food. When you *feel* like exercising, do it. Be flexible to allow different kinds of movement into your life. Exercise can be integrated into your life, and it needn't be painful and a struggle. Make it fun and enjoyable, or it will be counterproductive. What begins as frenzied determination soon gives way to boredom or hatred for whatever program you are in. You are naturally rebelling against the rigid structure you have imposed. Instead of setting strict rules, follow your heart, and soon exercise will be a pleasant, healthy part of your life.

Exercise is like good food. The more involved you become with food awareness, the better you feel about yourself. The more positive and lighter you feel, the more you will desire good things for yourself. Good food and exercise will naturally find their way into your life when you follow this program, and the best part of it is they are not something you *have* to do, but what you truly *want* to do.

the true cause of fat ๖

The second technique for losing unwanted fat is to understand the true cause of fat. Fat is not caused by overeating; in fact, it isn't related to food at all. Fat has to do with how we use, or don't use, our inner power.

The truth is, within each person there is an inexhaustible abundance of creative power. The source of this power is God, or the universe, and each one of us is a vessel or channel for this energy. This means the universe's divine love, wisdom, and intelligence are available to us all the time if we choose to accept it, listen to it, and follow it in our lives. God, or the universe, is speaking to us all the time through our intuitive senses. We all have intuitive feelings, which, if we listen carefully, tell us the right thing to do in every situation.

For example, my intuitive thought was: food is here on the earth to nourish us. It is good, healthy, and here for me to enjoy. I believe we all feel this way, and that's the reason why we feel angry when we start counting calories and placing heavy restrictions on our food. The anger is a natural reaction against a wrong idea.

The more receptive we are to our inner voices, the more our lives are enriched with the natural abundance and goodness the universe intends for us. When we turn away from the power and don't follow our intuitive senses, our lives begin to reflect a lack of energy, and instead of goodness and abundance, we create struggle, conflict, and unhappiness.

When we choose not to accept our power, we become weak and vulnerable. The mind/body sets up various defense mechanisms to protect us while we remain in this vulnerable position. Some people build mental walls around themselves; others build actual physical barriers, becoming recluses; still others create walls of fat. All these walls, or defenses, are ways in which we subconsciously wait until we decide to accept our power. The extra weight falls away when we accept our power.

Women have particular difficulty accepting this inner power. We can feel it, but we are often frightened by it. Rather than accept and deal with it, we often choose to give up our own power and be "taken care of" by the men in our lives. I believe that more women are overweight than men because women are more intimidated by their power than men, who have traditionally been taught it was necessary to use their power for survival.

THE FEAR OF BEING THIN. I came to recognize finally how my fat was working to protect me against my own fears. My biggest fear, I discovered, was not of being fat, but of being thin! Every time I became thin, I noticed I received a lot of male attention. This made me very uncomfortable; I was afraid I might give in to some of this attention and perhaps ruin my marriage.

This fear of my own sexual power always led me to take on those protective layers of fat again. If I had some extra padding, I was less attractive, received less attention, and no longer had to worry about what to do with this power.

Once I exposed my fear and became more conscious of it, I became less afraid. I started to take responsibility for my sexual power, and instead of fearing it, I began enjoying it. I realized the male attention was coming to me because I was exuding an attractive vitality. By stripping away the fat, I was not just exposed and conscious, I was more powerful! I no longer felt any pressure to *do* anything about the attention given to me. I could just enjoy it, be playful with it, and let it pass by.

WAITING CAN PUT ON WEIGHT. There was another element to my fat. I was frustrated by circumstances in my life that kept me from using my creative energy. I have always been a very creative person, but I allowed my own creative needs to be put aside while I began raising my family. My excuse was I couldn't do both, so I chose to be caretaker of the family until the children were old enough for me to return to my career. During this period, I literally gained "wait."

"Weighting" is a way of holding back our creative power. Many women believe they must make a choice between their own personal power and the needs of others. It is my belief that you can and should do what feels right for you.

There are times in all our lives when we want to act on a particular goal or project, but something happens to postpone it. When waiting is inevitable, surrender to it. It is an opportunity to develop patience and objectivity toward the project. Step back and observe your feelings, motivation, and desires regarding the project. There is a natural flow between the creative and receptive cycles in our lives, and they each need their proper time.

ACCEPTING OUR FAT. After I came to these realizations, I accepted my fat. I stopped seeing it as an enemy, and I began to love myself, even with the extra weight. As I followed my inner voice more and more, my old pattern of letting things slide, or waiting to follow through on my ideas, was replaced by a desire to act quickly and responsibly. And then I began to really lose weight!

While you are going through the mental and emotional transformations as you deal more and more with the real cause of your fat, give yourself approval for all the good work you are doing on yourself. Treat yourself to the things you enjoy: time alone, relaxation, favorite activities. If you have been waiting until you lose weight to buy a nice wardrobe, don't. Get yourself a few nice items that fit you *now*. Don't live in the future, because it will surely take care of itself if you are dealing with your weight consciously.

affirmations ✖

In the Bible it says, "In the beginning was the Word, and the Word was with God, and the Word was God." This passage explains that before there was a physical creation there was the thought of the creation. The thought (or Word) is the same as God (with God), because it is the creative force, which can manifest what it sets out to do.

This creative force is the power within each one of us. *Our thoughts are creative, and they produce results*! Positive thoughts create positive results, and negative thoughts create negative results. Once thoughts are created, they are set into motion and continue producing results until they are unthought. We use affirmations to "un-think" thoughts we no longer want to have.

Affirmation means "to make firm." By repeating a thought over and over, we make this thought firm. Affirmations can be positive or negative. "I enjoy eating desserts, and I am losing weight" is an example of a positive affirmation. Another is, "I am a good person, and I deserve to enjoy eating." Examples of negative affirmations might be, "I have the worst luck; nothing good ever happens to me," or "Desserts make me fat."

Listen to your inner dialogue the next time you wish to eat a dessert. Do you hear yourself putting the dessert or yourself down? Do you get pictures of yourself getting fatter by eating sweets? Do you think of yourself as weak and out of control? Write down your observations. Are your thoughts about yourself and desserts positive or negative?

Affirmations, positive or negative, are mental commands to your subconscious mind, where all your thoughts are stored. Each time a positive command is given, it strengthens similar positive thoughts. Likewise, negative commands strengthen already existing negative thought forms.

Therefore, in order to clear away old negative thoughts about ourselves, our weight, and the food we eat, we replace them with positive ones in the form of affirmations. By repeating new, positive affirmations you are giving energy to new mental patterns, and ignoring the old ones. The old thoughts eventually fade away from lack of attention, and the new thoughts take their place.

WORKING WITH THE SUBCONSCIOUS. We can create a wonderful, positive life for ourselves by working with the subconscious.

The subconscious mind is like a child: whatever you tell it, it believes. If an idea is fed into it in a strong persistent way it will begin to act out the idea and bring it into reality.

An interesting thing about the subconscious is that it doesn't understand negatives. In other words, if you say "I don't want to be overweight," it will interpret this as "I want to be overweight." It is programmed to receive the positive already. Therefore, when creating affirmations or personal goals, phrase them carefully in the positive. The above could be reworded, "I am achieving my ideal weight."

Here is something else to remember when making your own affirmations. Phrase them in the present, as if they are already happening, or about to happen. "I will be thin" or "I want to be thin" must be rephrased to be "I am thin" or "I am becoming thin."

The subconscious is a powerful friend. It works in mysterious ways, and the secret of its power has yet to be fully explained. But the truth remains, *it works*! Therefore, don't be concerned about *how* your desires will be fulfilled. Continue repeating your affirmations, and let the subconscious do the rest.

To give you an example: I was working with the affirmation, "Desserts make me healthy and strong." After a little while, I noticed I wanted to make my own desserts with good nutritious ingredients. Also, I would find myself in the store reading labels, and choosing the healthiest desserts. This was not conscious; I found myself doing these things quite spontaneously. It was only later, in looking back, that I realized the subconscious had subtly maneuvered me into making the right choices to materialize my affirmation.

FAITH. Faith is necessary in the beginning because it may take time before you see results. The amount of time it takes depends on the amount of resistance you have to the new affirmations. In some cases, results are immediate. However, in the case of negative thoughts that have existed for years, even back to childhood, it will take more time.

Have faith your affirmations are working. They are not simplistic, naive, wishful, or blind positive thinking. When I first started using them, a part of me didn't really believe they could work. I found myself saying "I am getting thinner every day," but deep down I was running another thought, "I don't really believe this is going to work. How can I get thinner just by thinking it?" Do you see what I did? These doubts, or negative thoughts wiped out the good work I was doing with the affirmation. Remember, thought *is* creative, and it will produce results. Ask yourself, what kind of results do I want, positive or negative?

PERSISTENCE. There were many times I would repeat an affirmation to myself as I looked in the mirror, and would feel discouraged. I might be saying. "My legs are becoming more slender and more shapely every day," but there would be the old thought fighting for control. After all, the old thought ("My legs are flabby") had been accustomed to quite a bit of attention. And to make matters worse, the mirror was reaffirming the old thought.

At times like this, be persistent. Without judging the old thoughts, watch them play through your mind. This is the old you putting up a fight for survival. Persist in affirming your positive thoughts, without condemning the old. It is natural for the positive thoughts you have been feeding your mind to force out the old, because there really isn't room for both. Realize your old negative thoughts are on their way out, and be thankful.

Sometimes the negative playback gets so strong that there is no room for anything positive. This happens to me occasionally, usually after a particularly positive period when I am feeling real changes taking place. Then all of a sudden I am bombarded with the old thoughts, sometimes for days. Fighting back with positive thoughts doesn't seem to work. It only creates a struggle. Here are some affirmations that work for me during these stressful times. They take the focus off food and body, and bring it back to the power within, which is creating all the changes in the first place.

1. I trust the Universe is taking care of me and all I need to do is relax and let it do its work.

2. I am now open and receptive to the Universe.

3. I am ready to receive the power and love of the Universe more and more every day.

4. Universe, release the barriers that keep your light from shining through me.

WAYS TO USE AFFIRMATIONS. Affirmations work best in the form of a spontaneous inner dialogue between your intuitive self and the old self. Your intuitive self *knows* you are beautiful, radiant, and perfect. The old self believes you are unattractive or overweight. Get in touch with your intuitive self and direct loving, healing thoughts to the old self.

If this feels strange to you, use the affirmations in the following sections. They will get you started in the right direction. After you get the hang of it, create your own. Talk to yourself as you are driving to work, working in the kitchen, and so forth. Do this when you feel down about yourself, if you can; but also do it when you feel good.

Repeating to yourself is the easiest way to use affirmations. One way of repeating is to make a tape and then listen to it. Set aside five or ten minutes a day, preferably in the morning when you awake, and in the evening just before bed. Bedtime is a perfect time to listen to affirmation tapes, because as you drift off to sleep, you are open to the new thoughts on a very deep level.

After using an affirmation for a few weeks, put it aside and work with another. This will prevent you from going unconscious, that is, not noticing what you are saying anymore due to overrepetition. The following are several other methods I recommend to vary your practice.

Write down an affirmation over and over, until you lose interest in the meaning. By involving your hand, there is added concentration and body involvement. Also, I recommend doing this in the morning or evening.

Say the affirmation in front of a mirror. Repeat the affirmation while looking at yourself, and continue saying the affirmation over and over until you can say it without grimacing. When you can say it with honesty and sincerity, you can stop.

Have another person sit facing you. Repeat the affirmation to the person. Then have the person repeat it back in the second person. For instance, you might say "I am achieving my ideal weight."

The person would then repeat back, "You are achieving your ideal weight." Continue this until you can feel it truly.

⌇ Write down an affirmation in a double column notebook. Put the affirmation in the left column, and leave the right column open for any comments, thoughts, feelings, or doubts that come up while you are writing. This is an excellent way to catch sight of the resistance you may have to the affirmation. Write the affirmation ten times or more, if possible.

⌇ Repeat the affirmation in the first, second, and third persons. For example, "I am achieving my ideal weight," "You are achieving your ideal weight," and "[Your name], is achieving her (or his) ideal weight." Say the affirmation with conviction and feeling, as you would like to hear others speak of you. Hearing the affirmation as others would say it makes it easier to accept.

I have provided lists of affirmations below. As you read through them, check off any that ring a bell for you. These relate directly to your negative thoughts and will be of the most benefit. Although these are just a small sampling, they should give you the idea of how to make your own affirmations once you get going. I have limited the lists to affirmations that deal with self-esteem, body/weight, and food, but you can make up affirmations about anything in your life. Once you get familiar with these, you will see how easy it is to create them for all aspects of your life.

SELF-ESTEEM AFFIRMATIONS. These affirmations build a positive self-image, create a feeling of well-being, and lay a foundation on which to build other affirmations later. These affirmations are perhaps the most important ones, because loving and feeling good about yourself are the keys to creating other positive things in your life.

1. My inner light is getting brighter and brighter.

2. Goodness dwells within me, and I like to spread it around.

3. I feel safe in my relationship.

4. I feel more alive and happy with every breath I take.

5. It's O.K. for me to be a strong, powerful person and still receive love.

6. It's O.K. to have many men attracted to me sexually. I can say no if I want to.

7. People like me and I like them.

8. People enjoy being with me, it makes them feel good.

9. I love and forgive myself.

10. I am strong and can cope with this problem.

BODY/WEIGHT AFFIRMATIONS. The following affirmations deal directly with those old thoughts about our body and weight. Most of us have a large negative storehouse of tapes we run about how we look, and how we *think* we look. Most people are not happy with their bodies, so these affirmations are specifically geared to establishing a more positive body image.

1. My body is pleasing to myself.

2. My body is pleasing to others.

3. My physical body is my most valuable possession.

4. My body is a reflection of divine beauty, wisdom, and intelligence.

5. Every day my body expresses more health, strength, and beauty.

6. I deserve to have the naturally beautiful body I desire for myself.

7. I can lose weight just by the power of my mind.

8. I am now eating my way to thinness.

9. It is easy for me to lose weight.

10. This process of losing weight is taking the right amount of time.

FOOD AFFIRMATIONS. The frustration we have felt toward fat has most often been directed toward food instead. As a result, we have a lot of negatives about food. These affirmations will liberate you to enjoy any of the foods you wish to eat.

1. I deserve to eat any food I want and still be slender.

2. I am becoming radiant and vital with all the good food I eat.

3. I am open and willing to receive the rich abundance the earth has to offer.

4. All the food I eat is healthy, and it is helping me achieve my ideal weight.

5. I am losing my extra weight while eating the foods I enjoy.

6. Desserts make my body healthy and radiant.

7. I love food, and I can take it or leave it.

8. I can eat (bread, ice cream, cake, etc. You fill it in) and be slim.

9. Food is safe and pleasant for me.

10. I enjoy making my own desserts because I know I am giving myself the very best, and I deserve it.

the turning point ✦

The process of gaining and losing weight has been a long one for me. It has taken many years to unravel my own inner confusion, to find the right techniques, and to get the desired results. For each of us, there is a turning point when we suddenly see clearly and finally decide that *now* we are going to make the change. I would like to share with you a friend's own story of how that turning point came to her. Karen Darling is a weight-loss counselor living in Ashland. Her own struggle with fat and the successful outcome is related below in her own words.

"Spring, 1966 . . . I remember standing in front of the Safeway Bakery, making every possible effort to suppress the rage that was boiling up in me. I really wanted a glazed twist, but I also wanted my bulging thighs to shrink.

I was faced with the same old, frustrating decision I had to make dozens of times a day. And usually the glazed twist (hot fudge sundae, hamburger, or french fries) won the contest. But this day something felt different. I really was fed up with the feeling of powerlessness.

I said to myself; "I used to be thin, I deserve to be thin once more, and more importantly, I deserve to eat the foods I enjoy and still be thin." After this bold statement to myself, I marched right over to the counter and ordered a twist to go. I was amazed that I only bought one. I turned on my heel, and with my head held high I marched to my car and ate my beloved twist.

I did more than just eat it, however. I enjoyed the taste, savoring every sticky morsel. Feeling not a shred of guilt, I took my sweet time to finish it.

This experience was a turning point in my compulsive eating career. This was the day I started to shed my extra pounds and my negative beliefs about food.

As the weeks and months went by, I continued my practice of eating whatever I wanted. But the amount I wanted was different from before. I still enjoyed the same variety of foods as always, including the rich, high-calorie goodies that are always no-no's on a dieter's list. Now I couldn't finish one complete sundae, let alone two or three as was my habit before.

I was miraculously losing weight, maybe a pound or less a week. During the year that followed my "enlightenment" at the Safeway Bakery, I went through many positive personal changes, but best of all my size 16 figure was now a size 6. And, I ate anything I wanted."

The key for Karen was in her feeling of powerlessness. We all feel powerless when we believe food is making us fat. When we believe food can do all these things to us, we give it tremendous power over ourselves. When Karen finally became so fed up with her lack of power, she decided to create the reality *she* wanted. That reality for her, for me, and I believe for all of us, is to eat what we want and still be slim. That day in the Safeway Bakery turned Karen toward taking full responsibility for her body and food. I believe there is such a turning point for everyone.

My own understanding about fat continues to grow and expand all the time. Even as this book is going to press, there is more I would like to share. The truth is, the more aware I become through using these techniques, the deeper my understanding grows. I am finding this wonderful process of becoming more aware is not confined to food, it involves all aspects of my life.

I encourage you to work with the simple guidelines in this chapter. These guidelines—eating with awareness, understanding the cause of your fat, and using affirmations—will give you a healthy, positive attitude toward food, and especially desserts, in addition to a more slender body.

As you prepare to enjoy your desserts, remember to eat only *what* you want *when* you are truly hungry, and enjoy the flavor of every bite, then stop when you are full. As you begin to eat what you want, you may want to eat all the junk food you can. This is natural after all the self-denial and guilt you have experienced in the past. Don't worry, this period usually lasts only a short time.

As you feed the mind more positive messages, the body will automatically begin to gravitate toward more positive, life-giving foods. And this is where these recipes come in! These desserts will not only satisfy your sweet tooth, but also give you the best ingredients, flavor, and nutrition. As a result, you will increase your health and vitality, and best of all, you will enjoy them *without* guilt!

SUGGESTED READING

Karen Darling, *Weight No More*. Whatever Publishing Company, Mill Valley, California, 1984.

Shakti Gawain, *Creative Visualization*. Whatever Publishing Company, Mill Valley, California, 1978.

Susie Orbach, *Fat Is a Feminist Issue*. New York: Publishing Group, Berkley, 1978.

Leonard Orr and Sondra Ray, *Rebirthing*. Celestial Arts, Millbrae, California, 1977.

Sondra Ray, *The Only Diet There Is*. Celestial Arts, Millbrae, California, 1981.

❧ *Looking Ahead* ❧

Honey & Spice IS MORE THAN JUST A DESSERT BOOK offering whole-some, delicious recipes. It also offers recipes for those on sugar- and fat-restricted diets, along with nutritional information about the foods used in the recipes. I would like to take you on a tour of the book to show how it is divided, and what each part presents to you. By looking ahead in this way, the book will become more useable.

Part One, *Dessert Foods & Health*, presents an overview of the main nutrient groups in dessert cookery. The first chapter, *Honey & Other Sweeteners*, provides information about honey, its many vari-eties, its historical uses as both food and medicine, and its nutri-tional benefits. Also discussed are date sugar, fructose, malt syrup, maple syrup, molasses, and table sugar.

Chapter Two, *Whole Grain Flours*, gives a history of flour mak-ing, and outlines some of the benefits of using unrefined, whole grain flours in baking. Included is a list and description of the vari-ous whole grain flours available for the interested baker.

Chapter Three, *Butter & Oils*, describes the hydrogenation process by which margarine is made. A look at how oils are refined and processed is presented, along with a list of some of the more available unrefined oils and their uses in baking.

Chapter Four, *Milk & Milk Products*, looks at the various varieties of milk, how they are processed, and which are best to use. Included is some research information about the chemical additives used in making commercial ice cream.

Chapter Five, *Eggs*, concentrates on the positive benefits of eggs in the diet. Some new research on cholesterol is presented to offset the bad publicity the egg has received over the years.

Chapter Six, *Fruits, Nuts & Seeds*, describes current practices used in bringing fruit to market, and keeping it fresh. A list of nuts and seeds, and their health benefits is presented.

Chapter Seven, *Spices, Flavorings & Salt*, looks at the history of spices, and lists the various dessert spices with descriptions and uses. The section on salt looks at the varieties available, and demonstrates which are best to use.

Part Two, *The Natural Pantry*, lists all the major dessert ingredients used in the recipes, and gives a brief history of these foods and their health benefits. Nutritional charts are given for many. Although some of the facts have been presented in Part One, *Dessert Foods & Health*, this information is more complete. Ingredients are listed alphabetically for easy kitchen reference, and give you nutritional information at a glance. Although it would have been easier to put the nutritional charts together in one chart at the back, as most books do, I wanted to have the individual information immediately available to the cook. So if you are making an apple pie, for example, you can look up apples, honey, and crust ingredients separately and read about the wonderful benefits your body will be receiving by eating the dessert you have chosen to make.

Part Three, *Recipes*, speaks for itself. However, there is an organization to the recipe chapters which is especially useful. The first chapter presents desserts requiring absolutely no, or very little preparation. These desserts are closest to their natural state, fresh and uncooked. Each subsequent chapter generally involves a little more preparation, and in most cases, more cooking. Also, the recipes at the beginning of each chapter are generally easier to prepare and as the chapter progresses, the recipes entail a little more preparation.

Dessert Cheeses, Fruits & Nuts presents desserts in the Continental tradition. Fresh fruits, dessert cheeses, and nuts served with tea are perfect for busy cooks. These uncooked, unsweetened desserts are also the easiest to prepare. Wine suggestions are given with each type of cheese.

The recipes in the next chapter, *Fruit Desserts*, range from simple fresh fruit salads requiring only the slicing and mixing of fruit, to fruit gelatins which only take about ten minutes to make, to elegant baked fruits.

Parfaits & Puddings offers both blended and chilled desserts and some recipes that require some cooking with thickening agents. In either case, these recipes are simple and easy to prepare.

Frozen Desserts are most appropriate for hot weather, but for many of us, ice cream is an all-year-round favorite. You can use the basic recipes in this chapter: Grape Ice, Blackberry Frozen Yogurt, and Banana Nut or Peach Ice Cream, to create your own flavors by substituting other fruits. An electric ice cream maker speeds up the preparation time so that in twenty minutes you can be done with many of these recipes.

Cookies & Candies require more preparation time, but with a cake mixer or food processor they can be made very quickly and efficiently. This chapter is popular with children, and because the recipes are so easy to make, it is a wonderful way to get them started in the kitchen.

Cakes & Breads involve more ingredients, more preparation, and longer baking times than most of the preceding recipes. These desserts are not only filling, they will give you nutritious energy that lasts for hours while the body processes the complex carbohydrates in the ingredients.

Toppings & Fillings provides an assortment of recipes from homemade yogurt, granola, and date sugar, to cake frostings and fillings. Most of these recipes are very quick and simple to prepare, and add the final touches of elegance to other desserts. For easy reference, I have given the page number of the appropriate topping or filling suggestions along with many of the recipes that require them.

Pies & Pastries probably take the most time to prepare, and they are the last recipe chapter. Fruit or cream fillings and the crust require some planning ahead, but once started, these recipes can be prepared in about 30 minutes. That's pretty good for a homemade, quality dessert!

Honey & Spice also offers a special feature in the recipe section for those who wish or need to eliminate *all* sweeteners from their diet, even honey, molasses, maple syrup, and malt syrup. Why, you may ask, would anyone want to do that? Read on . . .

desserts for the
sugar-restricted diet ✋

In 1900 the average consumption of white sugar in the United States was 9 pounds a year per person. Now, it is up to 150 pounds per person. A large portion of this nation's sugar consumption comes from bakery products, such as jams, jellies, candies, and soft drinks. A smaller, but not insignificant, amount comes from hidden sources, such as packaged, canned, and frozen foods.

Could this rising rate of sugar consumption be responsible for the fact that one out of every four Americans has hypoglycemia? This modern malady is statistically related to the use of sugar and is practically unheard of in cultures that use few sugar products. Many doctors and nutritionists believe that hypoglycemia is caused by stress and the overuse of sugar. This overuse overstimulates the glands involved in the metabolism of sugar, causing these glands to malfunction or break down completely. The cure for hypoglycemia is dietary and calls for total abstinence from sugar and other refined foods.

As the evidence has mounted against the dietary value of white sugar, certain advertisers have suggested that raw or brown sugar is healthier and more nutritious. In the following chapter,

Honey & Other Sweeteners, some information about how white sugar is processed will clarify this issue. The bottom line is, sugar is sugar, and it is best to leave it alone if you are hypoglycemic.

Several years ago I was suffering from very bad, frequent headaches, among other unpleasant symptoms. When my doctor confirmed I was hypoglycemic, I began following a fairly strict diet outlined in Paavo Airola's book, *Hypoglycemia: A Better Approach*. I did this for a couple of months, until the symptoms disappeared. Then I gradually began to vary my diet.

Naturally, the first things I introduced back into my food program were desserts. I did this carefully, and in moderation, and I still do. I was surprised to find that the honey and natural sugar desserts from these recipes were easy for my body to assimilate. However, when I occasionally ate refined sugar desserts, the negative effects were noticeable.

Although doctors say there is no difference between honey and refined sugar in the way the body uses them, there is a real difference for me. Naturally, the best desserts are those that contain complex carbohydrates: fruits, nuts, seeds, and whole grains. Not only do these foods offer the most nutrition, but also their complex carbohydrates take longer to break down and enter the bloodstream. These foods provide hours of sustained energy, whereas a candy bar may give only a short rush followed by a sharp drop in energy level.

For those on sugar-restricted diets, whether the cause is hypoglycemia or diabetes, there are *over 140 recipes* with either no sweetener (including the dessert cheeses) or an "unsweetened variation." Whenever possible, I have given an "unsweetened variation" at the bottom of the recipe, suggesting a substitution for the sweetener. You will see that among the main substitutes, frozen, unsweetened fruit juice concentrates (such as orange and apple) are possible substitutes, and date sugar is another.

Some recipes, including the ice creams and many of the cookies, cakes, and pies, cannot be changed without totally altering the desired flavor or texture. Therefore, the variations offered do not have the same flavor and texture as the original recipes, yet they do offer tasty alternatives for those wishing to eliminate unnecessary sweeteners.

If you have any tolerance for honey or maple syrup, you might want to try one recipe at a time and see if it agrees with you. You may notice, as I have, that unrefined wholesome ingredients mixed with small amounts of unrefined sweeteners, can be gentle on your system and satisfying to your sweet tooth.

desserts for sodium- and fat-restricted diets ✌

I don't usually salt my food and often omit the salt in dessert recipes. I feel that the smidgeon of flavor salt adds is not really worth the health risks. I have noticed that the more I do away with salt, the more I enjoy the healthy nutritious ingredients I choose to use in my desserts.

If you are on a sodium-restricted diet, please use the recipes and omit the salt. In the *Cookies & Candies* chapter, I have also included recipes for homemade baking powder and baking soda. These are simple to make and cut down on your salt intake considerably.

Over the years I have gradually replaced whole milk products with low-fat or skim milk substitutes. You will find that the recipes call for low-fat yogurt, cottage cheese, or milk. If you prefer, use the skim milk products. By adding a little noninstant skim milk powder to skim milk, it will thicken a little and be a bit richer in flavor. (You will have to use a blender for this).

In some cases, such as with ice creams, I enjoy using whipping cream and half and half for rich flavor. However, milk can be substituted to make a tasty ice milk. The addition of extra skim milk powder in these recipes will also put more richness back into the flavor.

For those who must avoid high-fat foods, I have offered recipes for "Mock Sour Cream," "Mock Whipping Cream," and "Mock Cream Cheese." You will find these in the *Toppings & Fillings* chapter.

And now, it is with great pleasure that this book of dessert recipes and nutritional information is offered to you. May you enjoy happiness, good health, beauty, and vitality with every dessert you eat!

It is most certain that 'tis easier
to preserve Health than to recover it, and
to prevent Diseases than to cure them.
　　—Dr. George Cheyne
　　　An Essay on Health and Long Life, 1725

Dessert Foods & Health

This book is designed to provide an alternative to devitalized snacks and desserts. The major attraction of these recipes lies in the wholesomeness of their ingredients. It is clear that the more wholesome the ingredients, the healthier the dessert will be. Use the best ingredients nature has to offer and you'll never be disappointed in the fresh, alive flavors or the health benefits that will come your way. A little background information about the major dessert food groups will illustrate the importance of choosing quality food products.

I have researched these foods in order to help clarify some of the more confusing food issues: for example, margarine vs. butter, and eggs vs. cholesterol, to name a couple, plus some of the common practices in the food industry which may be hazardous to health. This research developed from my own desire to find the answers to the question, "which are the healthiest food choices we can make?" Hopefully these discussions will be useful to you as you make your own choices.

Honey & Other Sweeteners

THE RECIPES IN THIS BOOK WERE INSPIRED by my own preference for honey, yet my intent is not to persuade anyone to use honey exclusively, or to replace all sugar in their diet with honey. Rather, it is my feeling that honey is a delightful food to be enjoyed for its own merits. Honey is truly one of nature's gourmet foods for the discerning palate. It is a delicacy that offers as many varieties as there are flowering plants; not only does every region produce its own local favorites, but every country has specialty honeys to offer the international market. Later on in this section, I will discuss various honeys available from around the world, and provide a short list of a few honeys available in this country.

I was introduced to honey at an early age. My maternal grandfather, Papa Joe, was a mild-mannered, artistic man who raised bees in his backyard in St. Louis. He was a man rooted to the past in some ways. He preferred whole grain bread and used honey on his grapefruit. He believed that honey had some healing properties which he partook of daily. He ate fresh garlic, too, in the European tradition. None of these practices were in vogue during his time, yet he continued them for as long as I knew him. Even though I was too young to understand much about the raising of bees, Papa Joe and his honeybees made a lasting impression on me.

In my own way, I have followed in his footsteps. I began using honey because I believed it was the healthiest sweetener available, and through my own explorations with honey and whole grain flours, this book was born.

honey: the oldest sweetener ✒

Our earliest records of honey go back to prehistoric times, around 15,000 B.C. A rock painting found in the Queves of Arana near Valencia, Spain, shows two men stealing honeycomb while the bees fly all around them. From these early times up to the eighteenth century, honey was the only sweetener used, and it was a very precious commodity. Religious wars and the urban development of the late Renaissance period made honey scarce, and from

1600 to 1900 very little honey was available. In the 1700s, the cheaper sweetener made from sugarcane made honey a luxury item.

In my readings about honey, I found a great deal of interesting information. The ancient people of the world regarded honey in the highest sense. It was a magical food not only used as an everyday food, but also in festive and religious ceremonies. For example, honey is mentioned frequently in the Old Testament as a respected food. The promised land of the Jews was known as the "Land of Milk and Honey." Special religious practices called for the use of honey: it was eaten in early Christian baptismal ceremonies, before Christian fast-days, and before the Jewish New Year. Honey was regarded as an aphrodisiac, and a giver of health, vitality, eloquence, and luck. It was considered a sacred substance that symbolized love, wisdom, and purity. Its use as a medicine goes back to ancient Egypt. Here is some of the honey chronology.

EGYPT. As early as 2500 B.C., beekeeping was a popular industry in Egypt. The temple at Abusir has the Egyptian methods of beekeeping accurately recorded on the walls. Smoking the bees to subdue them, and the extraction, filtering and packing of honey are shown in detail. In some parts of Egypt today, beekeeping practices are still very similar to the ancient methods.

Honey was used as a food in everyday life, and a beer made from wheat, barley, and honey was drunk during feast times. Honey was a significant part in wedding and religious ceremonies because it symbolized fidelity, devotion, and good health.

Honey was also used as a medium of exchange, and often given as gifts to the Pharaoh by visiting dignitaries. The bee's superior industry and organization was so highly respected by the Egyptian ruling class that the bee symbol was used on official papers requiring the Pharaoh's signature.

GREECE. Although the ancient Greeks didn't have the same respect for the attributes of honeybees as the Egyptians, honey was an important food in their culture. Honey was an ingredient of Ambrosia and nectar, the food and drink of the Greek gods, and so it was equated with youth, vitality, and longevity. The Greeks also believed honey improved beauty, health, and wisdom. For all these reasons, honey was a popular food with the people, athletes, and warriors.

By about 400 B.C., there were already 20,000 hives in the ancient Greek state of Attica. The honey from this region was reputed to have special medicinal and nutritional qualities. Mount Hymettus near Athens was also well-known for its particular kind of honey, which is available even now.

ROME. Beekeeping was practiced throughout the Roman empire, which assured the Roman people of a honey harvest practically all year around. Honey was enjoyed by the ancient Romans as a food and in their beverages. A particularly popular drink served at Roman feasts was made from honey, milk, and poppy juice. This drink produced a euphoric state. In Rome, honey was also used in religious rites and as a medium of exchange with which to pay taxes and to barter.

EARLY AMERICA. Until the seventeenth century, there were no honeybees in North America. They were brought over by settlers from England, France, Holland, and Spain, and multiplied quickly, even following the pioneers on their long trek overland to the West Coast.

HONEY IN MODERN TIMES. Until 1940, the honey sold in American groceries was a blend of various home-produced honeys, packaged and sold as a blended product. World War Two brought food rationing, including the rationing of every kind of sweet. This gave people an economic interest in beekeeping, and local cottage industries thrived. Honeys were usually available only through the beekeepers, and were labeled according to the major flower (flora) source available to the bees. Clover, hawthorn, lime, and blackberry honeys were available, and the public began to appreciate the subtle differences in aroma and flavor. During this period honey was sold at a premium, and people were prepared to pay for it.

When rationing ended, the normal trading between countries resumed and quantities of foreign honeys were available at lower prices than ever before. Honey farming steadily continues to increase in Australia, America, Mexico, and South America, and today these countries are the largest exporters of honey. New Zealand still exports fairly large quantities of honey, but not as much as before the war. China is exporting quite a bit, followed by Poland, Spain, Hungary, Romania, Greece, and France. As a result of the increased worldwide honey production, there are many exciting varieties of honey available.

honey for health ✌

Although honey is no longer used as a popular medicine, primitive, ancient, medieval, and modern man have used it to treat similar ailments. Honey can be an effective treatment for cuts and burns and for gastric, intestinal, and respiratory disorders. It is also used in surgical dressings, as a tranquilizer, and as a salve for skin diseases and inflammation of the eyes and eyelids.

The healing properties of honey were discovered early in history. Primitive and ancient cultures experimented with the roots and leaves of native plants to heal their bodies. Even today many "folk remedies" are used in rural areas where oral traditions have kept practices alive, and where industry and sophisticated technology have not yet penetrated.

The Hindus and Chinese used honey as an ointment on smallpox patients to speed healing and to prevent scarring. An ancient Egyptian document, the *Papyrus Ebers*, refers to the wonderful healing properties of honey for both internal and external uses and documents its use as a surgical dressing, and to relieve the inflammation of the eyelids and eyes. Hippocrates, the "father of medicine," believed in the therapeutic use of honey, recommending its use to clean sores and ulcers, to soften hard ulcers of the lips, and to heal carbuncles and running sores.

One of the books of the *Koran* contains this passage specifically relating to the bee and the medicinal property of honey:

Thy Lord has taught the bee saying, provide thee houses in the mountains and in the trees, and in the hives that men do build for thee. Feed, moreover, on every kind of fruit, and walk the beaten paths of the Lord. From its belly cometh forth a fluid of varying hues, which yieldeth medicine for men. Verily in this is a sign for those who consider.

During the Middle Ages and up to this century, the country people of Central and Eastern Europe used honey medicines for various kinds of wounds, boils, burns, and ulcers, and drops of warmed honey were used to treat earaches.

Honey is also used as a folk remedy for hay fever. The treatment usually involves locating the pollen causing the allergic reaction and feeding the patient honey from that pollen. Hay fever patients are also advised to chew on honeycombs before and during hay fever season, and to take honey mixed with apple cider vinegar three or four times a day. Honey is also used in cough syrups and cough drops. An old-fashioned remedy for coughs is made with honey, lemon juice, and glycerine, while Eucalyptus honey is considered the best for treatment of sore throats.

from hive to table ꒰

The honeybee has a very efficient, highly organized society, which hasn't changed since primitive times. There is a definite division of labor within the hive, and each bee's place in the society is set at birth. These divisions consist of the queen, drones, and worker bees.

The queen bee is the largest bee, and the only one who can reproduce. She develops from the same kind of egg as a worker bee, but a special food, royal jelly, is fed to the young to produce a queen. Her main function is to lay eggs and oversee the hive.

The drones are male bees and their sole function in life is to reproduce with the queen bee. They must be fed by the worker bees and have no sting. Once a drone mates with the queen, he dies. If the hive can't support all the bees, the workers will push unwanted drones out to fend for themselves.

The worker bees are unfertile females. They are the tireless ones who gather the honey, care for the young bees and the queen, and construct and maintain the hive.

Worker bees forage the fields for the nectar found in flowering plants. Nectar is a thin, watery, sugary fluid stored in nectaries, which are usually located in the base of the flowers. Nectars vary in their proportion of sugar and water. The bees choose the flowers with the sweetest nectar every time.

The bee extracts the nectar from the flower and stores it in a small internal honey sac. This is where the nectar undergoes its first change. Enzymes and juices begin to convert the sucrose into simple sugars, and by the time the honeybee returns to the hive, the nectar has become honey, which consists of two simple sugars, dextrose and levulose.

Back at the hive, the worker will unload the unripe honey to other worker bees if she is very busy or she may deposit the honey droplet into a cell herself. The workers evaporate the water content from the unripe honey by exposing it to the warm, dry air currents in the hive and fanning it with their wings. When only 18 to 20 percent of the water remains, the honey is ripe enough and is sealed in a cell with a waxen cap. Here it continues to ripen until eaten by the colony as food or collected by the beekeeper.

COMPOSITION OF HONEY. Honey is a complex substance, and its composition varies depending on flora, location, soil, and even climatic conditions. Therefore, clover honey from Texas will have different characteristics than clover honey from California. The main differences are attributed to the composition of the soil on which the plant is feeding and on the varieties of other plants growing in the same area and producing nectar at the same time. The bees invariably mix the nectars as they go about collecting from many plants growing in an area. For this reason, clover honey can vary in color and taste. For instance, clover blossoms blooming in an area where blackberry blossoms are also producing nectar will produce a different clover honey than that produced in an area where clover blossoms and orange blossoms are producing nectar at the same time.

Soil composition affects the chemical composition of honey in that some soils are acid, some alkaline, and they all vary according to their mineral content. The traces of potassium, ash, nitrogen, sulfur, manganese, and iron found in honey reflects the relative mineral richness of a particular soil. Generally speaking, the darker honeys have the highest mineral content. For instance, buckwheat and heather honeys contain four times as much iron as the light honeys, such as clover and sage.

The following information has been prepared by the *American Honey Institute* to show the average chemical composition of honey:

Principle Components	Percent
Water	17.7
Levulose (fruit sugar)	40.5
Dextrose (grape sugar)	34.0
Sucrose (cane sugar)	1.9
Dextrins and gums	1.5
Ash (silicon, iron, copper, manganese, chlorine, calcium, potassium, sodium, phosphorus, sulfur, aluminum, magnesium)	.18

The remaining components of honey are cluconic, citric, malic, succinic, formic, butyric, lactic, pyroglutamic, and amino acids; minute amounts of protein; and pigments, such as carotene, chlorophyll and chlorophyll derivatives, and xanthophylls; flavor substances derived from terpens, aldehydes, alcohols and esters; sugar alcohols such as mannitol and dulcitol; tannins; inhibine, which is a bactericidal substance; enzymes; and minute quantities of the vitamins thiamine, riboflavin, niacin, biotin, pyridoxine, and pantothenic acid.

POLLEN. Pollen is a fine powdery or granular substance produced by many plants to fertilize the female part of the flowers. This fertilization, or pollination, initiates seed and fruit development, and without this process, most plant life could not continue to exist. Pollination is carried out naturally by the wind, honeybees, and other insects.

Pollen is the primary part of the honeybee's diet. As the honeybee gathers nectar from the flowers, the hairs on her body brush against the pollen-loaded anthers. The bee mixes this pollen with her own enzymes and compacts it together into "pollen baskets" on her hind legs. Back in the hive, the pollen is stored along with the honey. When honey is extracted from the hive, the raw honey contains a large amount of pollen, but this is usually filtered out by well-meaning people who think the pollen is "scrap material."[1]

Pollen is a very complex food. It is a complete food consisting of the essential amino acids, enzymes, growth hormones, steroid hormones, and a gonadotropic hormone which stimulates the sex glands.[2] The vitamins present in pollen are provitamin A (carotenoids), thiamine (B_1), riboflavin (B_2), niacin (B_3), pantothenic acid (B_5), pyridoxine (B_6), Vitamin B_{12}, biotin, and vitamins C, D, E, and K. There are 28 minerals found in the body, 14 of which are essential vital elements present in such minute amounts they are called trace elements. Pollen contains all of these 28 minerals.

Pollen has received some attention from health food faddists in the last several years, but it has been used as a food for centuries. Pollen has been used to enhance beauty, regenerate the body, treat hay fever, prostate troubles, hemorrhoids, asthma, allergies, digestive disorders and intestinal putrefaction, chronic bronchitis, and to retard the aging process. It is used by many athletes to increase their strength, vitality, endurance, and stamina.

Dr. Paava Airola, considered during the past decade to be America's foremost nutritionist and the world's leading authority on holistic health and biological medicine, said, "Pollen is the richest and most complete food in nature. It increases the body's resistance to stress and disease and also speeds up the healing process in most conditions of ill health. It also possesses age-retarding and rejuvenative properties."[3]

Dr. Remy Chauvin, a French researcher, reports that pollen has an antiputrefactive factor similar to that of fermented or lactic acid foods. It also destroys harmful bacteria in the intestines and improves assimilation and elimination.

The United States Department of Agriculture conducted experiments based on the theory that bee pollen contains an anticarcinogenic principle that can be added to food. In 1946, they reported that pollenized food—1 part in 10,000—either prevented or delayed the appearance of mammary tumors in mice and existing tumors were reduced in size.[4]

Since the value of pollen as a food has been recognized, pollen is often harvested separately from the honey. Raw honey purchased through a local beekeeper will most likely contain a high percentage of pollen. Honey containing pollen can be used in beverages, cereals, baked goods, and on fruit.

If you wish to obtain bee pollen, you can get it from a local beekeeper in loose, granule form. This pollen should be refrigerated and stored in an air-tight container. One teaspoon a day is enough to start out, then if you wish, gradually build up to two or three teaspoons a day. Health food stores also carry bee pollen in tablet form, and these come sealed in vitamin-type bottles. There are different qualities, so check labels carefully.

CHARACTERISTICS OF HONEY. Once honey has been removed from the hive, temperature, humidity, and the way the honey is handled will affect its color, texture, and clarity.

ᴥ Honey is hygroscopic. This means it has a great affinity for water and it will draw moisture out of the air or out of any material containing moisture. It is this property which makes honey bactericidal. All organisms must retain a certain amount of moisture in order to survive. When honey draws the moisture out of bacteria, they die. This hygroscopicity makes honey an excellent surgical dressing for wounds, cuts, burns, and other skin irritations.

Honey-baked goods will retain moisture and stay naturally fresh for long periods because of this property. Fruitcakes made with honey can be wrapped in tinfoil and allowed to mature for months, if they are sealed in airtight containers. A caution about cookies made with honey: they will soften if left open to the air but can be crisped again in a warm oven.

❧ If you keep honey in your pantry you may notice the texture changes as the honey gets older. You might notice crystals forming, and in time the whole jar may become solid with crystals. This process is called *granulation* or *crystallization*, and the resulting honey is "candied." This happens to almost all honeys with age and cool temperatures.

Honey granulates, or candies, at temperatures between 50° and 65°F. Granulation doesn't affect the flavor or content of the honey, so it is still good after it crystallizes. In some countries, granulated honey is considered a delicacy.

Granulation depends on the proportions of levulose and dextrose in the honey. Honeys with a high levulose content, like tupelo and sage, usually don't granulate. Honeys high in dextrose, like alfalfa and clover, granulate quickly. Crystallized honey can be reliquefied by placing the container in a pan of hot water. Keep the temperature under 200°F in order to retain the color, flavor, and vitality of the honey.

❧ Honey may also change color with age. Honey stored over a period of years will darken. This color change may also occur if the honey is stored at a temperature higher than 70°F (room temperature).

❧ Most honeys contain sugar-tolerant yeasts derived from the nectar and pollen. When honey is stored at 50°F or below, these sugar-tolerant yeasts are kept inactive. However, at temperatures around 60°F, honey and especially granulated honey, becomes affected by the action of these yeasts. Well-ripened honey won't ferment unless it is exposed to air long enough to absorb enough moisture to activate the yeast. Honey with less than 18 percent moisture will rarely ferment if stored in an airtight container. Honey that has been diluted with water or any other liquid will ferment unless refrigerated. Yeasts can be destroyed by heating the honey at 145°F for one hour. After this, store the honey in an airtight container.

🦐 The whitish, foamy layer sometimes seen on top of honey is produced during the pouring process and in no way affects the purity of the honey.

LABELING OF HONEY. When buying honey, it is helpful to understand the terms used on its label. There are two kinds of honey: comb honey and extracted honey. *Comb* honey consists of sections of the wax hive structure with the honey stored inside. *Extracted* honey is the liquid that has been drained from the comb and is stored in jars or tins. *Filtered* honey has been put through various filters to remove pollen grains and generally clarify it. *Unfiltered* honey is packaged just as it is found in the comb and probably contains the most nutrients. *Organic* honey is specifically derived from organically grown, unsprayed flowers. All honey is "pure"; no refining, additives, or chemical preservatives are needed since bacteria cannot live in honey.

Honey is either blended or unblended. *Blended* honey is a mixture of honeys gathered from different flowers. This may happen naturally as the bees gather nectar from a variety of wild flowers, or the beekeeper may blend several honeys to produce better flavors. *Unblended* honey comes from one kind of flower. This is also called uniflora honey.

HONEY AND ITS COLOR. Honey color ranges from very light to very dark. The lightest honeys are generally favored as table honey. However, the famous heather honey of Europe is quite dark, and it is a very popular table honey there.

The best honeys in the United States are usually referred to as "water-white." Clover honey is considered a typical white honey by which others are judged.

White Honeys. In the North, white comes from all the clovers—white, alfalfa, crimson, mammoth, alsike, and sweet—and from basswood, raspberry, willow-herb (fireweed), milkweed, Canada thistle, apple, cucumber (pickle), and Rocky Mountain beeplant.

In the South, white honey is derived mostly from gallberry (holly), sourwood, tupelo, mangrove, cotton, palmetto, bean, huajilla, catclaw, huisache, mesquite, and California sage.

In the American tropics, white honey comes chiefly from log-wood or campeche.

Amber Honeys. Amber honeys come from many sources; a few of the more familiar ones are goldenrod, wild sunflower, heartsease, Spanish needle, sumac, poplar, gum, eucalyptus, magnolia, marigold, horsemint, horehound, and carpet-grass.

Dark Honeys. These bring to mind the buckwheat honey of the United States and Europe, and heather honey, which comes only from Europe. Buckwheat honey is not as good as clover, either in density, color, or flavor, yet many people like it as much or better than white honey. In France there is a demand for buckwheat honey by bakers who make a particular bread with it.

Heather honey is a dark, rich, strong-flavored thick honey. Heather honey from Scotland is more expensive than the heather honey from England, because it is gathered from another species of flower.

VARIETIES OF HONEY. Uniflora honeys are those made of the nectar gathered from one type of flower. There is such a wide variety of uniflora honeys that you could never tire of the subtle and varied flavors the honeys of the world have to offer.

Australia is the largest honey producer today. The climate is ideal for the making of honey: sunshine, high temperatures, and dry conditions cause plants, and especially trees, to store nectar in large amounts. Like most honey-producing countries, Australia has a clover honey, the best of which comes from Queensland. Yellow-box, blue and red Gum, muggamugga, iron bark, and eucalyptus honeys are also produced there.

New Zealand produces a fine clover honey and a manuka honey that is exported to Germany in large quantities. Tasmania is best known for its leatherwood honey.

Most Mexican honey comes from the Yucatan and Campeche areas. Yucatan honey is usually a blend of main crop honeys. Uniflora honeys of importance are spring apple blossom and Guadalajara. Mexican honey is becoming more popular, especially in Europe, because it is both flavorful and inexpensive.

Honeys from Guatemala and Jamaica are also inexpensive because the equipment and techniques used to collect and extract the honey are somewhat primitive. The honeys, however, have very good flavors and when the packers filter and process them, the resulting honey is on a high standard.

Europe has a variety of superior honeys. France is known for its rosemary, heather, lavender, jasmine, acacia and sycamore honeys. Hungary, Romania, and Yugoslavia produce the finest acacia honey. The two main honeys from Spain are orange blossom and lavender. Poland produces a wonderful lime honey. Greece still produces Hymettus honey, collected from Mt. Hymettus, where in ancient times the honey was renowned. Another lovely honey from Greece is the lemon blossom. From Scotland we have the finest heather honey, while England also produces a good heather honey in the northern counties.

The following is a list of some of the varieties of honey available today.

Acacia or Huajilla Honey. This beautiful water-white honey comes primarily from Texas. It is almost as clear as water, mild in flavor, and delicate in aroma.

Alfalfa Honey. Most alfalfa honey has a pleasant, slightly minty flavor. It is thick and rich, and the color varies from water-white to light amber, depending on the humidity, season, and character of the soil. This honey has a tendency to granulate, although it will stay liquid for a season if kept in a warm room. When granulated, it is fine and creamy and is often sold in solid form in cartons.

Aster Honey. Pure aster honey is white, but usually it is amber or yellow from goldenrod or other late-blooming autumnal flowers. It has a pleasant aromatic taste and it is so thick that extraction is often difficult. Although the newly gathered honey has a rank odor, the fully ripened honey has a fine flavor and good body. It also granulates quickly and has a fine grain when crystallized.

Basswood Honey. Besides alfalfa, sage, and white clover, basswood furnishes more honey than any other plant or tree in this country.

Basswood honey is white and has a strong aromatic or minty flavor. Pure basswood honey has a very strong flavor and is best blended with milder flavored honey.

Buckbush Honey. This honey is made from the nectar of flowers from a branching shrub common in Washington and Idaho. The extracted honey is water-white with a very pleasant flavor and is slow to granulate, sometimes remaining liquid for up to three years.

Buckwheat Honey. This honey is a dark purple and looks like sorghum molasses. The flavor is very strong and somewhat unpleasant to those who are not buckwheat honey fanciers.

Campanilla Honey. This honey is also known as white bellflower, campanilla blanca, Christmas pop, and aguinaldo de pascuas, and it is an important crop to the beekeepers of Cuba. The honey is similar to alfalfa or sage in color and flavor.

Canada Thistle Honey. This light-colored honey has a delightful flavor and is equal to the best clover honey on the market.

Cotton Honey. The cotton plant is a valuable honey plant cultivated mainly in the "cotton belt" states of North and South Carolina, Georgia, Tennessee, Alabama, Mississippi, Arkansas, Louisiana, and Texas. Cotton honey is light in color and mild in flavor. It granulates easily into a very fine, white candy.

Dandelion Honey. Dandelion is a valuable honey plant in Spain, Holland, Austria, Germany, and Norway. In the United States, dandelion honey is sometimes put on the market, but it doesn't have a fine flavor, so it is most often used as a breakfast honey. It is a deep-yellow honey which usually crystallizes within a week or two after extraction.

Eucalyptus Honey. Most of this honey comes from the blue gum species grown primarily in Australia, New Guinea, and California. It is an amber honey of inferior quality, and is usually only used commercially. Other species, such as the sugar gum, mahogany gum, and the white iron bark are reputed to produce fine honeys of exquisite flavors.

Fireweed (Willow Herb) Honey. Fireweed grows mostly in the lumbering regions of northern Wisconsin, Minnesota, Michigan, Canada, Washington, and New England, in areas that have been burned over. Unfortunately this plant's growth is confined almost entirely to areas where forest fires have occurred. The honey is water-white, has a superb flavor, and is sweet, with a slight suggestion of spice.

Gallberry Honey. This honey is also known as inkberry and evergreen winterberry. It grows in sandy coastal soil from Massachusetts to Georgia and Florida, and along the Gulf Coast to Louisiana. The honey is light amber, very heavy and very mild and pleasant in flavor. When it is pure and well-ripened, it won't granulate.

Goldenrod Honey. Goldenrod is a valuable honey plant in New England and Canada. It produces thick, heavy honey with the golden-yellow color of the blossoms. When thoroughly ripened, the quality is rich and pleasant. Although its flavor is stronger than that of white clover, it is a very popular honey in New England. After extraction, it granulates to a course grain in about two months.

Heartsease Honey. This plant is widely distributed over eastern and central North America, particularly in Illinois, Kansas, and Nebraska. The extracted honey varies in color from a light to a dark amber. The flavor is very good, although it is not quite up to that of white honey. The comb honey is almost as white as that of clover. Heartsease honey granulates in very fine crystals. When liquifying this honey, take care not to overheat, since it is injured more easily by overheating than any other honey.

Horehound Honey. This is an important honey plant in Texas and California. Its flavor seems to depend on locality, with some people reporting it to be bitter; others, sweet. In California, the dark amber honey is too strong for table use, but it is used in the medicine industry.

Locust Honey. This is one of the finest honey trees of the eastern and southern states. The honey is milk-white, heavy bodied, and mild in flavor.

Logwood Honey. Logwood trees are found in the West Indies and Central America, and there are areas in the tropics where this tree is the predominating growth. When in full bloom, miles and miles of the countryside are adorned with the logwood's beautiful golden flowers and delicate, pleasing perfume. In Jamaica, logwood is the principle source of honey, in both quality and quantity. The honey is almost water-white, is very dense, and has a peculiarly pleasing flavor that seems to be the essence of the fragrant blossom.

Mangrove Honey. Black mangrove is an evergreen maritime shrub or tree grown in southern Florida. The honey is white and somewhat thin, and has a sweet, mild flavor.

Marigold Honey. Although marigolds are found all over the United States, they are not a significant source of honey except in Texas. The extracted honey is rich and of a golden color. The comb honey is also golden yellow.

Mesquite Honey. This tree is common in southern Texas, New Mexico, Arizona, and Mexico. Mesquite honey is light amber, and the quality is good. Many people consider this honey a good everyday table honey, because you don't get tired of its flavor. In the Hawaiian Islands, mesquite is the chief source of floral honey. It is known as algarroba, or keawe. On the western side of the Islands, there are vast forests of algarroba trees covering thousands of acres of land. The honey is water-white and about as thick as white clover honey. It has an agreeable, although peculiar, flavor. It is suitable to use for table honey, although it granulates soon after extraction.

Milkweed Honey. There are almost 2000 species of milkweed plants. Milkweed is a honey plant in such states as Massachusetts, North Carolina, Tennessee, Texas, Nebraska, California, and Michigan. It is an excellent honey, either white or tinged with yellow, and it has a pleasant fruity flavor with a slight tang. It is very thick and heavy and is good for table use.

Mustard Honey. Wild mustard, or charlock, belongs to the same family as the turnip, cabbage, radish, and rape. Native of Europe, it has become naturalized all over the United States, and is often abundant in grain fields. The honey is mild in flavor and light in color and is comparable to sage honey. Although not as heavy as alfalfa, it has the same tendency to granulate quickly.

Orange Honey. Most of the pure orange honey comes from southern California where the trees are sufficiently abundant to yield honey unmixed with nectar from other sources. Orange honey is also cultivated in Florida, Louisiana, and Texas. Orange honey is light amber, clear, and heavy. The delightful flavor and aroma are reminiscent of the fragrant blossom.

Palmetto Honey. The cabbage palmetto tree grows on the east and west coasts of Florida. It produces honey that is almost water-white, translucent, and extremely mild in flavor. It is an excellent honey to blend with other honeys.

Pennyroyal Honey. This is an important honey plant in southern Florida, but not a very dependable one. In January, when the nectar flows, unfavorable weather will stop the secretion of nectar and prevent the flight of the bees. Only a small quantity of this honey reaches the market, but it is excellent quality, light in color, and delicious.

Raspberry Honey. This is an important honey plant wherever raspberries are cultivated on a large scale for market. Connoisseurs praise this honey for its exquisite flavor, which is reminiscent of the berry itself, and for all the qualities that are so desirable in clover honey. Raspberry honey has such a delicate comb that it almost melts in the mouth.

Sage Honey. This honey is a product peculiar to California. The entire sage region lies south of a line drawn from the coast through San Luis Obispo and Tehachapi. The honey is obtained mainly from the white and black sages (also known as ball, button, and blue sage). Sage honey is water-white, thick and heavy, and does not granulate.

Sourwood Honey. Also known as the sourgum and sorrel tree, sourwood grows in the rich eastern forests from Pennsylvania southward to Florida and Louisiana. Sourwood honey is a medium amber color, and of an excellent quality.

Sumac Honey. Sumac shrubs, small trees, or vines grow in southern New England, especially in Connecticut. The scarlet sumac yields a rich, but mild honey that will suit the most sensitive taste. When pure, the honey has a golden color. If properly ripened, it has no noticeable odor, but it is very heavy, and waxes instead of candying.

Tupelo or Gum Honey. The tupelos are the most valuable honey-producing trees in Florida, if not in the entire United States. Tupelo gum is the source of the "tupelo honey" found in the market, and this special variety is the greatest honey-producer of all the tupelos. It is white, very thick, and delicious. If it is unmixed with other honeys, it will not granulate.

White Clover Honey. In the central and eastern states no other honey plant is so universally known as white clover. It is the honey with which all other honeys are compared. It is a delicious white honey of the finest quality, with a very sweet mild flavor, excellent for all uses.

Yellow Box Honey. This honey comes from the yellow box plant in Australia. This is a mild, light yellowish-colored honey, which takes months to granulate. It is ideal for breakfast cereal, sweetening fruit drinks, or in delicate-flavored cakes.

other sweeteners ॐ

In addition to honey, other sweeteners can add interesting flavors to desserts. Maple syrup adds such a delicate, characteristic flavor to cakes and cookies. Molasses gives a rich, full-bodied flavor to breads, cakes, and cookies. Date sugar is crunchy, with a slight "brown sugar" flavor. Rice syrup is another sweetener, which is not very sweet at all, and can be used in the same way as honey. The same goes for malt syrup, but it has a stronger, malty flavor, and it is a bit sweeter than rice syrup. Many of these sweeteners can be interchanged, and I encourage you to experiment with them. The following is a list of these other sweeteners with brief descriptions of their uses.

DATE SUGAR. This sweetener is made from dried ground dates. It is an unrefined carbohydrate containing vitamins and minerals. It is especially high in potassium. A recipe for homemade date sugar is provided in the *Toppings & Fillings* chapter, but it is much easier to buy date sugar at a natural foods store. Date sugar is very crunchy with a brown sugar flavor, making it a good sweetener to add to crumb toppings. The date sugar crystals don't dissolve in heated water, so it isn't a suitable sweetener for sauces, gelatins, or fillings. However, it is appropriate for cookies and cakes. To cut down on the sweetness, sometimes I like to substitute one-third of the recipe's honey for date sugar.

FRUCTOSE. This is the latest wonder food being substituted for white sugar in soft drinks, candies, and cakes. It is also being used to sweeten "natural" sodas and dessert products and is sold by the pound in many natural food stores. Fructose is much sweeter than ordinary table sugar, so less is required, which automatically reduces the calories and grams of carbohydrate in many recipes. This feature makes fructose an attractive alternative sweetener for dieters and diabetics.

Fructose is a simple sugar which is one of the sugars found in fruit, so many people think this makes fructose more natural than white sugar. However, the truth is, commercial fructose is *not* made from fruit and is even more processed than white sugar.

There are two forms of fructose sold commercially: crystalline fructose and high-fructose corn syrup. Crystalline fructose is made from white sugar (sucrose). Sucrose is a complex sugar consisting of one molecule of fructose and one molecule of glucose. To produce crystalline fructose, the white sugar goes through further refining to split the bond between the fructose and glucose. This is done by an ion-exchange process with a column of calcium salts which uses a large amount of energy. Then the two simple sugars are mechanically separated.

High-fructose corn syrup is made first by an acid hydrolization and acid enzyme treatment which leaves very few nutrients. Fructose is created by adding enzymes to the corn syrup. This enzyme action takes place at 212°F and produces a corn syrup containing 42 percent fructose. The enzymes are removed by filtration and some of the syrup is sold at this point while the rest is processed further to remove glucose. The resulting syrup is 90 percent fructose.

Fructose, like other refined sugars, contributes to diabetes and raises the serum triglycerides and cholesterol levels. It also interferes with the white blood cells' ability to destroy harmful bacteria.[5] I have experimented with fructose and I am not impressed. It does have the familiar crystalline form of white sugar and it is easy to use, but be aware that it is sweeter when cold than when hot. Fructose is definitely a very refined sweetener and from a health viewpoint, less desirable than honey and the other sweeteners used in the recipes.

MALT SYRUP. This is a very thick, but not too sweet, syrup made from fermented, germinated barley (and sometimes corn). It has a very mellow flavor. Diluted with fruit juices, it makes a nice pancake syrup. It is often stocked in health food stores. If honey is too sweet for you, try substituting malt syrup in any of our dessert recipes, in the same proportions as honey.

MAPLE SYRUP. This delicious sweetener is getting harder to find and more expensive to buy. Pure maple syrup is expensive, because it comes only from certain maple trees grown in the colder winter climates, and it takes time and care to make the syrup. The syrup is made right where the trees are grown, in less-than-modern facilities. When purchasing maple syrup, make sure you are getting *pure* maple syrup. Check the labels carefully. By law imitation maple syrups can contain a minimum of 10 to 13 percent real maple syrup and therefore cost only a fraction of the "real thing."[6] Maple syrup contains calcium, potassium, sodium, phosphorus, and small amounts of iron and vitamin B_{12}.[7]

MOLASSES. Molasses is a by-product of sugar production. Briefly, this is what happens. Sugar canes are harvested and brought to a local factory where they are chopped and crushed to remove the juice. This juice, which is only 12 to 13 percent sucrose, is filtered and passed through heating vats. Lime is added to coagulate and separate out any undesired matter. The resultant syrup, or cane molasses, is then poured into vacuum pans, where it is cooked until crystals begin to form. The molasses and crystals mixture is spun in a centrifuge to separate the crystals from the syrup. This first extraction is blackstrap molasses. The process of boiling, crystallizing, and spinning is repeated, and the resulting crystals are raw sugar. Raw sugar is light brown, is 96 percent sucrose, and contains many impurities.

The *raw sugar* is shipped to factories in the United States for the last refining process. There, the raw sugar is cleaned by washing and filtering, the color is removed by passing it over charcoal, and it is crystallized and dried. The resulting white sugar is 99.9 percent sucrose.

Brown sugar is sometimes made by cutting short the refining process so that the sugar retains some of the molasses syrup. Other brown sugars are made by adding brown caramel to the pure white crystals. These sugar products are 96 to 99.9 percent sucrose and have lost some of the nutritional constituents of the original cane.[8]

The nutritional differences between raw, brown, turbinado, yellow, and white sugars are negligible. The raw sugar varieties only look healthier because of their light brown color.

This little diversion from molasses is intended to give an overview of the whole process of which it is a part. Blackstrap molasses, which is the first extraction, is the healthiest molasses, containing only 35 percent sucrose and small amounts of iron, calcium, sodium, potassium, and a few of the B vitamins. Blackstrap molasses is a very dark, thick syrup with a distinctive, somewhat bitter taste. It was widely used as a folk medicine and healing tonic. However, since crude or Barbados molasses is sweeter and doesn't have a bitter taste, it is preferred in desserts.

SORGHUM. People from the Southern states are most familiar with this sweetener, but occasionally you can find it in other regions as well. It is made from sorghum, a grain similar to corn. It is a very thick syrup rich in calcium, phosphorus, and iron.[9] Sorghum is not as sweet as honey, but it is sweeter than malt syrup.

NOTES

1. American Professional Marketing, Inc., "The Bee Rich Honeybee Pollen Story," 4233 Charter Ave., P.O. Box 19140, Oklahoma City, OK 73144.

2. Paavo Airola, *Rejuvenation Secrets from Around the World*, Phoenix, Arizona: Health Plus, Publishers, 1974, p. 44.

3. *Ibid.*

4. Journal of the National Cancer Institute, Vol. 9, No. 2, October 1948, pp. 119–123.

5. Janice Fillip, "The Sweet Thief," *Medical Self-Care*, Fall 1981, pp. 12–19.

6. John Yudkin, *Sweet and Dangerous*, New York: Van Rees Press, 1972, pp. 28–29.

7. Beatrice Trum Hunter, *The Great Nutrition Robbery*, New York: Charles Scribner's Sons, 1978, p. 112.

8. United States Department of Agriculture, *Nutritive Value of Foods*, Home and Garden Bulletin No. 73, prepared by Agricultural Research Service.

9. *Ibid.*

Whole Grain Flours

THE ESSENTIAL INGREDIENT of any cake or pastry is the grain. At the heart of the grain or seed is the embryo, sometimes called the germ. The germ is the most vital part of the plant, for only it is capable of producing a new plant, and it contains most of the vitamins and minerals in the grain. The endosperm surrounds the germ and contains gluten-forming proteins and starch. Around the endorsperm is a layer of aleurone, another protein, then several layers of bran. A thin husk surrounds the entire seed.

A grain of wheat contains sixteen minerals: carbon, chlorine, fluorine, hydrogen, iodine, iron, lime, magnesium, manganese, nitrogen, oxygen, phosphorus, potassium, silicon, sodium, and sulfur. Wheat also supplies the B vitamins, niacin, riboflavin, and thiamin.[1] In general, flours that retain most of the original nutrients of the grain are the best choice for our dessert pantry.

the flour story ❧

The milling technique used by the Egyptians in 4000 B.C. was quite simple. Millers removed the husk, and used huge stones to pulverize the germ and the endosperm. The grinding released the wheat germ oil into the flour, thereby coloring and flavoring the flour slightly. Because the flour was used immediately to make bread, there was no opportunity for the wheat germ oil to turn rancid or for nutrients to be lost. Moreover, since only the husk was removed, the flour and the bread made from it contained all the nutrients in the grain.

The Egyptians' primitive technique was unacceptable to European bakers and grocers, whose bags of flour turned rancid when left on the shelf too long. This problem was solved by the roller mills of the mid-nineteenth century. These mills crushed rather than ground the seed, then separated and sifted out the germ from the kernel, thus removing the source of the oil that could turn rancid and, unfortunately, many of the precious nutrients in the grain.[2]

Twentieth-century technological advancements have resulted in advanced roller milling machinery that removes most of the bran and the germ and blows off the remaining bran and aleurone layers. The resulting powder is bleached until it is beautifully white and will last forever on a shelf. However, in the process, the minerals and B vitamins are substantially reduced.

A study at the University of California has found the following nutritional losses for different wheats.[3]

Minerals	Approximate Loss in Roller Milling
Minerals Present in Different Wheats	
Manganese	98%
Iron	80%
Magnesium	75%
Phosphorus	70%
Copper	65%
Calcium	50%
Potassium	50%
B Vitamins Present in Different Wheats	
Thiamin	80%
Niacin	75%
Riboflavin	65%
Pantothenic Acid	50%
Pyridoxine	50%

The study also reported losses in the B complex vitamins found most abundantly in the wheat germ and bran, namely biotin, inositol, folic acid, choline, and paraminobenzoic acid. Unsaturated fatty acids and vitamin E, which are richly supplied by the wheat germ and to some extent, the bran, are also drastically reduced during roller milling.[4] The best proteins are found in the germ and bran, and these too are removed, leaving poor proteins in the remaining white flour.

The recognition of serious vitamin loss in the processing of white flour led to an attempt to improve its nutritional quality. By 1938, the idea of food enrichment was endorsed by the AMA through the Council on Food and Nutrition and the Council on Pharmacy and Chemistry. As the enrichment program exists today it specifies the addition of synthetic thiamin, riboflavin, niacin, vitamin D, and calcium to help maintain a minimum standard.

However, other important nutritional elements are not covered by the enrichment program. For example, the vitamins biotin, pyridoxine, and pantothenic acid; the minerals phosphorus, potassium, manganese, and copper; and the amino acids lysine and tryptophan are lost in milling.[5] Although they are essential to the health of the human body, they are not restored to the flour by the enrichment program.[6]

There is also concern about the bleaching of flour. Bleaching prevents souring and infestation by weevils, and also speeds up the natural aging process of flour, which improves its bread-making qualities. None of these advantages, however, outweighs the health hazards created by using bleaching agents.

Bleaching agents have been under close scrutiny for years. The use of nitrogen peroxide as a bleaching agent was banned by early twentieth-century legislation, but this ban was disputed and often disregarded by millers.[7] Because the law was difficult to enforce, use of nitrogen peroxide continued.[8] In 1920, nitrogen peroxide was replaced by agene (nitrogen trichloride), which unfortunately was introduced without proper testing. By 1949 researchers had found agene to be a dangerous chemical capable of producing abnormal behavior in animals,[9] and was finally banned. Later tests showed agene to be definitely harmful to humans,[10] specifically causing myopia and allergies in children.[11]

Agene was replaced by chlorine dioxide, which has been found to destroy all the vitamin E that remains after the milling process, and also to form toxic side products with the oil's essential fatty acid (EFA) and the amino acid methionine.[12] However, use of chlorine dioxide continues today.

I strongly recommend using unbleached white flour for your baking needs: it is readily available at all markets, it has all the same baking and cooking properties as bleached white flour, and it is healthier.

VARIETIES OF FLOUR. Because of their superior quality, I use whole grain flours, particularly whole wheat flour, in these recipes instead of white flour. I also often use soy milk powder and soy flour. Although whole wheat and soy flours are "heavier" than all-purpose or cake flour, the results are still pleasing and tasty.

I occasionally use other varieties of flours, such as millet, barley, oat, and brown rice flour. Each of these flours has its own distinctive flavor and way of enhancing baked goods. The following section will provide you with basic information about the many flours available to you, while specific nutritional information is supplied in *The Natural Pantry* section.

I hope you will be inspired to try them in these recipes. If you do, use only a couple of tablespoons of these specialty flours in place of the whole wheat flour until you become familiar with the flavor and properties of the flour. Many of these flours can be purchased in supermarkets; some may be available only at your health food store or farmer's market.

Arrowroot Flour or Powder. Arrowroot flour comes from the tuberous root of a South American plant. It is unrefined and nutritious, and is an excellent substitute for cornstarch. It is also a popular thickening agent for cream sauces and clear, delicate glazes. Allow 2½ teaspoons to 1 cup liquid. To substitute for flour, use 1½ teaspoons arrowroot to 1 tablespoon flour. To substitute for cornstarch, use 1½ tablespoons of arrowroot to 1 tablespoon of cornstarch.

Barley Flour. This flour is ground from the barley grain. It is white and flavorful, and because of its light color, it makes excellent white or cream sauces and can be used as a thickening agent where a light color is desirable. Barley flour contains no gluten, so it should not be used alone in breadmaking. In cookie recipes where whole wheat flour is used exclusively, try using ½ barley flour and ½ whole wheat. To substitute for all-purpose flour, use ½ cup barley flour for each cup of white flour.

Bran Siftings. When the whole wheat flour is milled and sifted, the residue is bran siftings. It has a high fiber content and a little added to breads, cakes, muffins, and cookies provides bulk and relief from chronic constipation. Add 1 to 2 tablespoons of bran siftings to some of the cookie or bread recipes in this book.

Brown Rice Flour. Ground brown rice produces a dense, heavy flour. The flavor, however, is very sweet and tasty. Used in small quantities, rice flour enriches baked goods, and it is an excellent thickener for gravies, sauces, and puddings.

Buckwheat Flour. Most Americans are familiar with this flour as the principle constituent of buckwheat pancakes. It is a dark, heavy flour and has a rich flavor. Buckwheat flour is very fine, and too much will produce a very heavy, dense product. Use this flour sparingly in cookies, breads, muffins, and cakes. For a good texture, use ¼ cup buckwheat flour to ¾ cup of other flours.

Carob Flour or Powder. Also known as St. John's Bread, this chocolatelike flour comes from the pod of the carob tree. It is nutritious and low in fat and can be substituted for chocolate by those who are allergic to chocolate. The toasted carob powder has the best flavor.

Cornmeal. This is coarsely ground corn, and is available as white or yellow cornmeal. I prefer the yellow cornmeal, as freshly ground as possible. Cornmeal adds texture and a cornlike flavor to breads, muffins, and cakes, especially those containing apples, raisins, carrots, or dates.

Graham Flour. Graham flour is stone ground whole wheat flour that is coarsely milled and contains the whole wheat berry. This flour adds more texture and weight to recipes that use whole wheat flour.

Millet Flour. Millet flour is a light yellow color, mild in flavor. Millet is a well-balanced grain, easy on the stomach, and excellent to use in cases of stomach disorders. The flour makes a pleasant, nutritious addition to cakes and batters. It is the main ingredient in the crepe batter in the *Fruit Desserts* chapter.

Oatmeal. There are two kinds of oatmeal. The first kind is steel-cut oatmeal, also known as "Irish" or "Scotch oatmeal." It is made of hard pieces of cracked oats and requires cooking. The second kind is rolled oats, which are flattened flakes. These can be eaten raw when combined with a liquid or can be lightly cooked. Rolled oats are the variety used in baking cookies and breads.

Oat Flour. This is made from ground oat groats. It is a beige-white flour and makes light, fine-textured cakes, cookies, and breads. Oat flour is best combined with wheat flours. It can be up to ⅓ of such a mixture.

Rice Bran. A by-product of processing brown rice, rice bran consists of the outer bran layers and is rich in nutrients. Add rice bran to cookies, cakes, and breads in small quantities to start with. It is recommended that you begin by adding 1 tablespoon of rice bran and omit an equal amount of flour.

Rice Polishings. A by-product of processing brown rice into white rice, rice polishings consist of the inner bran layer and are very rich in nutrients. Add one or two tablespoons to cookies, cakes, and breads instead of the same amount of flour.

Rye Flour. The whole rye berry is ground into rye flour to produce a dark, dense flour, which is used primarily in breadmaking. I have also used rye flour in muffin batters, and it is very tasty.

Rye Meal. This is coarsely ground rye flour, used in making pumpernickel-type breads. The consistency is similar to cornmeal.

Soy Flour. Soy flour is made from roasted soybeans ground to powder and is very high in protein. Soy flour is not a true flour, but a

Food	Grams of Protein per Pound of Food
Low-fat soy flour (or grits)	225
Full-fat soy flour (or bean meats)	182
Peanut butter	118
American cheese	109
Navy beans	100
Lean beefsteak	90
Halibut	86
Lean pork chops	82
Salmon	80
Frankfurters	68
Eggs	59

highly concentrated vegetable protein. The table on the previous page, prepared by the Soy Flour Association, shows how soy flour ranks among other protein foods.

Not only is soy flour the richest in protein of all the foods listed, but also it is one of the richest sources per pound of the entire vitamin B complex. In addition, soy flour has high quantities of calcium, phosphorus, potassium, copper, magnesium, and iron.

Tapioca Flour. Tapioca flour is made from the Brazilian cassava root and is popular for making very clear glazes. Tapioca flour sauces don't break down and become watery after freezing, so this is an excellent thickener to use when baking in quantity with freezing in mind. Tapioca flour should never be boiled: this makes it stringy. Cook the tapioca in fruit juice or water up to the boiling point, and when the first bubbles begin surfacing, immediately remove from the heat. The mixture will look thin and milky. Allow it to cool, stirring only every few minutes. After it has cooled several minutes, add it to the food you are glazing.

Wheat Germ. This is the very perishable inner germ of the wheat kernel. Buy it in vacuum-packed containers to ensure freshness, and once opened, store it in the refrigerator. Very nutritious, wheat germ can be used instead of bread crumbs, added to cereal, soups and stews, casseroles, baked goods, and sprinkled on desserts.

Whole Wheat Flour. When buying whole wheat flour, make sure it is marked *100 percent whole wheat*. Check carefully because bags of flour in the supermarket are often a mixture of 40 percent whole wheat and 60 percent white flour. Also, make sure it is "stone ground." Although stone-ground flour is more expensive, stone grinding is the best milling process available. In other processes, such as high-speed roller, hammer, or steel plate milling, the oil released from the germ is heated and may turn rancid. This action flavors and spoils the flour.

If you are interested in making your own freshly ground flours, hand and electric grinders are available for home use. Hard Red Spring and Hard Red Winter Wheats are the best varieties for baking: both are higher in protein and rise better than other wheat varieties. Buying wheat in bulk is also a good way to cut costs. However, avoid buying grain at feed stores. Although prices are lower, the risk of contamination is higher. Many of these feeds are actually "treated seeds," which means they were treated with a possibly poisonous chemical to prevent insect damage during planting. Also, feeds meant for livestock and poultry often contain impurities, such as bugs, worms, and dirt, and do not meet the standards of cleanliness required for human consumption.

Health food stores usually carry a good supply of bulk whole grains suitable for grinding, plus a variety of stone-ground flours. If possible, always try to get "organic" whole grain flour, grown without chemical fertilizers or sprays.

NOTES

1. Edward E. Marsh, *How To be Healthy with Natural Foods*, New York: Arc Books, Inc., 1967, p. 109.

2. Beatrice Trum Hunter, *Consumer Beware! Your Food and What's Been Done to It*, New York: Simon and Schuster, 1971, p. 288.

3. Eleanor Baker and D.S. Lepkovky, *Bread and the War Food Problem*, Riverside: College of Agriculture, University of California, June, 1943.

4. *Ibid*.

5. A.M. Copping, "The Nutritive Value of Wheaten Flour and Bread," *Nutritional Abstracts*, Review, Vol. 8, 1939, p. 555.

6. Hunter, *op.cit.*, p. 291.

7. *Ibid.*, p. 293.

8. Oscar E. Anderson, Jr., *The Health of a Nation*, Chicago: University of Chicago Press, 1958, pp. 269–270.

9. Sir Edward Mellanby, "Diet & Canine Hysteria Experimentally Produced by Treated Flour Preliminary Report," *British Medical Journal*, Vol. 2, 1946, pp. 885–893.

10. "Flour Bleachers and Improvers," *British Medical Journal*, No. 5252, Sept. 2, 1961, pp. 631–632.

11. B.S. Platt, "Fourth International Congress of Nutrition, Paris," *The Lancet*, Vol. 2, 1957, p. 288.

12. T. Moran et al., "Interaction of Chlorine Dioxide with Flour: Certain Chemical Aspects," *Nature*, Vol. 171, 1953, p. 103.

Butter & Oils

BUTTER AND OILS ARE ESSENTIAL INGREDIENTS to most desserts. They add richness to the flavor and lightness and flakiness to the texture of pies, pastries, and cakes. Fats are much maligned because they are so high in calories. However, fats are a great source of energy for the body and serve many valuable purposes. They retard the hunger process because they take longer to digest than carbohydrates or proteins. They carry essential fatty acids and help in the transport and absorption of fat-soluble vitamins. They also lubricate the gastrointestinal tract.

Fatty tissue surrounds all vital body organs and is interlaced throughout muscle tissue. It holds the nerves and organs in place and protects them against injury. Fat layers in the body act as insulators to keep us from losing body heat and help us maintain body temperature.

The major food sources of fat are used frequently in preparing desserts: butter, margarine, vegetable oils, cream, homogenized milk, milk products, egg yolk, nuts, avocados, and whole wheat cereals. Below is a list of the fat content of some of these foods, shown as percentages of total weight:[1]

Food	Fat Content
Oils	100%
Butter, margarine	80%
Most nuts	60%
Peanut butter	50%
Cheese	30–35%
Milk	2–4%
Most bread, fruit, vegetables	under 1%

For the recipes, butter and unrefined vegetable oils are used exclusively, because they are the healthiest and least processed of the shortenings available. Margarines and hard vegetable shortenings should be avoided.

butter ✺

Butter has been manufactured by man for more than 5000 years. It was used first as a medicine and later as a food. Farm-made butter has always been made from fresh, sweet cream, and its color depended on the season. During the summer months when the cows were eating fresh green plant matter, the butter was a deep yellow because of the presence of more carotene (a fat soluble pigment) in the cream. During the winter months when the cows were eating dry feed, the butter was a much lighter color. Carrot juice was often added to the winter cream to give the butter a deeper color.

Butter today is not always a wholesome farm product. Sometimes stale cream is used instead of sweet cream and calcium carbonate or sodium bicarbonate is often added to give the cream a fresher taste.[2] The costly method of coloring the butter with carrot juice has been replaced with cheaper coal tar dyes.[3] Some of these dyes may be carcinogenic and are currently under investigation by the FDA. Most producers add salt to butter to retard the growth of yeast and molds. This lengthens its shelf life and makes it nearly impossible to tell how old the butter is.

Despite all this, you can still shop wisely for good quality butter. Unsalted, sweet cream butter is preferable. Although more perishable, this kind of butter has fewer additives.

margarine ✺

By the early 1800s the search began for a butter substitute, because butter often turned rancid. One experimenter created a product called oleomargarine, named after its principal ingredient, oleo oil, which was extracted from beef tallow. Shortages in the animal fat used to make oleomargarine led to the use of vegetable oils and a new process called hydrogenation.

Animal fats, such as butter or lard, are hard and congealed because they are saturated, that is, the carbon linkages in their molecular chains are bound by hydrogen atoms. Fats from vegetable sources are usually liquid and are called oils. They are unsaturated, or polyunsaturated, because their carbon linkages are not all bound by hydrogen atoms. The makers of oleomargarine found that adding hydrogen atoms to liquid, unsaturated vegetable oils turned these oils hard. This process, called hydrogenation, made it possible to replace animal fats with cheaper, more plentiful vegetable oils.

Margarine was not popular at first, oddly enough because it was less expensive than butter and was therefore considered inferior. In addition its cold cream or lardlike appearance was very unappealing. This changed in 1952 when colored margarine was made legal in most states.

Soon the food industry giants became involved in the manufacture of margarine. They made packaging more attractive and launched big advertising campaigns emphasizing "spreadability." Then they began to "educate" the public about cholesterol and heart disease. Large companies even suggested that the polyunsaturated oils used in margarine would reduce cholesterol levels and thereby cut the risk of coronary disease. Doctors became the main target of this advertising, and soon many doctors were suggesting that people with heart problems replace butter with margarine and go on polyunsaturated diets. The campaign was apparently a success. Sales boomed as more and more people switched from butter to margarine.

Despite the real and claimed advantages of margarine, there are some compelling reasons for questioning their use. Scientists taking a closer look at hydrogenation have found that during this process the normal *cis* fatty acids are changed into unnatural, "upside-down" molecular structures called transisomers, which make polyunsaturated margarines solid at room temperature. However, transisomers are not normally found in human tissues and do not behave as normal fatty acids.

Experiments with animals by Dr. F. A. Kummerow, professor of food chemistry at the University of Illinois, have shown that margarines containing a high level of transfatty acids are more likely to cause heart disease than cholesterol-rich animal fats such as butter or cholesterol-rich foods such as eggs.[4] Some margarines produced in the United States contain from 36 to 40 percent transfatty acids, while some margarines produced in other countries may contain even higher percentages.[5]

There are other reasons for concern about hydrogenated oils. Some of the more highly unsaturated fatty acids in oils cannot be produced by the body and must therefore be supplied in the diet. These are called essential fatty acids (EFA). Dr. Hugh Sinclair conducted clinical experiments with both animals and human beings at the Laboratory of Human Nutrition, Oxford University. The results showed that hydrogenated oils produce a deficiency of EFA either by destroying them or by producing abnormal toxic fatty acids that have an anti-EFA effect.[6]

The research also concluded that a deficiency of EFA contributes to neurological diseases; heart disease; arteriosclerosis; skin disease; and degenerative conditions, such as cataract, arthritis, and cancer. Based on this information, it seems that quality butter offers far fewer health risks than margarine.

oils ಸ

Oils that have been processed as little as possible are healthiest. About 4000 years ago, the Assyrians and Chinese pressed their own oil by roasting sesame seeds, grinding them, and leaving the crushed seeds in a bowl until the oil separated. The result was a rich, cloudy, crude oil that retained the aroma and flavor of the seed.

This is not the kind of vegetable oil you will find on most supermarket shelves. These refined oils have been extracted at extremely high temperatures (350°F or more). This process is undesirable because oils extracted at such high temperatures are harder for the body to break down and may clog cell membranes.

The more widely used solvent process is the most economical since only 1 to 2 percent of the original oil is lost. The relatively small loss makes these oils less expensive than the unrefined cold-pressed oils.

SOLVENT METHOD. In the solvent method, a solution of hexane or benzine (both petroleum products and now believed to be carcinogenic) is mixed with the ground oil-containing seeds. The mixture is then boiled to drive off the solvent. The use of these petroleum products has raised doubts about their safety:

> "Since various petroleum constituents . . . produced cancer in man and experimental animals, the presence of such chemicals in food appears to be objectionable, particularly when such materials are subject to high temperatures."[7]

The refined oil is further treated with caustic soda, lye, or other strong alkalis, and is then filtered. In some cases, a sodium hydroxide solution is added to keep the oil from darkening, but usually the bleaching is achieved by mixing in bleaching earth, fuller's earth, or clay. After refining and bleaching, the oil has an unpleasant odor and taste, so it is deodorized at high temperatures. Finally, the oil is stripped by steam distillation, cooled, and further filtered. Phosphoric, citric, or tartaric acids may be added to give the oil a longer shelf life. Salad oils and mayonnaise may be "winterized" to keep the oil from solidifying under refrigeration, that is, the oil is cooked slowly over a long period, solids are removed, and then it is filtered again.[8]

COLD-PRESSED OILS. I believe it is best to choose wholesome oils closest to their natural state. Health food stores, or the health section of some large supermarkets, are the best places to buy unrefined, cold-pressed vegetable oils. Truly cold-pressed oils are made by hydraulic pressure. Very few oils can be made in this way: sesame seed oil and olive oil are the best known.

Most of the unrefined oils, although also labeled "cold-pressed," are made by the pressure method of extraction. During this process the ground or flaked seeds, nuts, or fruit are placed in a large cylinder, and a large screw presses them against a back plate. The mixture reaches temperatures at least 130 to 150°F, and must be even greater for the manufacture of corn germ and soy oils. For soy oil at least, this high heat is desirable, since it destroys a digestion-inhibiting substance.

The flavor, aroma, and nutritional sediment left with this process make these oils far superior to purified oils. In terms of food value, these relatively unrefined oils provide a good source of unsaturated fatty acids. Some of the more highly unsaturated fatty acids, such as linoleic acid, cannot be produced or built up in the body from other fatty acids, so they must be supplied in our food. If the body is supplied enough linoleic acid, however, it can manufacture the other essential fatty acids. Corn, cottonseed, and soy oil are very good sources of linoleic acid, along with most vegetable oils (but not coconut oil).

Unrefined oils provide other nutrients; chlorophyll, vitamin E, carotenoids; and minerals, such as copper, magnesium, calcium, and iron. Lecithin, vitamin E, and sesamol are natural agents also contained in corn, safflower, and soy oils. Unrefined oils also ensure a better assimilation of vitamins A, D, and E and help the body use calcium, a mineral known to be especially effective in relieving stress.

Remember that these oils have a much shorter shelf life than refined oils and should be used within a short time after their purchase. Refrigeration or storage in metal containers in a cool, dark place will help retard spoilage. The following is a list of the best oils for baking.

Corn Oil. Peruvians began cultivating corn and pressing its oil thousands of years ago. Corn oil is the most unsaturated of all the grains. High in linoleic acid, it also contains amounts of oleic, linolenic, and arachidic acids. Corn oil is also a very good source of phosphorus and the fat-soluble vitamins A, D, and E. It has been found to correct the over-alkaline system and restore its proper acid balance. It is a light and easily digested oil.

Olive Oil. The ancient Mediterranean cultures regarded olive oil as a food and medicine. For the Hebrews, it was a symbol of prosperity. Although it is low in linoleic acid, olive oil's rich oleic acid content (80 percent) makes it completely digestible. It increases the absorption of the fat-soluble vitamins A, D, E, and K. *Virgin oil*, also called lucca oil, is taken from the first cold pressing of the olives. This is the best and most expensive oil, and has a greenish tinge and rich scent. *Grades 1 and 2 olive oil* are edible oils in which cold-pressed oil is blended with hydraulic extractions. Since olive oil has a distinctive flavor which is not suitable for dessert-making, mix it with safflower oil to make its flavor milder and also to increase its linoleic acid content.

Peanut Oil. This oil has a high content of oleic and linoleic acids. The best quality peanut oil is cold-pressed and will remain liquid at room temperature without clouding over as some oils do. It has a bland taste and stores well in cool conditions.

Safflower Oil. This oil was cultivated by the ancient civilizations along the Nile and down through Ethiopia. It contains up to 80 percent linoleic acid. The seeds must be husked, then pressed with hydraulic machines. Chemical solvents are sometimes used. Cold-pressed safflower oil is the best quality available, but because of the laws regarding labeling, you will have to ask your supplier which method of extraction was used. Safflower oil is considered by many to be the best baking oil because of its mild flavor and light color.

Sesame Oil. A popular cooking oil for centuries in Africa and the Far East, sesame oil contains approximately 40 percent linoleic acid and 50 percent oleic acid, and a good amount of lecithin. Since there are no husks to remove from the seeds, extraction is very simple. The best grade oil is obtained in a single cold-pressing. This oil is clear, with a pale yellow color. The seed pulp is then heated and two further pressings are made under hydraulic pressure. This process yields a much darker, inferior oil. Good quality sesame oil can enhance some desserts, such as cookies and cakes, and it doesn't turn rancid, even in hot weather.

Sunflower Oil. This oil has a very high linoleic acid content, and also contains oleic and palmitic acids. The oil is rich in vitamins E, A, and D. Sunflower oil is a mild, light yellow oil which is quite suitable for baking.

NOTES

1. Ronald M. Deutsch, *The Family Guide to Better Food and Health*, Creative Home Library, Des Moines, Iowa: Meredith Corporation, 1974, p. 67.

2. Gary Null with Steve Null, *The New Vegetarian*, New York: William Morrow and Company, Inc., 1978, p. 98.

3. *Ibid.*, p. 98.

4. F.A. Kummerow et al., *Swine as an Animal Model in Studies on Atherosclerosis*, Urbana: Burnsides Research Laboratory, University of Illinois, 1974.

5. Beatrice Trum Hunter, *The Great Nutrition Robbery*, New York: Charles Scribner's Sons, 1978, p. 70.

6. Dr. Hugh Sinclair, *Drug Trade News*, 1 July 1957.

7. P.R. Peacock, "The Carcinogenic Action of Heated Fats and Lipoids," *British Medical Bulletin*, 1947, Vol. 4, p. 364.

8. Beatrice Trum Hunter, *Consumer Beware! Your Food and What's Been Done to It*, New York: Simon and Schuster, 1971, p. 219.

Milk &
Milk Products

Sausalito Bay   7/14/80

MILK AND MILK PRODUCTS, such as yogurt, ice cream, sour cream, and whipping cream, are delicious and attractive dessert additions. They add extra sparkle and interest to pies, cobblers, cakes, baked fruits, and gelatins. Besides their creamy, rich visual appeal, some of these ingredients actually enhance the overall nutritional value of the dessert. Milk, yogurt, yogurt cheese, and cottage cheese in particular can transform ordinary desserts into protein-packed energy foods. On the other hand, although sour cream and whipping cream are an elegant way to dress up desserts, they do not add significantly to nutritional content. For this reason, they will not be discussed in this section, even though they are used in many of the recipes.

milk ✍

Milk has often been referred to as a perfect food, because it has all the amino acids to make it a complete protein. For this reason it is of particular importance to vegetarians. Because it contains the amino acids often lacking in vegetable proteins, it is an excellent complement to these foods.

The protein in milk, casein, is important for building muscle tissue and supporting growth throughout the system. Milk has a high content of calcium and phosphorus, both of which are essential for good bone and tooth structure. The ratio between them in milk makes them highly usable, and their absorption by the body is aided by the fat content in milk. Milk is a good source for the fat-soluble vitamins A, D, E, and K, plus the water-soluble B vitamins, especially riboflavin. However, milk does not provide much vitamin C, iron, or copper.

RAW MILK. At present there is some controversy about the value of raw milk versus pasteurized milk. Pasteurization destroys harmful disease bacteria commonly found in milk. However, consider the following information from the National Health Federation.

❧ Raw milk contains all the enzymes important to its digestion and absorption, whereas pasteurized milk loses more than 90 percent of these enzymes during the heating process.

❧ In raw milk, 100 percent of the amino acids remain intact, whereas lysine and tyrosine are changed by heating during the pasteurization process resulting in less availability of the whole protein complex to the body.

❧ All 18 saturated and unsaturated fatty acids are available in raw milk, whereas they become altered by the heat in pasteurization, especially the 10 essential unsaturated fats.

❧ There is 100 percent vitamin and mineral retention in raw milk, whereas two-thirds of the fat-soluble vitamins and 80 percent of the water-soluble vitamins are lost during pasteurization. Calcium loss by heat may be as high as 50 percent, depending on the temperature.[1]

The main objection to raw milk is the possibility that it may contain disease bacteria. If you buy uncertified raw milk from a farmer, there is certainly some risk involved. But certified raw milk must meet rigorous government standards for maintenance of proper sanitary conditions, inspection of cows and milk samples, and inoculation of cows against disease. Certified raw milk seems the best choice, but if it is unavailable in your area, pasteurized milk is certainly preferable to no milk at all or soft drinks and imitation or sugar-fortified fruit drinks.

SKIM MILK. Skim milk is popular because it has fewer calories than whole milk. The process used to remove the fat content of the milk also removes the fat-soluble vitamins, but most of these lost vitamins are usually replaced.

DRIED MILK. I recommend the *noninstant* skim milk or whole milk powder. Dried milk contains an abundance of fat free protein; vitamins B_1 (thiamin), B_2 (riboflavin), B_6 (pyridozine), and B_{12}; choline; inositol, niacin, pantothenic acid, para-amino-benzoic acid, biotin, and folic acid. An analysis of powdered milk indicates it has a high mineral concentration of calcium, chlorine, cobalt, copper, iodine, iron, magnesium, manganese, phosphorus, potassium, sodium, sulfur, and zinc.[2]

Only ½ cup of dried milk powder supplies 35 grams of high quality protein to the diet, the equivalent protein of six eggs. It can be used as a protein booster for baked desserts, breads, casseroles, soups, blended drinks, cookies, candies, cakes, and icings.

Dried milk can be stored for long periods, but it is best to use it one to two months after purchase. Dried milk should always be stored in airtight containers in a cool place. To make your own milk from the powder, mix ½ to ¾ cup of the milk powder with 1 quart of water. Use a blender, electric mixer, or egg beater for best results.

GOAT'S MILK. The mineral and protein composition of goat's milk is closer to that of human milk than that of cow's milk. Since the time of Hippocrates, goat's milk has been recommmended for infants, invalids, people with stomach ulcers, or those allergic to cow's milk, because it is so easily digested. It is easy to digest because it has very small fat globules about the size of those in homogenized cow's milk. Goat's milk has more calcium and vitamin A, and a little less protein than cow's milk. It is available in most health food stores.

OTHER MILK VARIETIES. I do not recommend using evaporated, condensed, imitation, or filled milks for the following reasons.

Evaporated milk has 60 percent of its water removed during a heat-vacuum evaporation process. The concentrated milk is then homogenized and sterilized, and emulsifiers and stabilizers are usually added. Vitamin D is added and then the milk is sealed in a tin container, minus many of its important nutrients.

Sweet condensed milk has 50 percent of its water removed, but it is not sterilized. Instead, approximately 44 percent sugar is added to preserve the milk, and then it is canned. Both evaporated and condensed milk may contain relatively large amounts of lead, a toxic metal often introduced into the milk by outdated canning equipment. In 1973 the Consumers Union found that six well-known brands of canned milk had lead levels almost as high as the maximum daily allowance set for children one to three years old by the Department of Health, Education and Welfare. A follow-up report in 1974 showed a drop in the lead content, but significant residues of lead were still present.[3]

Imitation milk is usually a combination of water, corn syrup, hydrogenated coconut oil, sodium caseinate (a protein derived from soybeans or milk), potassium phosphate, stabilizers, emulsifiers, synthetic vitamins and minerals, and artificial flavorings and colorings.

Filled milk has the butterfat removed and replaced with vegetable fats. It is a combination of skim milk and vegetable fat or nonfat milk solids, water, and vegetable fats. It is less expensive than whole milk and appeals to people on low-cholesterol diets. However, the vegetable oil chosen to replace the butterfat is usually coconut oil, which is high in saturated fatty acids. Therefore filled milk is higher in saturated fat than whole milk with butterfat. The coconut oil in filled milk can also cause diarrhea and low growth rates in infants.[4]

cottage cheese ✍

This is an unripened, "fresh" cheese made from whole or skim milk. While it has a high protein content, it is very low in saturated fats. Creamed cottage cheese contains 2 percent fat, and the uncreamed kind has practically no fat. Cottage cheese is also the best buy of all the cheeses in terms of amount of protein per dollar spent. When served with fresh fruit or fruit gelatins, it is an excellent protein snack or dessert.

yogurt ✍

Like cottage cheese, yogurt is an excellent addition to the diet as a natural accompaniment to fresh fruit salads and fruit sauces.

Yogurt is a fermented milk product with a thick creamy texture and a tart taste. Often dry milk powder is added to commercial yogurts to give them a thicker texture. This makes the protein content in yogurt higher than that in milk. Yogurt has a few advantages over regular milk: the protein is more easily digested, the calcium is more readily assimilated, and yogurt manufactures healthy amounts of B vitamins in the intestinal tract, which keeps it clean and toned.

The lactic acid, carbonic acid, and alcohol created during the yogurt fermentation process, have a stimulating effect on the stomach and intestinal tract. Moreover, the bacteria used to make yogurt produce a natural antibiotic condition in the intestines that is generally resistant to harmful bacteria.

There is some evidence that yogurt contains a property that lowers blood cholesterol. Dr. George V. Mann, of the Vanderbilt University Medical School, found that the members of the Masai tribe had a low blood cholesterol level even though their diet was essentially made up of saturated fats and foods high in cholesterol content.[5] Their diet also consisted of large amounts of whole milk yogurt. When the researchers fed the Masai larger quantities of whole milk yogurt, they found that their blood cholesterol levels were lowered even more. They concluded that there is some cholesterol-inhibiting factor within the yogurt; but it has not yet been identified.

When buying yogurt, choose the low-fat varieties. Avoid fruit-flavored yogurts that contain sugar and artificial flavorings. There are, however, several delicious yogurts made with honey and natural fruit flavors. Most yogurts contain a thickening agent; those using dry milk powder for this purpose are best. You can make your own yogurt by following the recipe for *Homemade Yogurt* in the recipe chapter, *Toppings & Fillings*.

Yogurt cheese, made from yogurt, is a very good substitute for cream cheese. It has a similar thick, creamy consistency, but many fewer calories. To make yogurt cheese, follow the recipe given in the same chapter, *Toppings & Fillings*. Yogurt cheese can be added to frostings and gelatins or spread on sweet breads.

ice cream ✍

Ice cream provides about the same amount of nutrients as an equal amount of milk, but has more than twice the calories. Commercial ice creams are a tribute to our sophisticated chemical technology. It is legal for the makers of ice cream to use more than twelve hundred stabilizers, emulsifiers, neutralizers, and artificial flavors and colors.[6] Most of these additives are chemicals and some create exciting new flavors, but their effects on the human body have not been conclusively studied.

Emulsifiers and stabilizers are used to make the smooth texture of ice cream. In the past, natural foods such as eggs, milk protein, fat, lecithin, gelatin, agar-agar, or seaweeds were used. Since these ingredients are getting more costly, they have gradually been replaced by inexpensive ingredients, such as polyoxyethylene and carboxymethylcellulose. Both have been labeled potentially cancer-inciting substances. Another ingredient, propylene glycol alginate, has also been used in germicides, in antifreeze substances, and as a paint remover.[7]

Vanilla is another costly ingredient that has been replaced in less expensive ice creams. Vanillin, a synthetic substitute, not only is less costly to make, but also is much stronger in flavor. Other synthetics used to replace real vanilla are vanildene ketone and piperonal, a well-known louse killer.[8]

Chocolate is a very popular flavor originally made from a cocoa extract. However, when an ice cream is labeled "artificially flavored," its "chocolate" flavor may come from amylphenyl acetate, vanillin, aldehyde C, veratraldehyde, n-butylphenyl ethylacetal, and propylene glycol.[9] Artificially flavored "strawberry" ice cream may contain Corp Praline, alcohol, propylene glycol, glacial acetic acid, aldehyde C, benzyl acetate, vanillin, methyl heptine carbonate, methyl salicylate, ionine beta, aldehyde C, diacetyl, and anethol.[10] Other flavors have been duplicated in the laboratory to give us imitation flavorings whose chemicals are suspect. A few of the flavors to avoid are: banana, cherry, pineapple, and black walnut.

Commercial ice cream makers also use a variety of chemicals to color their products. Red Dye 2, also known as amaranth, has been a controversial food additive for some time. For example, in 1970 Russian scientists published two new studies incriminating Red 2. One of the studies showed that the red dye caused cancer in rats.[11] The other study showed that Red 2 caused birth defects, still-births, sterility, and early fetal deaths in rats given the dye in exceedingly small amounts.[12] The FDA dismissed the Russian paper on Red 2 as inconclusive and stated that the dye had been tested many times and found "clean." Actually the FDA's tests, conducted in the early fifties, *did not* find "no effects." Many of the rats tested with the dye had formed tumors.[13] Since then, further testing has resulted in the establishment of new safe limits of the red dye, and it continues to be used widely throughout the food industry, along with other artificial colors used in the making of ice cream.[14] These dyes are being tested by concerned scientists, and although they have not been banned, the potential health risks presented by them must not be taken too lightly.

I recommend choosing from the several brands of natural ice creams on the market. These are usually made with honey and natural colors and flavors. Their stabilizers and emulsifiers are also made from natural sources, such as carrageenan, agar-agar, gum acacia, guar seed gum, gum karaya, locust bean gum, gum tragacanth, and gelatin. These natural additives are preferable to their synthetic and potentially carcinogenic counterparts.

The healthiest, most natural ice cream is the kind you make at home with honey, fruits, nuts, and spices. By combining fruits, or using the many extracts available, you can create your own exotic flavors. To make your own ice cream, buy one of the many reasonably priced ice cream makers. If you wish to follow their recipe booklet, you can substitute honey for sugar by cutting the sugar proportions in half. A helpful hint: by adding a little skim milk powder to your mix (see our recipes for proportions), you will have a thicker ice cream that won't melt as quickly. Another tip: I have found that the subtle flavors of fresh fruits and honey are enhanced by "aging" overnight.

NOTES

1. National Health Federation Bulletin, issued to the public through Alta-Dena Dairy, Los Angeles, California.

2. Edward E. Marsh, *How to be Healthy with Natural Foods*, New York: Arc Books, Inc., 1967, p. 30.

3. Rodger P. Doyle and James L. Redding, *The Complete Food Handbook*, New York: Grove Press, Inc., 1976, p. 24.

4. "Milk: Why is the Quality so Low?" *Consumer Reports*, January, 1974, p. 75.

5. George V. Mann and A. Spoerry, "Studies of a surfactant and cholesteremia in the Masai," *American Journal of Clinical Nutrition*, 27:464, 1974.

6. Gary Null with Steve Null, *The New Vegetarian*, New York: William Morrow and Company, Inc., 1978, p. 109.

7. Beatrice Trum Hunter, *Consumer Beware! Your Food and What's Been Done to It*, New York: Simon and Schuster, 1971, p. 250.

8. *Ibid.*, p. 252.

9. Joseph Merory, *Food Flavorings: Composition Manufacture and Use*, Westport, Connecticut: Avi Publishing Co., 1960, p. 170.

10. *Ibid.*, p. 186.

11. A.I. Shtenberg and E.V. Avrilenko, "Effect of Amaranth Food Dye on Reproductive Function and Progeny Development in Experiments with Albino Rats," *Vop. Pitan*, 29, 66, 1970.

12. M.M. Andrianova, "Carcinogenic Properties of the Red Food Dyes Amaranth, Ponceaux Sx, and Ponceaux 4R," *Vop. Pitan*, 29, 66, 1970.

13. Jaqueline Verrett and Jean Carper, *Eating may be Hazardous to Your Health*, New York: Simon and Schuster, 1974, p. 124.

14. Wilhelm Hueper, "Potential Role of Non-Nutritive Food Additives and Contaminants as Environmental Carcinogens," Symposium on Potential Cancer Hazards from Chemical Additives, *Archives of Pathology, American Medical Association*, Vol. 62, 1959, pp. 235–237.

Eggs

EGGS ARE A WONDERFUL DESSERT INGREDIENT. They make the texture of cakes and custards light and add richness to their flavor. Most importantly, they are an almost perfect source of protein, because their amino acid makeup meets the needs of human growth and health. They are also one of the easiest proteins to digest. Eggs are an excellent source of unsaturated fatty acids, iron, phosphorus, trace minerals, vitamins A, E, K, and B complex, including B_{12}. Next to cod liver oil, eggs are the best source of vitamin D.

All these reasons make eggs a desirable food for most people. Yet, while egg consumption was as high as 400 eggs per person per year in 1945, it is now under 275 eggs per person per year.[1] What has led to the decline in the egg's popularity?

cholesterol ✒

In 1960, a 14-year study of a middle-class suburban community concluded that cigarette smoking, high blood pressure, and high blood cholesterol were important risk factors in the development of heart disease.[2] Since one egg contains 275 milligrams of cholesterol, the American Heart Association recommended that people reduce their egg consumption. This was followed by a surge of negative advertising designed to scare people away from this high quality protein food.

Later research isolated *several* dietary risk factors for coronary heart disease: overeating, excess dietary fat, low ratio of polyunsaturated fatty acids in the diet, excess dietary cholesterol, excess dietary sucrose, high consumption of common salt, deficiency of dietary fiber, and softness of the water supply.[3] Moreover, although most of the dietary cholesterol in Western society is derived from eggs, there has been no evidence relating the number of eggs consumed to the risk of coronary heart disease. In support of this, there was an interesting study involving eight severely burned patients whose cholesterol level was below normal. For one month they were given 35 eggs to eat each day, for the purpose of providing concentrated protein and calories to help speed recovery. During and after the egg diet, their cholesterol levels remained normal, and they showed no side effects.[4]

What is cholesterol? Is it really a villain? On the biochemical level, cholesterol is just a normal constituent of the blood and tissues and can be found in every animal cell. It performs necessary functions in the synthesis of the sex and adrenal hormones, production of bile acids, formation of cell membranes, and construction of new tissues. Some cholesterol is naturally manufactured by the human body, while some is supplied by the diet. The ordinary American diet supplies 600 to 900 milligrams a day, whereas a "low" cholesterol diet supplies about 300 milligrams a day.

Research has shown that adults eliminate up to about 800 milligrams of cholesterol daily, which would balance the amount normally supplied through diet and manufactured in the body. Problems arise when the diet or the cholesterol-making mechanism supplies more cholesterol than is needed. Medical scientists believe that this may be a genetic disorder. Research has shown that people with high blood cholesterol resulting from faulty cholesterol regulation also tend to develop heart disease more often than people with normal levels.

Populations eating a diet rich in fiber, particularly from cereals and legumes, usually have a lower blood cholesterol concentration and a lower mortality rate from coronary heart disease than populations eating a typical Western diet, usually relatively low in fiber.[5] There is also some evidence that the blood concentration of cholesterol in healthy persons can be reduced by increasing consumption of foods rich in fiber.

FOODS THAT REDUCE CHOLESTEROL. Another way to reduce blood cholesterol is to eat foods of plant origin, because fruits, vegetables, cereal grains, legumes, and nuts do not contain cholesterol. Instead they have plant sterols, which have been shown to reduce blood cholesterol. Indeed, recent studies have shown that some foods specifically function to keep cholesterol in check. Eggplant, onions, garlic, yogurt, pectin, and lecithin-containing foods, such as soybeans, are particularly effective in lowering cholesterol levels. The biochemical agents responsible for this action do function differently in each of these foods, but their effect is the same. Most important, these agents are not destroyed by heat during cooking.[6]

For instance, eggplant contains an element that binds the cholesterol in the intestines and carries it out of the system so that it can't be absorbed; garlic and onions have active ingredients that check cholesterol levels; and it is believed that yogurt bacteria produce a substance that blocks cholesterol production in the liver.[7] Lecithin lowers the LDL (low-density lipoproteins), the constituents that get stuck in the arteries and are the harmful agents in cholesterol. Lecithin provides HDL (high-density lipoproteins), which take the LDL out of the arteries and into the liver. There they are processed for the digestive tract and excreted.

Pectin limits the amount of cholesterol absorbed from fat-rich foods. Recent studies have shown that 12 grams of pectin taken daily with meals decrease cholesterol in the blood by 8 percent.[8] Apples eaten whole are high in pectin and might be an excellent dietary aid to reduce cholesterol levels.[9] Citrus fruits also contain pectin. Since it is found in the white membrane of the fruit, it is best to eat whole fruit.

selecting eggs ﾗ

Thanks to new information about cholesterol and how to control it, we no longer feel that we must give up eggs to be healthy. Here are some useful hints about selecting and buying eggs.

ﾗ Health-minded people seem to prefer brown, fertile, organically grown eggs. The color of the eggshell, however, depends entirely on the breed of chicken, and has no bearing on nutrition. Fertile eggs may contain a little more protein due to added nutrients in the embryo, but this would be an insignificant amount since the embryo is so small.

ﾗ Eggs from organically raised chickens are worth the extra money they might cost. These eggs usually have darker yellow yolks due to their more natural living conditions. Organic eggs may not be higher in nutritional value, but they *are* free of chemical residues. Your local farmer's market or health food store probably carries organically grown eggs. If you live near a rural area, check around for a small egg operation or for farmers that raise chickens without chemical feeds and treatment. For those people who have room in their backyards and live in places where ordinances allow it, there is nothing easier than raising your own hens. They are sturdy birds with minimal needs and make interesting pets for children.

✑ When buying eggs you should check all the eggs in the carton for any cracks. Cracked eggs should not be used, even in cooking, because there is a greater chance that they may be contaminated by disease bacteria, particularly salmonella.

✑ Eggs must be graded before they are packed for sale. The grades refer only to the condition of the shell and the interior proportions of yolk to white. For instance, Grade AA or Fresh Fancy eggs have centered, firm, small yolks and thick whites, while Grade A eggs have less centered yolks and thinner whites. Where appearance is important, A or AA eggs are best for frying and poaching. However, Grade B eggs are quite adequate for cooking and baking.

NOTES

1. Gary Null with Steve Null, *The New Vegetarian*, New York: William Morrow and Company, Inc., 1978, p. 118.

2. *Ibid.*, p. 119.

3. *Diet and Coronary Heart Disease*, Report of the Advisory Panel of the Committee on Medical Aspects of Food Policy (Nutrition) on Diet in Relation to Cardiovascular Cerebrovascular Disease, Great Britain Department of Health, 1974, p. 18.

4. Null, *op. cit.*, pp. 120–121.

5. *Diet and Coronary Heart Disease, op cit.*, p. 18.

6. *Indian Journal of Nutrition and Dietetics*, Vol. 2, 1975.

7. George V. Mann, *Atherosclerosis*, Vol. 26, No. 3, 1977.

8. P.N. Durrington, *Lancet*, August 21, 1976, Great Britain.

9. Dr. Fisher, "Nutrition," *Diet and Cholesterol in Cardiovascular Disease*, Heart Disease Research Foundation, 1974.

Fruits, Nuts & Seeds

FRUITS, NUTS, AND SEEDS ARE TRADITIONALLY used to add color, texture, and their own distinctive flavors to accent the world of dessert cookery. More importantly, however, they can be used as the main ingredient in today's desserts. Continental desserts of fresh fruits and nuts, and simple but elegant fruit salads—these can be the perfect end to rich gourmet meals.

fruits ✌

The natural sweetness and high vitamin and mineral content of fruits make them excellent snack, breakfast, and dessert foods. Fruits are rich sources of vitamin C, and many are abundant in vitamin A. Although they are low in protein, fruits supply us with important trace minerals.

Another important constituent of fruits is fiber. This is the structural part of plants called cellulose, and it is essential to any good diet. In addition to its effects in controlling blood cholesterol, cellulose provides bulk and stimulates the peristaltic action of the intestines. This "roughage" cleans and tones the intestinal tract, preventing sluggish elimination.

Fruits also supply us with carbohydrates, which are the fuel of life. We get the majority of our calories from the sugars and starches in carbohydrates, some of which are used to build up the more complex compounds used in various metabolic processes. The American diet is high in carbohydrates, but many are not necessarily good for us. Fruits, however, are a wonderfully healthy way to incorporate the benefits of natural carbohydrates into our bodies. Nutritional information for individual fruits used in these recipes can be found in the following section, *The Natural Pantry*.

selecting fruit products ✌

There are several ways to liven up your diet with fruit. Fresh fruits are excellent for any time of day or evening. They are light, nutritious, and naturally sweet. Frozen fruits can be used in cooking and baking when certain fruits are out of season, and once thawed, some frozen fruits can be eaten as you would fresh fruit. Canned fruits and juices, provided they are unsweetened, are wonderful ways to bring fruit into the winter menu. Juices are also healthy thirst-quenchers for the summer. Dried fruits are best consumed during the winter when fresh fruits are less available or very costly. They can be mixed into hot or cold cereals, baked goods, puddings, or they may be stewed in water or juice.

FRESH FRUIT. Fresh, ripe fruit is the healthiest choice for desserts, whether eaten whole or sliced into fruit salad, since the nutritional content is not altered by cooking. Remember that unripened fruits have less vitamin content than tree or vine-ripened fruit. Also, vitamin losses occur when fruits are shipped long distances or stored for a time before they reach the market. For these reasons, it is wise to buy only fresh fruits in season, and preferably only those locally grown.

The food industry has developed various practices and treatments to prolong and enhance the attractiveness of fresh fruit. Some of these practices are harmless, but others may be or have been proved to be actually dangerous. The following practices apply to fresh fruit at various stages of its growth, ripening, and storage.

Ripening with Gas. Many fruits give off ethylene gas during the ripening process. This gas has a stimulating effect on the ripening of other fruits. For instance, bananas ripen faster when stored with apples. Therefore the food industry uses this gas to ripen fruits, such as bananas and tomatoes, which are picked unripe in order to withstand the time they must spend in transport. Since ethylene is a natural product of ripening, it is unlikely this would produce any harmful effects.

Mature fruits ripened with ethylene do not show significant nutritional differences from naturally ripened fruits. However, when immature green tomatoes are ripened in this way, their vitamin C content is only half as much as that of a naturally ripened fruit. Consumer Union reports that 80 percent of the tomatoes produced in Florida are picked green and reddened with ethylene gas, while

Mexican tomatoes are usually picked after the fruits have begun to ripen.[1]

Hormone Sprays. Hormone sprays are widely used to increase the size of fruit. Grapes, tomatoes, strawberries, blueberries, cranberries, apricots, peaches, pears, apples, guavas, and cherries are often subjected to this treatment.[2]

Gibrellic acid, one such spray, is used to increase the size of fruit. For example, Thompson seedless grapes sprayed with gibrellic acid increased in size by 28 percent.[3] Although it is found naturally in most seeds and fruits, a synthetic form is used as a hormone to induce faster growth. Sometimes fruit is labeled "gibbed" or "ungibbed" to indicate whether it has been treated. At this time, there has not been enough research to indicate whether this process causes health hazards.

The decrease in honeybees, due to increased use of pesticides, has led to the use of synthetic hormone sprays that allow the fruits to "set" even without pollination of the flowers. Research studies linking the sprays to birth defects have not yet prevented the widespread use of these harmful chemicals in the food industry.[4]

Pesticides. Another common practice in the food industry is the use of pesticides to insure the growth of larger food crops. The federal "safe" standards for the amount of allowable pesticide residues on produce are being questioned by scientists. They are concerned that not enough testing has been done to determine if current levels are really safe. Often government standards do not take into account that residues build up in the body over a period of time and may accumulate to unsafe proportions. Although pesticide residues are legally subject to checks, Ralph Nader's study group report on the Food and Drug Administration found that only 0.7 percent of the 2.5 million interstate produce shipments between 1963 and 1966 were inspected.[5] It follows that with such a loose inspection system we cannot be sure that no produce containing residues above the allowable limits reaches the markets and eventually, our tables.

Storage. All green plants growing under natural conditions in the sunshine take in carbon dioxide and give off oxygen. After harvest and during ripening, however, fruits reverse this process, breathing in oxygen and exhaling carbon dioxide. This biochemical change eventually causes the fruit to decay. Refrigeration slows down this process, but the change continues, only at a slower rate.

Fruit growers discovered that they could reduce breathing in cold storage by lowering the oxygen level and adding nitrogen to the atmosphere for some fruits and carbon dioxide for others. This procedure results in less ripening and decay, and since both gases are harmless, the storage of fruit in a controlled atmosphere seems to be generally quite safe. Most apples sold between November and August have been stored in this manner. Pears and strawberries are also often stored in a controlled atmosphere. Nutritionally, these fruits hold up better than those stored in plain air.

Another practice in the food industry to keep fruit looking better longer may not be as safe. Many fruits are coated with wax to reduce the wrinkling caused by water loss. Waxed fruit retains its flavor and texture longer than untreated fruit. Apples, oranges, tangerines, lemons, grapefruit, and cantaloupes are commonly waxed. Dr. Wilhelm C. Hueper, former director of the Environmental Cancer Section of the National Cancer Institute, claims these waxes may cause stomach cancer and that "consumers of food stuff coated with paraffins or waxes are at a risk."[6] Unfortunately, since federal regulations do not require waxed fruits to be labeled, it is difficult to tell if wax has been applied. Of course, fruits whose skins can be removed present no problem.

The safest, healthiest fruits you can buy are organic. This means that they are grown in soil fertilized by natural waste materials and without the aid of pesticides. Although these fruits may not be as large and blemish-free as those produced by agribusiness, organic fruit growers are endeavoring to farm in harmony with environmental ecology, and it is worth supporting them. If organic fruits are not available, take special care to wash all fresh fruit, but avoid soaking it in warm water since this practice leaches out nutrients.

FROZEN FRUITS. Frozen fruits have almost as many vitamins and minerals as fresh fruits. Fruits used in freezing are generally of higher quality than those used in canning, and they are picked ripe and frozen immediately. This insures that the fruits retain most of their nutrients, color, and flavor. However, their crisp texture is usually lost.

CANNED FRUIT. Canned fruits are subjected to long periods of heat during cooking, processing, and storage. This destroys much of the nutritional value, bright color, and live quality found in fresh fruits. If you find it necessary to buy canned fruit, choose fruits canned in their own juice. If *no* sucrose or corn syrup has been added, the fruits will still have a surprising amount of nutrients left. Avoid fruits packed in light, heavy, or extra-heavy syrup. The proportion of sugar to water varies in these syrups, but they all contain a high percentage of sugar to fruit.

FRUIT JUICES. I frequently use fruit juices as a liquid sweetener in my recipes. Fresh-squeezed orange juice is more nutritious than the frozen kind, and is recommended for gelatin recipes where no cooking is involved. Frozen and bottled juices are fine for desserts requiring cooking, but they should be 100 percent pure juice, with no added sweeteners or preservatives. Unfiltered juice is usually so labeled and is preferable to filtered juice because less of the fruit pulp is processed out, so it has a higher vitamin and mineral content. Shake unfiltered juice well before using to spread those vitamins and minerals around.

DRIED FRUITS. Dried fruits are high in iron and vitamins C and A. They are much sweeter than fresh fruits and are more suitable as natural sweeteners for snacks and desserts, and in breakfast cereals and breads. The high concentration of fruit sugar and the stickiness of these fruits can cause tooth decay, so brush teeth carefully after snacking on these foods.

Fruits dried naturally in the sun or in a dehydrator darken in color and become very hard. To make these fruits more attractive, most commercial fruit processors use sulfur compounds to lighten the color of apricots, golden seedless raisins, and some figs and peaches. Both sulfur dioxide and sulfite are used as color preservatives and must be revealed on the label. Although they have been tested and determined safe in the quantities used, more research is being done, and it may be advisable to avoid fruits dried with these additives.

Sorbic acid, or potassium sorbate, is used as a preservative in dried fruits that have been partially rehydrated to make them softer. At this time, it is considered a safe food additive and must also be shown on the label.

The process used to make "moist pack" dried fruits seems to be much safer and offers a more natural alternative to the consumer. In this process, dark-colored fruits, which contain no sulfur, are partially rehydrated and then pasteurized. Pasteurization eliminates the need for any preservatives and makes the fruit more palatable. You can easily rehydrate your own dried fruits at home by soaking them in warm water. The leftover, nutrient-rich water can be recycled into hot cereals, breads, etc.

nuts and seeds ✌

In addition to flours made from whole grains, seeds and nuts also play an important part in our desserts. Not only do they impart their own characteristic richness and flavor, but they also add a protein boost to desserts. The newest research from the Max Planck Institute (of nutrition) in Germany shows that soybeans, sesame seeds, pumpkin seeds, almonds, and peanuts each contain all the essential amino acids, making them complete proteins.[7] Other seeds, nuts, and grains, which are considered incomplete proteins because they lack one or more of the essential amino acids, can be combined with either eggs or milk to complete the protein. Therefore desserts containing seeds and nuts can provide us with both pleasing taste and body-building proteins.

Seeds and nuts also supply minerals and trace elements, such as magnesium, manganese, iron, zinc, copper, molybdenum, selenium, chromium, fluorine, silicon, potassium, and phosphorus. They are particularly abundant in vitamin E and the B complex vitamins. These nutrients are important in preventing premature aging and stress-related problems.[8]

Seeds, nuts, and grains are also excellent sources of the essential unsaturated fatty acids, linoleic and linolenic acids (called the "vitamin F factor"). These foods also contain pacifarins and auxones. Pacifarins are antibiotic substances that increase the body's natural resistance to disease, and auxones play a part in cell rejuvenation and in synthesizing vitamins within the body.[9]

Most important, seeds, nuts, and grains supply us with a good amount of lecithin, a natural substance that is very important to the maintenance of healthy nerves, brain tissue, and glands. Lecithin keeps fat moving freely through the blood without forming deposits on arterial walls. It also insures better use of vitamins A, D, and E and helps the body use calcium. Lecithin is an important factor in relieving stress. When a generous amount of lecithin is added to the diet over an extended period of time, it prevents fatigue caused by destruction of nerve sheaths, promotes greater energy in older people, reduces cholesterol level in the blood, improves resistance to pneumonia, and prevents artery and liver impairment.[10]

To get the best health benefits from seeds and nuts, they should be purchased raw and unsalted. They are a delicious addition to most desserts and they also go very well with fresh fruit. Alone or combined with dried fruits of all kinds, they make excellent snacks that can be packaged ahead of time and taken on hikes, to the movies, or to work or school.

VARIETIES OF NUTS AND SEEDS. The following is a list of various nuts and seeds which are delicious eaten raw or used in your dessert cookery. More specific nutritional information on many of these items is detailed in Part Two, *The Natural Pantry*.

Almonds. Although native to North Africa and western Asia, almonds are cultivated throughout the Mediterranean region. There are two kinds of almonds: bitter and sweet. Bitter almonds are inedible. Sweet almonds are the ones we use as food. The flour made from the nutmeats is high in protein and can be used by people who must restrict starch in their diet. Almond oil is used as an extract for flavorings. Because the almond skin contains tannic acid, some people believe the nuts should be eaten only after blanching. This is easily done by pouring boiling water over the nuts, soaking for about 10 minutes, and removing the skins.

Brazil Nuts. This South American nut is a favorite of Europeans and Americans (who import more than half the entire South American production). Brazil nut trees produce large woody nuts, which weigh two to four pounds and contain 12 to 25 hard seeds—the Brazil nut as we know it. The woody outer shell is used for cups and other utensils. The Brazil nut has a hard triangular shell. Inside, it is creamy white, with a rich, oily flavor.

Cashews. Cashew nuts grow on medium-sized trees native to the Central and South American tropics, but cashew production is greatest in India, Mozambique, and Tanzania. Cashews grow in a most curious manner. A single kidney-shaped, olive-colored nut hangs beneath a bright orange, pear-shaped fruit three times its size. The fruit is called a cashew apple and is usually not eaten. The nut shell has an oily substance so toxic and irritating that it must be burned off before one can touch it. The nut must then be boiled or roasted and a second shell removed before it can be eaten. Cashews are very rich: about 45 percent fat and 20 percent protein. They have a very sweet flavor when eaten raw, while roasting brings out a deeper, richer flavor.

Coconut. The coconut palm tree is native to Malaysia, southern Asia, and tropical South America. The coconut is a seed: the largest known to man. When the nut is still green, the inside is a white creamy substance that can be eaten with a spoon. When it ripens, the outside becomes brownish, harder, and woody, and the coconut meat is formed. There are many food elements in the brown skin, so this should be eaten too. To open a coconut: pierce the eyes (the three soft spots at the end of the shell) and drain out the milk. Then tap the nut all over with a hammer until the shell cracks. Coconut is best eaten fresh and shredded or grated into puddings or gelatins. Dried coconut shreds are used to flavor cookies and cakes.

Hazelnuts. Hazelnuts and filberts are so closely related that they are considered interchangeable. The hazel is a small tree. The nuts, like acorns, grow in little cups of a rich, medium-brown color, which came to be known as hazel. When the nuts are fully ripe, the husks turn brown and the nuts fall down and will rattle when shaken. They should be gathered only at this time. England, Turkey, and Spain are the leading producers of hazelnuts. American hazels grow mainly in Washington and Oregon but bear small nuts of little commercial value. Hazels are a very nutritious eating and baking nut.

Peanuts. Peanuts are really legumes, like peas, but are more often eaten as nuts than as vegetables. Peanuts are very nutritious; high in protein, iron, and vitamins. A pound of peanuts has the same or more body-building nutrients than a pound of sirloin, and twice as many calories. If you buy peanuts in the shell, after you eat the nuts, feed the shells to your house plants; they are a great soil enricher. Buy shelled or unshelled peanuts unsalted. The shelled nuts go rancid quickly, so it is best to purchase them in vacuum-packed tins. Buy 100 percent old-fashioned peanut butter, unsalted is preferable, with no sugar added.

Pecans. Pecan trees grow wild throughout the Mississippi Valley region and the river valleys of Texas. They were first cultivated in El Paso at the end of the seventeenth century, and the largest-producing cultivated areas are in the South. Pecans are now the first in economic importance of the native North American nut trees and the fifth leading tree nuts of the world. Most commercial varieties are olive- or oblong-shaped and have brown, polished shells (some are dyed red). The best quality pecans are thin-shelled and easy to crack. Pecans are delicious eaten raw, or baked in pies, breads, and candies.

Pine Nuts (Pignoli). These nuts have been harvested from pine trees in dry southern European countries since prehistoric times. The most popular edible seeds are those from the Mediterranean stone pine, which have been relished since the time of ancient Rome. The cones must be exposed to the sun to open the scales so that the seeds can be extracted. Pignoli are a luxury nut, mostly due to the difficulty of extracting the very small nuts. They are usually sold shelled, have a slight pine taste, and are very rich in texture. They are primarily used in cooking.

Pistachios. This nut originated in Syria and has grown in the Mediterranean region for at least 5000 years. The leading producers of the nuts today are Iran, Turkey, and India. Although there is some cultivation in California and Oregon, most pistachios are imported and for that reason they are expensive. The pistachio fruit is reddish and wrinkled, and inside is the hard, double-shelled, oval nut. Pistachios are naturally white, but are sold covered with a red, blue, or green dye. Natural, undyed pistachio nuts, plain or salted, can be obtained at some natural food or Middle Eastern specialty stores. Traditionally they are used to flavor ice cream, Indian halvah, and Turkish delight.

Poppy Seeds. These small slate-blue seeds have an agreeable nutty flavor and no narcotic properties. The use of poppy seeds as a condiment on bread spread to Europe from Asia Minor during the Middle Ages. Poppy seed is available as a condiment in whole form, to be used as a topping for rolls, breads, cookies, cakes, and baked goods and as a garnish. Toasting or baking the seeds brings out the pleasant nutty flavor and crunchy texture. The crushed seeds can be mixed with sweetening and used as a filling for pastries and coffee cakes.

Pumpkin Seeds. These large seeds are familiar to everyone who has carved a pumpkin. Spread them on a cookie sheet, bake them at 325°F for about 15 minutes, and you will have a bowlful of delicious seeds for the whole family to peel after dinner. They are rich in nutrients and are an excellent snack food. Ground pumpkin seed meal can be added to cereals, fruits, or desserts as a topping. They also make a nice addition to crumb toppings used for pies, apple betty, and so forth.

Sesame Seeds. These very small seeds come from the Middle East and India. Sesame seeds can be purchased hulled or unhulled. The unhulled seeds are usually brown, with a slightly bitter taste. The hulled seeds are white, delicate in flavor, and perishable. Sesame seeds are rich in nutrients, and the vitamin E content strengthens the nerves and heart. The oil of the seeds is wonderful in salad dressing and in cooking and baking. A popular way to use sesame seeds is to sprinkle them over rolls, breads, and cookies just before baking. After baking, the flavor resembles that of toasted almonds. Sesame seed meal can be made in a blender or grinder and used as a dessert topping, or in cakes, cookies, breads, and candies.

Sesame Tahini. This is the paste made from finely ground sesame seeds. It is very creamy, oily, and rich. Tahini makes an excellent spread for bread, and is a good butter substitute: it offers unsaturated fatty acids, vitamins, minerals, and plenty of protein. You can mix it with honey to make the Middle Eastern candy, halvah.

Sunflower Seeds. The white, brown, black, or black-and-white-striped seeds of the sunflower plant are really dried fruits. Sunflower seeds were supposedly introduced to Europe from the area of New Mexico by the Spanish in the beginning of the sixteenth century. It is said that sunflower seeds are chewed extensively by the Russians. Those who chew them are supposed to have excellent teeth, due to the seed's exceptionally high content of vitamin D, vitamin B complex, and vitamin E. They can also be used in cookies and breads. The seeds are highly perishable, so it is best to use them right away.

Walnuts. The most important species of walnut trees are the English and Eastern Black. English walnuts, also known as Persian walnuts, grow in many European countries and on the West Coast of the United States. Most commercial production of walnuts is from the English species. The hard-shelled oval or round nuts develop from catkins in clusters of three or four. Husks open in the fall and nuts drop to the ground. They should be picked immediately and dried in a single layer in a shaded, airy place. The rich and oily nut is used in candies, ice creams, and baked goods.

NOTES

1. Rodger P. Doyle and James L. Redding, *The Complete Food Handbook*, New York: Grove Press, Inc., 1976, p. 40.

2. *Ibid.*, p. 41.

3. *Ibid.*

4. *Ibid.*

5. Turner, James S., *The Chemical Feast: The Ralph Nader study group report of food protection and the Food and Drug Administration*, New York: Grossman, Publishers, 1970, pp. 145–146.

6. Doyle and Redding, *op. cit.*, p. 42.

7. Resolution #80, *International Society for Research on Diseases of Civilization and Environment*, Belgium.

8. Paavo Airola, *Hypoglycemia: A Better Approach*, Phoenix, Arizona: Health Plus, 1977, p. 82.

9. *Ibid.*, p. 83.

10. Edward E. Marsh, *How to be Healthy with Natural Foods*, New York: Arc Books, Inc., pp. 95–96.

Spices, Flavorings & Salt

the wharf   7/16/80

ONCE ALL THE MAJOR INGREDIENTS of a dessert are mixed together, a touch of the right spice or flavoring will add character and zest to the recipe, and turn a standard dessert into something unusual and unforgettable. Each person has their own preference for a particular spice or two, and many of us tend to use the same ones over and over. This chapter not only gives a little history, but also gives a list of dessert spices and their uses for those who wish to venture beyond the familiar into flavors yet unexplored.

spices ✌

The first records of the use of spices and herbs date back to ancient Egypt, around 2600 B.C. During this time, onions and garlic were used as medicinal aids to preserve the strength of the thousands of workers building the great Pyramid of Cheops. Later, spices became essential ingredients in the embalming process, which involved cleaning and rinsing the abdominal cavity with fragrant spices, such as cumin, anise, marjoram, cassia, and cinnamon, to preserve the body against decay. Spices and aromatic gums collected from desert shrubs were also used by the Egyptians as anointing oils and incense to banish evil spirits, unpleasant odors, insects, pests, and serpents from their homes and public buildings.

A medical papyrus discovered by the German Egyptologist George Ebers contains extensive information about Egyptian practices in internal medicine and surgery. This document, written around 550 B.C., lists more than 800 medicinal drugs, including many of the herbs and spices used commonly today, such as anise, caraway, cardamom, cassia, coriander, fennel, fenugreek, garlic, mustard, onions, poppy seed, saffron, sesame, and thyme.

Spices were also used in ancient China, Mesopotamia, and India. When Alexander the Great conquered the Persian Empire, the trade routes brought these exotic commodities to Greece. From Greece the use of spices spread westward to Rome and then, during the Dark Ages, northward throughout Europe, preserved like many things by hard-working Benedictine monks. Spices were used to flavor food and beverages, to disguise bad tastes and odors, to make food more palatable and to help preserve meats.

When the Crusades reopened the Eastern trade routes, European eating and cooking habits were changed forever.

In America, herbs and spices were used as healing medicinal drugs until the end of the nineteenth century. Today, however, they are used primarily to enhance the flavor of foods and beverages. The effect of spices on health is now being tested, but more research must be done before any sweeping conclusions can be reached. Some effects have been noted, however. For example, studies of the gastrointestinal effects of spices reveal that the pleasing aroma and flavor they impart to food can lead to increased salivary and gastric flow and hence better digestion. There is also evidence that bile flow, essential to proper fat digestion, is stimulated by certain essential oils, such as oil of caraway.[1] Most pure ground spices have an insignificant sodium content, making them valuable in low-sodium diets where they may be used to flavor food to compensate for the lack of salt. The exceptions are allspice, celery seed, dehydrated celery and parsley flakes, and whole mace.[2]

The high price of spices has led some large companies to develop a line of artificial spices, including pepper, ginger, cinnamon, and nutmeg.[3] These spices are made by combining extracts of the real spice with cereal solids, emulsifiers, and other ingredients. The strength, color, and aroma of artificial spices is scientifically controlled in order to produce the consistent characteristics required by commercial food processors, such as bakers and snack manufacturers. These spices have an amazingly natural appearance, but science cannot duplicate all the secondary food factors in spices that function harmoniously to create balanced nutrition.

DESSERT SPICES. The following is a list of the main dessert spices along with a description of their flavors and uses. More detailed information about their history, health benefits, and their nutritional tables is given in Part Two, *The Natural Pantry.*

Allspice. This native of the West Indies and Latin America received its name because its flavor resembles a combination of cinnamon, nutmeg, and cloves. The full-grown aromatic fruits are picked unripe and dried. Allspice berries are sold both whole or ground. Whole berries are used in meat broths, gravies, and pickling liquids. Ground allspice is delicious in fruitcakes, pies, relishes, and preserves.

Anise Seed. This graceful annual herb of the parsley family is indigenous to Asia Minor, the Greek Islands, and Egypt. It is the source of one of the oldest aromatic seedlike fruits. Anise seed and anise oil are characterized by a strong, licoricelike flavor and odor. Anise seed is available either whole or ground. The whole seed may be used as a flavoring for cookies, cakes, and candies. Eaten whole after a meal, the seeds freshen the breath and improve digestion.

Cardamom. This tall herbaceous perennial belongs to the ginger family and is indigenous to South India and Ceylon. The fruit is a small ovoid green capsule containing 15 to 20 hard, brownish-black, angular seeds. The spice may consist of the whole fruit or the hulled seeds. Throughout the Arab countries, cardamom is the most popular spice, where it is used to flavor the traditional Cardamom coffee. In Scandinavia, cardamom is used in baking pastries, buns, and other baked goods. In India, cardamom pods are chewed after meals to help digestion and sweeten the breath. Cardamom seeds are characterized by a powerful aromatic odor and flavor. Their flavor is sweet and pungent. Cardamom is available in the pod (green or bleached), as the seeds with the outer shell removed, or ground.

Cinnamon and Cassia. Cinnamon is obtained from the dried inner bark of a moderate-sized, bushy, everygreen tree of the laurel family. The inner light-colored bark curls as it dries, taking on the appearance of a quill. These quills, or sticks, are an important ingredient in pickling, and are used to flavor stewed prunes, spiced peaches, and hot beverages. It is popular in Mexico for the brewing of hot chocolate. True cinnamon powder is tan, with a delicate aroma.

Today, most of what we call cinnamon is actually Cassia. Cassia bark resembles true cinnamon bark but it is coarser and thicker, with a more intense aroma, a higher essential oil content, and a less delicate flavor than cinnamon. Cassia powder is reddish-brown. It has almost entirely replaced cinnamon as a spice in this country.

Both spices are important in baking. In ground form they are used to flavor cakes, breads, buns, cookies, and pies.

Cloves. The dried, nail-shaped flower buds of an evergreen tree in the myrtle family come from the Spice Islands. The clove tree is rich in essential oils. The stems, buds, and leaves produce these oils, which are used in perfumes for soaps, in toothpastes and mouthwashes, and in medicine to aid digestion and relieve toothache.

Cloves are characterized by their strong, pungent, sweet flavor. In England cloves are mixed with apples in apple tarts; in France cloves and onions are basic ingredients for soup stock; in the United States cloves are used for studding ham and pork. Whole cloves are also added to both pickled fruits and sweet syrups. Ground cloves are popular in chocolate pudding, fruitcakes, and pies.

Coriander. This was one of the first herbs grown in America by the colonists, who introduced it to Massachusetts before 1670. Coriander seeds are globular, almost round, and brown to yellowish-red, with alternating straight and wavy ridges. The seed's essential oil is used today in perfumes, candy, cocoa, chocolate, baked goods, and liqueurs. Coriander seeds have become a favorite flavoring and food additive in many Latin American countries, especially Peru.

Coriander has a warm, distinctive, fragrant odor. Its pleasant taste is mild and sweet yet slightly pungent, somewhat reminiscent of a combination of sage and lemon. It can be obtained whole or ground. The whole seed is used in mixed pickling spice, while the ground form is used to flavor pastries, cookies, and buns.

Fennel. Common "garden fennel" is a tall, hardy, aromatic perennial of the parsley family, whose dried fruit is the spice fennel "seed." Fennel is closely related to dill, but is more aromatic, sweeter-smelling, and less pungent than dill seed. Dried fennel seeds are oval, greenish- or yellowish-brown in color, and resemble tiny watermelons. They emit an agreeable, warm, sweet odor, somewhat similar to that of anise. The seeds, available whole and ground, are used mainly to flavor bread, pastries, candies, and sweet pickles.

Ginger. This is the root of tropical plant grown in many hot countries. The root looks like a swollen fist and is called a "hand" of ginger.

Fresh ginger, available in most markets, can be peeled, minced, and added to cakes and breads. The dried root can be ground in a coffee mill just before using. The ground ginger bought in stores has lost some of its lovely aroma, so if you can grind your own, you are in for a treat. Ginger is used to flavor bread, cakes, puddings, pies, pickles, and syrups.

Mace. The nutmeg tree is indigenous to the Moluccas and other islands of the East Indian Archipelago. It produces two different spices: mace and nutmeg. When the fleshy fruit of the tree is ripe, it splits in half, exposing a scarlet membrane known as mace. The fragile, strongly aromatic, netlike membrane wraps around the nutmeg seed. When dried, mace is yellowish-brown in color. It has a sweet, warm, highly spicy flavor. Whole mace, known as "blades of mace," is not usually found in retail stores, but ground mace is readily available. Ground mace has an orange hue. It is a mild baking spice used to flavor pound cakes and donuts.

Nutmeg. The glossy brown, oval oily seeds of the nutmeg tree produce an essential oil used in baked goods, table sauces, confectionary, dentifrices, perfumes, and cosmetics. The flavor of nutmeg is warm and highly spicy, and in general tends to be sweeter and more delicate in aroma than mace. Nutmeg is available whole or ground. Fresh ground nutmeg is a treat on fruits, yogurt, and coffee drinks. Nutmeg is used to flavor eggnog, puddings, and fruit pies.

Star Anise. This small evergreen tree is native to southwestern China, and is entirely different from anise. However, the fruits of both plants contain essential oils of similar chemical composition and they taste very much alike, although star anise is harsher in aroma. In the Orient, the seeds are chewed after meals to promote digestion and sweeten the breath. Star anise is grown almost entirely in People's Republic of China.

flavorings ✺

In addition to spices, flavorings such as peppermint, anise, almond, lemon, and vanilla add interest to desserts. Vanilla is the most common flavoring, and like other extracts it is quite expensive.

Vanillin, the crystalline component of vanilla, was isolated as early as 1858. Because of shortages in the supply of vanilla beans and the cost of the pure extract, manufacturers have begun to produce artificial vanillin from lignin (in wood pulp), waste paper pulp, oil of sassafras, and coal tar.[4] In addition to the potential carcinogenic nature of these sources, artificial vanillin lacks the spicy flavor and delicate aroma of the pure extract from the vanilla bean and has a harsh odor and bitter aftertaste.

Since flavorings are used in such small quantities and only in special desserts, pure, natural extracts are worth the extra money they may cost. Flavorings are food, and we are best off when buying the natural, pure product.

salt ✒

In ancient times, salt was highly regarded both as a food and as a medicine. In these early cultures, diet and climate were the main influences on the amount of salt people consumed. Meat-eating nomadic tribes often had strict taboos against eating salt, because their animal diet provided them with plenty. However, vegetarian agrarian societies valued salt as an important part of their diet. In some of the oldest cultures, the sharing of salt was a token of friendship. In general, people living in colder climates consumed more salt, while those living in warmer climates used very little.

HEALTH CONSIDERATIONS. Today salt is used primarily to enhance the flavor of foods, but now there is much concern about its overuse. It has been linked with a variety of diseases, particularly heart disease. As a general rule, there are several good reasons why most people should use salt in moderation. Overconsumption of salt constricts the blood vessels, which makes the heart work harder to pump blood through its tightened capillaries and reduces circulation, thus lowering body temperature. Furthermore, salt dehydrates the blood cells and vessels, which causes shrinkage of the tissues. Finally, when the kidneys become clogged with salt, one may suffer lower backache, bags under the eyes, and a general bloated look.[5] However, salt in moderate amounts is necessary to allow the blood vessels to contract sufficiently to maintain body warmth and good intestinal muscle tone.

All salt originally came from the sea. When shifts in the earth's crust over 300 million years ago buried part of the sea, inland salt deposits were formed, such as those in Detroit. Over time, rainfall leached some of the trace minerals back out to sea. About 75 percent of salt is sodium chloride, and 25 percent consists of fairly large amounts of the minerals calcium, magnesium, carbon, sulfur, and potassium. Sea salt also has more than 30 trace elements.[6]

Today, 60 percent of America's salt comes from salt springs. These are places where underground fresh water washes over underground salt deposits, bringing the brine to the surface. Salt springs produce salt much more economically than do the sea salt factories, which account for only 14 percent of the salt manufactured. The remaining 26 percent of our salt comes from inland salt mines in Texas, Louisiana, and Detroit.[7]

REFINING AND PACKAGING. Although salt from all of these sources provides varying degrees of trace elements, most of this salt first goes to refining plants before reaching our tables. During the refining process, the salt crystals are made into uniformly fine crystals by heating them to 1200°F. This is followed by flash cooling. After refining, the resulting table salt is 99.9 percent sodium chloride. Depending on the brand, additives are combined with the salt to enhance its nutritional value and usability. For example, since most foods lack iodine, essential for the formation of thyroid hormones, iodine is added to salt in the form of potassium iodide. Natural salts do not have iodine, but iodized table salt may not either. As much as ⅓ of the potassium iodide may be lost within six weeks because the cardboard containers used in packaging are not very effective in keeping this volatile substance fresh. Since potassium iodide is very volatile, dextrose is added to prevent it from oxidizing when exposed to light. Since this combination of chemicals turns the salt purple, sodium bicarbonate must then be mixed in to bleach out the color. Finally, because the calcium and magnesium in salt attract water, causing it to cake, sodium silico aluminate is added to coat the salt crystals and make it pour easily.[8] Not only do you get several chemicals with your refined salt, but there are no minerals left. The added iodine may not even be intact. For these reasons, it is best to leave refined iodized salt out of the diet.

RECOMMENDATIONS. I recommend using natural salts for both baking and table use. These salts have larger crystals, and still retain some of their original trace minerals, because they are either sun-dried or kiln-dried under mild temperatures. Kosher salt is also an acceptable salt: its larger crystals are formed by a milder process than refined table salt, and some brands contain no additives. These salts have no chemicals to keep them "free-flowing," but a little rice added to your salt shaker will help absorb moisture. There is even a plus to this drawback. Since natural salt is harder to pour, there is less danger of pouring too much!

For persons interested in supplementing their iodine intake, there is another way to get iodine into the diet. Sea vegetables contain 4 to 8 percent salt, and plenty of iodine. The natural, complex sugars stored in the plant leaves stabilize the iodine after the seaweed is harvested and until it is eaten. Powdered sea kelp is probably the most practical way to use sea vegetables. Kelp can be stored in a salt shaker and used with meals. It has an unusual, pleasant flavor and provides iodine and other trace minerals. You can find sea salt and kelp at most health food stores.

NOTES

1. Frederic Rosengarten, Jr., *The Book of Spices*, Wynnewood, Pennsylvania: Livingston Publishing Company, 1969, p. 6.

2. *Ibid.*

3. *Ibid.*, p. 7.

4. *Ibid.*, p. 461.

5. Gary Null with Steve Null, *The New Vegetarian*, New York: William Morrow and Company, Inc., 1978, p. 199.

6. Jerome Irving Rodale, *The Complete Book of Food and Nutrition*, Emmaus, Pennsylvania: Rodale Books, Inc., 1967, p. 306.

7. "Salt: Walking the Briny Line," Talking Food Company, Charlestown, Massachusetts, 02129, Box 81, 1976.

8. *Ibid.*

The barren branches may appear inelegant:
They are, to the cook, the means to
make his fire.
   —Anwar-i-Suhaili

Sand Dunes   7/18/80

The Natural Pantry

The following section gives specific information on how to shop for natural food ingredients. The glossary lists all the foods used in the recipes. You will find the ingredients easy to find in most grocery stores. Some of the dry goods are best purchased in health food stores where more varieties and less-refined products are sold. I hope a little history and information about health-giving benefits, shopping, and nutrition will inspire you to bring these foods into your pantry on a regular basis.

In all cases where the nutritional information was available, a table has been compiled for the foods listed in this section. The following abbreviations are used in the chart: mg = milligrams, mcg = micrograms, g = grams, iu = international unit (the standard measurement for the oil-soluble vitamins A, D, and E).

In the nutritional information tables, a zero indicates the particular food does not contain any of the particular nutritive element listed. A dash indicates there may be some value present but it could not be measured.

Shopping for Natural Foods

MOST OF THE FOODS USED IN THESE RECIPES can be purchased at your supermarket. The next time you are shopping take along the following list, and become familiar with the location of these foods. If some of them are not supplied by your market, talk to the manager and ask about the possibility of stocking them. I have found these people to be very cooperative and willing to help. They also seem to appreciate customer feedback. Here are the basics of a well-stocked natural pantry, the beautiful "colors" you have to work with to mix up delicious, healthy desserts.*

Supermarket List

Fresh fruits
  apples
  oranges
  bananas
  lemons
  seasonal fruits such
     as peaches, pineapple,
     cherries, melons

Dried Fruits
  raisins
  dates
  figs
  currants

Fruit juices
  frozen juice con-
     centrates, such as
     apple and orange
  canned or bottled
     fruit juices, un-
     sweetened

Dairy products
  low-fat milk
  low-fat yogurt
  2% cottage cheese
  noninstant skim
     milk powder
  sweet cream butter
  eggs

Sweeteners
  100% pure honey
  100% pure maple syrup
  unsulfured molasses

Spices
  cinnamon, powdered
  coriander, ground
  cardamom, ground
  allspice, ground
  nutmeg, ground
  anise seed, ground or whole
  fennel seed, ground or whole
  cloves, whole and ground
  ginger, fresh and ground
  pure vanilla extract
  pure peppermint extract
  sea salt

Flours and grains
  whole wheat flour
  whole wheat pastry
     flour
  cornmeal
  wheat germ, vacuum-packed
  wheat bran
  brown rice
  rolled oats
  soy flour
  soy milk powder

* *The Natural Foods Primer,* selected sections from "Help! Now What", © 1972 by Beatrice Trum Hunter. Reprinted by permission of Simon & Schuster, Inc.

Supermarket List (continued)

Nuts and seeds
   vacuum-packed nuts,
      raw and unsalted
   fresh coconut
   sunflower seeds
   sesame seeds
   peanut butter, un-
      sweetened

Oils
   safflower oil, unrefined
   sesame oil, unrefined

As you will see, most of these foods can be found in your produce department or where you find dairy products, eggs, and baking supplies. Occasionally you may want to use canned fruit, such as pineapple chunks. Please check the labels and make certain your selection is unsweetened, packed in water or its own juice. The same is true for canned or frozen fruit juices. Choose only 100 percent real juice with no sugar added.

If you enjoy a little experimenting and wish to try new flavors, then a trip to your local health food store will expose you to products you won't be able to find in most supermarkets. The following is a list for the health food store:

Health Food Store List

Flours
   millet flour
   oat flour
   barley flour
   soy milk powder

Sweeteners
   sorghum
   malt syrup
   date sugar
   rice syrup

Juices, bottled
   boysenberry
   cherry cider
   papaya

Oils
   safflower, unrefined
   sesame, unrefined
   sunflower, unrefined

Miscellaneous
   agar-agar flakes or sticks
   noninstant whole or
      skim milk powder
   carob powder, toasted and
      unsweetened
   arrowroot powder

If you don't have a health food store, go to an independently owned market where you shop and are known. If the market doesn't carry some of the items, make a list. Speak with the owner about the possibility of stocking the items on your list that have a long shelf life and might also be purchased by others. Good items to start with are vacuum-packed wheat germ or sunflower seeds, unsweetened coconut shreds, herb teas, raw honey, carob powder, or arrowroot powder.

The following list of measure equivalents is included to help you in estimating your shopping needs.

Measure Equivalents

One pound of food	*Yield in cups*
Almonds, shelled	3½
Apricots, dried	3½
Brazil nuts, shelled	3
Butter	2
Cashews, shelled	3½
Cottage cheese	2
Natural hard cheese, grated	4
Corn flour	3–4
Cornmeal	3
Coconut, dried, shredded	4
Date sugar	2¼
Dates, pitted	2
Dates, whole	2½
Honey	1½
Figs, cut up	2⅔
Filberts, shelled	3½
Graham flour	3¾
Maple syrup	2
Molasses	1½
Oat flour	4½
Peaches, dried	3
Peanut butter	1¾
Peanuts, shelled	3
Pecans, shelled	3
Prunes, dried	2½
Raisins, dried	2½–3
Rice polishings	2

Measure Equivalents (continued)

Rye flour	6
Sesame seeds, whole	3
Soy flour	4
Sunflower seeds, whole	4
Vegetable oil	2¼
Walnuts, shelled	4
Wheat germ	4
Whole wheat flour	3½

how to store natural foods

Now that you have located the foods on your list, you need to store them carefully to preserve their nutritional value. If you have a good-sized freezer, you can use it to store some flours and extra butter bought on sale.

DRY GOODS. Set aside room in a cupboard especially for your flours, grains, nuts, seeds, and powders. If you are fortunate enough to have a pantry, this is ideal. Whatever space you choose, it should be dry and cool.

Clean, used mayonnaise jars are suitable containers for storing small quantities of dry goods. However, don't use the old lids. Use canning lids with rubber seals to make a more air-tight fit. Label the jars of flours and powders carefully, because they are sometimes hard to tell apart.

If you have bought more than a jarful of flour, pack the rest in small plastic bags, remove as much air as possible, seal well, label properly, and store in the freezer. This is important because it is hard to detect rancidity in flours (usually there is no noticeable smell or taste). The best procedure is to buy in small quantities and use right away, or store in the freezer as directed above.

DRIED FRUITS. Dried fruits that have not been treated with sulfurdioxide or fumigants are perishable and should be stored in the refrigerator. This is especially true in hot, humid weather when the fruit is susceptible to mold. If you do not have refrigerator space for your dried fruits, then buy in small quantities and store in air-tight containers in a cool, dry place.

Dried fruits have a high percentage of natural sugar, which helps to preserve them for long periods as long as they are kept cool. Occasionally these natural sugars will appear on the surface of the fruit as small, granular deposits. If this happens, the fruit has not spoiled, and can still be eaten. If the fruit has become especially dry and hard, it can be rehydrated by soaking in water.

NUTS AND SEEDS. Nuts have a long shelf life if they are left in the shell and stored in a cool, dry place in air-tight containers. If you are like me and don't like to shell nuts as you need them, purchase shelled nuts bagged or vacuum-packed, raw and unsalted.

If you want to roast nuts lightly, do this just before using them, since roasted nuts go rancid quickly. Once the container of nuts is opened, it is best to store them in the refrigerator or freezer.

Sunflower and pumpkin seeds are sold hulled in bags or vacuum-packed tins. Give them the same care as you would nuts.

Sesame seeds can be purchased hulled or unhulled. Unhulled seeds have a longer shelf life, but are more bitter than hulled sesame seeds. Both kinds should be stored in the refrigerator, but especially the hulled seeds, which have a shorter shelf life and should be used right away.

FRESH PRODUCE. Fruits and vegetables should be stored in the refrigerator to ensure crispness and freshness. Do not wash fruits until you are ready to use them, because they spoil quickly after contact with water. Berries, peaches, nectarines, and grapes are highly perishable and should be eaten within a couple of days.

Oranges and lemons retain their vitamin C content even when not refrigerated. However, once they are squeezed, the juice should be used right away.

Bananas, avocados, pears, and mangoes are best stored at room temperature. They will ripen faster in closed paper bags. Melons should also be ripened at room temperature.

EGGS. Fresh eggs should be refrigerated immediately because they are very perishable. They lose their flavor more quickly at room temperature, and moisture, bacteria, and molds may pass through the porous eggshell. It is also best to wash eggs, if you wish, just before using.

FRESH DAIRY PRODUCTS. Milk, butter, cream, and cheese should be refrigerated at 40°F to protect their flavor and food values. Cottage cheese and ricotta are the most perishable and should be stored with tight-fitting lids in the coldest part of the refrigerator. All fresh dairy foods should be tightly wrapped to prevent them from absorbing the flavors of other stored foods. Storage containers should not allow light inside because exposure to light decreases the riboflavin in milk.

Sweet butter is more perishable than salted butter so I store it in the freezer and remove a cube or two as I need it. Otherwise, butter should be stored in the coldest part of the refrigerator to ensure its flavor and freshness.

VEGETABLE OILS. It is best to buy crude, pressed oils in dark bottles or tins. If they are in clear glass, store them unopened in a cool, dark cupboard. Once opened, store them in the refrigerator in a dark bottle with a tight-fitting cap.

NATURAL SWEETENERS. Honey and molasses have a long shelf life even at room temperature after the jars have been opened. Honey tends to crystallize in a cold room, but this can be remedied by placing the honey jar in a pan of warm water and heating it slowly over low heat.

Maple syrup, once opened, will eventually spoil, so keep it refrigerated. If mold does form on the top, you can skim it off and the flavor of the remaining syrup will not be affected.

Store date sugar in an air-tight jar. To prevent it from drying out, place a piece of bread or apple in the container.

MISCELLANEOUS FOODS. Nonfat dry milk powder is very perishable. Even a small amount of moisture in an opened package can double the bacteria count. Store it in an air-tight jar and keep it refrigerated, or in a cool place. Plan on using it within a reasonable time.

Old-fashioned peanut butter should be refrigerated after opening to prevent the oil from going rancid. The oil may separate from the peanut butter, so you may have to stir it into the spread when you use it.

Carob powder, agar-agar, arrowroot powder, and vinegar do not have any special storage requirements. They may be kept in their original containers and stored in a cool cupboard.

A Glossary of Recipe Ingredients

AGAR-AGAR

This colorless and tasteless sea vegetable, also called *Kanten* in Japanese, is used as a jelling agent instead of gelatin or pectin. It can be bought in sticks, flakes, or powder. It is an excellent relief for constipation, because it absorbs moisture throughout the intestinal tract, provides bulk and lubrication, and increases peristaltic action. Recommended proportions: 3½ cups liquid (juice) to 2 tablespoons flakes (or 1 tablespoon granulated).

ALMONDS

The seed or nut of the almond tree fruit. A valuable food since Biblical times, the tree originally was a native of the eastern Mediterranean. The high fat, carbohydrate, and protein content make almonds and almond butter excellent muscle and body builders.

The calcium content is also valuable for teeth and bones. Almond oil was one of the earliest cosmetic aids, and is still a popular ingredient for face creams.

NUTRITIONAL INFORMATION

1 c. almonds, raw			
Calories	849	Pantothenic	
Carbohydrate g	27.7	acid mg	.668
Protein g	26.4	Vitamin C mg	t
Fiber g	3.85	Vitamin E iu	21.3
Saturated fat g	6.2	Sodium mg	6
Unsaturated fat g	67	Phosphorus mg	716
Vitamin A iu	0	Potassium mg	1098
Vitamin B$_1$ mg	.34	Calcium mg	332
Vitamin B$_2$ mg	1.31	Iron mg	6.7
Vitamin B$_3$ mg	5	Magnesium mg	386
Vitamin B$_6$ mg	.142	Copper mg	1.18
Vitamin B$_{12}$ mcg	0	Manganese mg	2.7
Biotin mcg	25	Selenium mg	2.8
Folic acid mg	.136	Zinc mg	—

ALLSPICE

A small purple berry that grows on a tree native to the West Indies. The berries are dried in the sun until they turn brown. Tastes like a mixture of cinnamon, nutmeg, and cloves. Mayan Indians used allspice berries to embalm bodies of important leaders. From the seventeenth through the nineteenth centuries the berries were used aboard ships to preserve meat during long voyages. Allspice berries are sold both whole or ground. Whole berries are used in pickling liquids. Ground allspice is used in flavoring cakes, pies, relishes, and preserves and in the preparation of sweet yellow vegetables.

NUTRITIONAL INFORMATION

1 t. ground allspice

Calories	5	Pantothenic	
Carbohydrate g	1.37	acid mg	—
Protein g	.12	Vitamin C mg	.75
Fiber g	.41	Vitamin E iu	—
Saturated fat g	.05	Sodium mg	1
Unsaturated fat g	.05	Phosphorus mg	2
Vitamin A iu	10	Potassium mg	20
Vitamin B_1 mg	.002	Calcium mg	13
Vitamin B_2 mg	.001	Iron mg	.13
Vitamin B_3 mg	.054	Magnesium mg	3
Vitamin B_6 mg	—	Copper mg	*
Vitamin B_{12} mcg	—	Manganese mg	*
Biotin mcg	—	Selenium mg	.06
Folic acid mg	—	Zinc mg	.02

*Present but value in mg unavailable

APPLES

Apples probably originated near the Caspian and Black seas in Southwest Asia. By the Stone Age, apples had already spread throughout Europe, and they were brought to America by the European colonists. I will list only a few of the more than 7000 varieties.

Red Delicious. The best eating apple. Grown in the states of Washington, Michigan, New York, and California. Crisp, somewhat tart, and red with five bumps on the bottom. They are fresh in September and October but are held in storage into May and June.

Golden Delicious. Yellow, sweet, and juicy, all-purpose. Excellent for fruit salads because the flesh doesn't brown as quickly as other varieties. Grown mainly in Washington, Illinois, and Virginia.

Rome Beauty. Bright red, medium to extra large. Good for baking. Fresh from September through November, but can be held in storage until June.

Jonathan. All-purpose, small to medium, bright apple. Grown in Michigan, Washington, and Illinois. Color ranges from red stripes over yellow or deep red to purple. Fresh in September and October but may be stored until May.

Winesap. Firm, crisp, juicy, tart eating apple. Also good for sauces and pies. Grown mainly in Washington and Virginia. Color is bright deep red with random areas turning to purple. Fresh from mid-September through mid-November. Available from storage until the end of June.

Gravenstein. Good eating apples. Mostly grown in Sonoma County, California. Medium large apple with yellow-green skin and red stripes. The early apples are green and are good for sauces and pies. Fresh in July, available through mid-September.

Newton Pippin. Firm, crisp apple grown mostly in California and Oregon. They are excellent for baking and pies when color is yellow-green. When yellow, they are best as an eating apple. Fresh in late September, but available until June.

McIntosh. All-purpose apple ranging in color from yellow green to red with light stripes of red to deep purple. Very juicy with firm skin. Best as an eating apple, and also good for sauces, pies, and baking. Needs less cooking time than other baking varieties. Grown in New York, New England and Michigan. Fresh from early September through October, but available until June.

Studies indicate that "an apple a day" will reduce skin disease, arthritis, and various lung problems. The pectin in apple peels reduces blood cholesterol and prevents protein matter in the intestines from spoiling. The malic and tartaric acids in apples help prevent liver disturbances, while the large variety of minerals and vitamins strengthens the blood.

NUTRITIONAL INFORMATION

	1 med., fresh	1 c. dried	1 c. unsweet- ened juice		1 med., fresh	1 c. dried	1 c. unsweet- ened juice
Calories	96	234	117	Pantothenic			
Carbohydrate g	24	61	29.5	acid mg	.19	—	.05
Protein g	.3	.9	.2	Vitamin C mg	7	9	2
Fiber g	1.8	2.6	.26	Vitamin E iu	1.33	—	—
Saturated fat g	—	—	—	Sodium mg	2	4	2
Unsaturated fat g	—	—	—	Phosphorus mg	17	44	22
Vitamin A iu	150	—	—	Potassium mg	182	484	250
Vitamin B$_1$ mg	.05	.05	.02	Calcium mg	12	26	15
Vitamin B$_2$ mg	.03	.1	.05	Iron mg	.5	1.4	1.5
Vitamin B$_3$ mg	.2	.4	.2	Magnesium mg	14.4	18.7	10
Vitamin B$_6$ mg	.05	.115	.075	Copper mg	.16	.2	.5
Vitamin B$_{12}$ mcg	0	0	0	Manganese mg	.126	—	—
Biotin mcg	1.8	—	1.2	Selenium mg	.9	—	—
Folic acid mg	.014	—	.002	Zinc mg	.09	—	—

APPLE CIDER VINEGAR

Vinegar was used by Stone-Age men who found it useful for preserving herbs, foods, and hides. It also made meat tender and killed germs. Apple cider vinegar has healing properties and has been used as a folk medicine and in naturopathic medicine to heal a wide variety of illnesses. Dr. D.C. Jarvis, in his book *Folk Medicine*, describes how he used apple cider vinegar to treat people suffering from arthritis, skin complaints, overweight, dizziness, and food poisoning. It is believed that the vinegar helps maintain the balance between acids and alkalis in the body.

There are many varieties of apple cider vinegar ranging in color from light yellow to amber brown. This variance in color is caused by differences in production methods. Some companies even add a small amount of burnt sugar caramel to make the vinegar brown. Always buy cider vinegar with a label stating clearly that it was made from the whole apple.

Cider vinegar is very rich in potassium, which is essential for a healthy nervous system, and is also high in phosphorus and calcium. It also contains small amounts of iron, chlorine, sodium, magnesium, sulfur, fluoride, silicon, and other trace minerals.

APRICOTS

The Chinese were probably the first to cultivate apricot trees over 4000 years ago. They were successfully introduced to the West in the late 1700s by Spanish missionaries. Today California produces 90 percent of the apricots grown in the United States.

Apricot season starts in mid-May and goes through August. Buy them when their color is golden yellow with a red overtone and velvety skin. The riper they are, the better the flavor.

The high potassium content in apricots helps keep heart muscles healthy, while iron and other minerals make apricots an excellent food to help people with anemia, tuberculosis, asthma, bronchitis, toxemia or blood impurities. Although high in natural sugars, they are fairly low in calories, which makes them a good dietary addition for weight-watchers.

NUTRITIONAL INFORMATION

	3 med., fresh	3 med., dried		3 med., fresh	3 med., dried
Calories	55	338	Pantothenic		
Carbohydrate g	13.7	86.5	acid mg	.26	.98
Protein g	1.1	6.5	Vitamin C mg	11	16
Fiber g	.7	3.9	Vitamin E iu	—	—
Saturated fat g	—	—	Sodium mg	1	34
Unsaturated fat g	—	—	Phosphorus mg	25	140
Vitamin A iu	2890	14.170	Potassium mg	301	1273
Vitamin B_1 mg	.03	.01	Calcium mg	18	87
Vitamin B_2 mg	.04	.21	Iron mg	.5	7.2
Vitamin B_3 mg	.6	4.3	Magnesium mg	13.7	806
Vitamin B_6 mg	.077	.22	Copper mg	.12	.455
Vitamin B_{12} mcg	0	0	Manganese mg	.2	.36
Biotin mcg	—	—	Selenium mg	—	—
Folic acid mg	.003	.018	Zinc mg	—	—

ARROWROOT

Arrowroot is a less refined thickener made from the starch of a root grown primarily on Saint Vincent Island in the West Indies. It is a fine powder that should be mixed in a little cold water to prevent lumping when added to cooking liquids. To substitute arrowroot for cornstarch, use 1½ tablespoons arrowroot to 1 tablespoon cornstarch. To substitute for flour, use 1½ teaspoons arrowroot to 1 tablespoon flour.

AVOCADOS

The avocado is a native fruit of Mexico and Central America. Cultivation of avocados began in Hawaii in the 1820s and at the beginning of the twentieth century in California and Florida. The great freeze of 1913 wiped out more than 100 varieties planted on California ranches. The one surviving was given the name Fuerte, meaning strength in Spanish.

Fuerte. This is a pear shaped avocado with a thin greenish skin stippled with yellow. This winter fruit is at its peak in January.

Bacon. Another winter variety, this large avocado has a full ovoid shape and fairly thin green skin. The flavor is rich and reminiscent of eggs.

Hass. This is the main summer variety. It is easily identified by its thick, rough, leathery skin, which is green when unripe and then turns black. It is available from June through late summer.

Buy fruit with a full neck, showing it was allowed to mature on the tree. If you select hard fruit, it will ripen at home in a few days on top of your refrigerator where it is an even warm temperature. To speed up the ripening, place the avocado in a paper bag or wrap in tin foil to confine the gases from the fruit, which help to ripen it.

Avocados take nine months to mature. They contain up to 30 percent of their weight in oil. They are also very high in protein and are chemically more like a nut than a fruit. Avocados can be used as a fruit or a vegetable. In our recipes, we find them a tasty addition to fruit salads and jellos.

NUTRITIONAL INFORMATION

1 med. avocado, raw

Calories	334	Pantothenic	
Carbohydrate g	12.6	acid mg	2.14
Protein g	4.2	Vitamin C mg	28
Fiber g	3.2	Vitamin E iu	—
Saturated fat g	—	Sodium mg	8
Unsaturated fat g	—	Phosphorus mg	84
Vitamin A iu	580	Potassium mg	1208
Vitamin B$_1$ mg	.22	Calcium mg	20
Vitamin B$_2$ mg	.4	Iron mg	1.2
Vitamin B$_3$ mg	3.2	Magnesium mg	90
Vitamin B$_6$ mg	.84	Copper mg	.8
Vitamin B$_{12}$ mcg	0	Manganese mg	4
Biotin mcg	—	Selenium mg	—
Folic acid mg	.102	Zinc mg	.7

BAKING POWDER

Made by combining baking soda and an acid ingredient, such as tartaric acid or tartaric acid with cream of tartar. When a batter containing baking powder is moistened, the soda and acid interact, releasing bubbles of carbon dioxide gas, that are sealed in by the heat. These small air pockets give lightness to quick breads, muffins, cakes, and cookies. They contain sodium aluminum and calcium acid phosphate. Ratio of baking powder is 1 teaspoon to 1 cup flour. Adding more baking powder would increase the loss of thiamin, a B vitamin. I recommend buying the fast-acting powders, or using our *Homemade Baking Powder* recipe if you wish to reduce salt intake. This recipe is in the *Toppings & Fillings* chapter.

BAKING SODA

Soda bicarbonate produces carbon dioxide gas when mixed and heated with acid substances such as vinegar, fruit, or buttermilk, this helps make light cakes, cookies, quick breads, and muffins. However, the alkali in baking soda destroys some of the B vitamins in the milk and flour. We can compensate for these losses by adding extra milk solids (dried whole or skim milk powder), yeast, or wheat germ to baked goods. If you wish to cut down on salt intake, I recommend our recipe for *Homemade Baking Soda* in the *Toppings & Fillings* chapter.

BANANAS

The tropical banana plant originated in Southeast Asia. Its botanical name, meaning "fruit of the wise men," was given to it because Indian gurus reportedly sat under the shade of banana plants while they meditated. The plants were introduced to the Canary Islands in the early 1400s and soon spread to the Caribbean Islands and Mexico.

Bananas are available year-round. They are picked green to withstand handling during shipping. Unlike other fruits this doesn't affect their flavor.

It is best to buy bananas in "green-tip" condition. This means the body of the banana is yellow but the tip is green. These will ripen at home in 2 to 3 days. After it is ripe, a banana can be refrigerated for several days. Even if the skin darkens, it will still be fine for eating. Bananas are best eaten when the yellow skin becomes flecked with brown spots. These flecks indicate the fruit sugar has fully developed and the fruit will taste sweet.

Avoid bruised fruit and fruit with dull, cloudy or smokey skin. Such fruit has probably suffered cold damage, and the ripening process won't continue.

Plantains are sometimes available in local markets. These bananas are larger than regular bananas and are a staple food in the tropics. When green, they are starchy and can be used in place of potatoes. As the plantain ripens it becomes softer and sweeter.

Bananas are so easily digested that they make excellent foods for infants and the elderly. They are recommended for people on low-sodium and low-fat diets. Bananas have also been used to provide relief for stomach ulcers, colitis, and diarrhea.

NUTRITIONAL INFORMATION

1 med. banana, raw			
Calories	127	Pantothenic	
Carbohydrate g	33.3	acid mg	.39
Protein g	1.6	Vitamin C mg	15
Fiber g	.8	Vitamin E iu	.6
Saturated fat g	—	Sodium mg	2
Unsaturated fat g	—	Phosphorus mg	39
Vitamin A iu	270	Potassium mg	550
Vitamin B_1 mg	.08	Calcium mg	12
Vitamin B_2 mg	.09	Iron mg	1
Vitamin B_3 mg	1	Magnesium mg	49
Vitamin B_6 mg	.76	Copper mg	.24
Vitamin B_{12} mcg	0	Manganese mg	.96
Biotin mcg	6	Selenium mg	1.5
Folic acid mg	.042	Zinc mg	.3

BARLEY FLOUR

Barley is the grain of a grass cultivated in China as early as twenty centuries before Christ. It was also widely used in ancient Egypt, Greece, and Rome. Barley was grown in Europe during the Middle Ages and was brought to North America by British and Dutch colonists. It is used here not for food, but for making beer.

Barley is a highly nutritious food, mild enough to help relieve stomach ulcers and diarrhea. It also helps prevent tooth decay and loss of hair and strengthens the nails of the hands and feet.

Health food stores usually carry barley flour that is made from pearled barley, which has the aleurone layers of protein removed during milling. If you can find a source that supplies natural brown barley flour, which has been hulled but not pearled, your baked goods will be higher in protein, vitamins, and minerals.

You can make your own flour by grinding the whole grain in a food mill or coffee grinder. Since I was unable to find nutritional information for barley flour, I have supplied it for the whole grain instead.

NUTRITIONAL INFORMATION

	1 c. pearled, pot, or scotch, dry	1 c. pearled, light, dry		1 c. pearled, pot, or scotch, dry	1 c. pearled, light, dry
Calories	696	698	Pantothenic		
Carbohydrate g	154	158	acid mg	—	1
Protein g	19.2	16.4	Vitamin C mg	0	0
Fiber g	2.14	.7	Vitamin E iu	—	—
Saturated fat g	.48	+	Sodium mg	—	6
Unsaturated fat g	1.52	2	Phosphorus mg	580	378
Vitamin A iu	0	0	Potassium mg	592	320
Vitamin B$_1$ mg	.42	.24	Calcium mg	68	32
Vitamin B$_2$ mg	.14	.1	Iron mg	5.4	4
Vitamin B$_3$ mg	7.4	6.2	Magnesium mg	71.4	71.4
Vitamin B$_6$ mg	—	.448	Copper mg	—	.8
Vitamin B$_{12}$ mcg	0	0	Manganese mg	—	3.36
Biotin mcg	—	—	Selenium mg	—	—
Folic acid mg	.04	—	Zinc mg	—	—

BLACKBERRIES

Native to Asia, Europe, and North America, blackberries grow so abundantly in the wild that cultivation is fairly recent. Blackberries are a member of the rose family, and their thorns and brambles are a nuisance to those wishing to pick the fruit. Each berry is actually a bunch of small fruits called drupelets.

Fresh from May through August, blackberries grow wild alongside highways, country roads, creeks, and railroad tracks. I suggest that you pick your own rather than buy them if you can. However, first check into local spraying practices as blackberries near roads are sometimes subjected to sprays that would be harmful if taken in large quantities. Blackberries are ripe when the fruit is dark purple or black and pull away from the caps easily when picked.

Good blood cleanser and general tonic. Recommended for constipation, anemia, obesity, weak kidneys, rheumatism, arthritis, gout, pimples, and other skin problems.

NUTRITIONAL INFORMATION

1 c. blackberries, raw

Calories	84	Pantothenic	
Carbohydrate g	18.6	acid mg	.345
Protein g	1.7	Vitamin C mg	31
Fiber g	5.9	Vitamin E iu	—
Saturated fat g	—	Sodium mg	1
Unsaturated fat g	—	Phosphorus mg	27
Vitamin A iu	290	Potassium mg	245
Vitamin B_1 mg	.04	Calcium mg	46
Vitamin B_2 mg	.06	Iron mg	1.3
Vitamin B_3 mg	.6	Magnesium mg	43
Vitamin B_6 mg	.07	Copper mg	.23
Vitamin B_{12} mcg	0	Manganese mg	.9
Biotin mcg	.6	Selenium mg	—
Folic acid mg	.018	Zinc mg	—

BLUEBERRIES

Blueberries grow wild in New England, the Pacific Northwest, Scandinavia, the British Isles, Russia, and South America. They have been known by many other names: huckleberries, bilberries, whortleberries, and hurtleberries. They have been cultivated in this country for 60 years.

Blueberries are fresh from May through September, but July and August are the peak times of production. They are produced mainly in New Jersey, Michigan, Maine, North Carolina, Washington, and Oregon.

Buy the fresh berries plump, and store in their container in the refrigerator. Use them right away as they will last only a few days.

Blueberries are a good blood cleanser and relieve anemia, constipation, diarrhea, obesity, menstrual disorders, and poor complexion.

NUTRITIONAL INFORMATION

1 c. blueberries, raw

Calories	90	Pantothenic	
Carbohydrate g	22.2	acid mg	.231
Protein g	1	Vitamin C mg	20
Fiber g	2.2	Vitamin E iu	—
Saturated fat g	—	Sodium mg	1
Unsaturated fat g	—	Phosphorus mg	19
Vitamin A iu	150	Potassium mg	117
Vitamin B_1 mg	.04	Calcium mg	22
Vitamin B_2 mg	.09	Iron mg	1.5
Vitamin B_3 mg	.7	Magnesium mg	8.7
Vitamin B_6 mg	1	Copper mg	.22
Vitamin B_{12} mcg	0	Manganese mg	.4
Biotin mcg	—	Selenium mg	—
Folic acid mg	.009	Zinc mg	—

BRAN

Bran is the partly ground husk of wheat or other grain, separated from the flour in the milling process. Bran provides bulk and fiber to the diet, which keeps the intestines toned and cleaned.

NUTRITIONAL INFORMATION

1 c. bran

Calories	121	Pantothenic	
Carbohydrate g	35.4	acid mg	1.65
Protein g	9	Vitamin C mg	0
Fiber g	5.2	Vitamin E iu	—
Saturated fat g	.42	Sodium mg	5.13
Unsaturated fat g	1.76	Phosphorus mg	727
Vitamin A iu	1650	Potassium mg	639
Vitamin B_1 mg	.41	Calcium mg	67.8
Vitamin B_2 mg	.49	Iron mg	8.49
Vitamin B_3 mg	12	Magnesium mg	279
Vitamin B_6 mg	.134	Copper mg	.9
Vitamin B_{12} mcg	0	Manganese mg	—
Biotin mcg	—	Selenium mg	35.9
Folic acid mg	.147	Zinc mg	5.59

BRAZIL NUTS

The edible seed of a tall South American tree, the brazil nut resembles a large coconut that contains many seeds inside. Their popularity is growing in the United States with half the entire crop coming here. There are many possible uses for this rich meaty nut. Chopped or ground, Brazil nuts can be used in cakes, cookies, and candies. Butter made from the nuts is a very nourishing food, especially good for those doing hard physical work. The calcium content of the nut strengthens bones and teeth.

NUTRITIONAL INFORMATION

1 c. brazil nuts, raw

Calories	916	Pantothenic	
Carbohydrate g	15.3	acid mg	.323
Protein g	20	Vitamin C mg	14
Fiber g	4.2	Vitamin E iu	9.1
Saturated fat g	18.7	Sodium mg	1
Unsaturated fat g	69.3	Phosphorus mg	970
Vitamin A iu	+	Potassium mg	1001
Vitamin B_1 mg	1.34	Calcium mg	260
Vitamin B_2 mg	.17	Iron mg	4.8
Vitamin B_3 mg	2.2	Magnesium mg	351
Vitamin B_6 mg	2.38	Copper mg	2.14
Vitamin B_{12} mcg	0	Manganese mg	3.9
Biotin mcg	—	Selenium mg	144
Folic acid mg	.006	Zinc mg	7.1

BROWN RICE

Rice has always been a staple in the diet of more than half the world's people. When the Japanese Navy introduced polished rice on board ship, thousands of sailors died of beri-beri. Dr. Robert Kunnels Williams, an American, received the American Chemical Society's Gold Medal for his research involving the first extraction of Vitamin B_1 (thiamin) from the rice bran and its successful use against beri-beri. In his speech to the society, he said, "Man commits a crime against nature when he eats the starch from the seed and throws away the mechanism necessary for the metabolism of that starch."[1]

Brown rice is the grain with only the indigestible husks removed. Since rice is susceptible to many diseases, it is often treated heavily with fungicides and pesticides. For this reason I recommend buying organic brown rice. You can get either the long grain or more chewy, short grain rice. The best ways to prepare brown rice is by boiling or steaming it for about 40 minutes.

NUTRITIONAL INFORMATION

1 c. brown rice, raw

Calories	704	Pantothenic	
Carbohydrate g	152	acid mg	2.1
Protein g	14.8	Vitamin C mg	0
Fiber g	1.6	Vitamin E iu	3
Saturated fat g	—	Sodium mg	16
Unsaturated fat g	—	Phosphorus mg	432
Vitamin A iu	0	Potassium mg	420
Vitamin B_1 mg	.68	Calcium mg	64
Vitamin B_2 mg	.08	Iron mg	3.2
Vitamin B_3 mg	9.2	Magnesium mg	172
Vitamin B_6 mg	1	Copper mg	.4
Vitamin B_{12} mcg	0	Manganese mg	3.2
Biotin mcg	18	Selenium mg	77.2
Folic acid mg	.032	Zinc mg	3.6

BUTTER

Made from milkfat, buttermilk, and water, butter usually has salt added and may contain a coloring agent. Fat content is 80 percent. Grade AA is made from fresh cream and is only slightly higher than Grade A in quality, whereas Grade B is made from sour cream.

Sweet butter contains about .01 percent salt as compared with 2 percent for salted butter. Salt is used as a preservative, but if used quickly, unsalted butter will not present any problems under refrigeration for a few weeks. Also, unsalted butter may be frozen for longer storage with little loss in flavor.

The fat in butter is over 60 percent saturated and except for Vitamin A, provides little additional nutritional value.

NUTRITIONAL INFORMATION

1 T. butter

Calories	102	Pantothenic	
Carbohydrate g	.1	acid mg	—
Protein g	.1	Vitamin C mg	0
Fiber g	0	Vitamin E iu	5.2
Saturated fat g	6.3	Sodium mg	2240
Unsaturated fat g	4.1	Phosphorus mg	36
Vitamin A iu	470	Potassium mg	52
Vitamin B_1 mg	+	Calcium mg	45
Vitamin B_2 mg	.001	Iron mg	0
Vitamin B_3 mg	—	Magnesium mg	4.5
Vitamin B_6 mg	+	Copper mg	.067
Vitamin B_{12} mcg	+	Manganese mg	.09
Biotin mcg	—	Selenium mg	—
Folic acid mg	—	Zinc mg	.2

CANTALOUPES

A variety of muskmelon with orange flesh and a sweet taste. Cantaloupes have yellowish or pale green skin and cream-colored raised netting. They should always be covered completely with this skin netting. Any smooth, slick areas on a melon means a poor choice. Test for ripeness by pressing gently to feel it "give" a little. A cantaloupe picked when fully mature will be smooth on the stem end.

NUTRITIONAL INFORMATION

¼ med. cantaloupe, raw

Calories	30	Pantothenic	
Carbohydrate g	7.5	acid mg	.25
Protein g	.7	Vitamin C mg	33
Fiber g	.3	Vitamin E iu	.14
Saturated fat g	—	Sodium mg	12
Unsaturated fat g	—	Phosphorus mg	16
Vitamin A iu	3400	Potassium mg	251
Vitamin B_1 mg	.04	Calcium mg	14
Vitamin B_2 mg	.03	Iron mg	.4
Vitamin B_3 mg	.6	Magnesium mg	17
Vitamin B_6 mg	.086	Copper mg	.05
Vitamin B_{12} mcg	0	Manganese mg	.04
Biotin mcg	3	Selenium mg	—
Folic acid mg	.03	Zinc mg	.06

Cantaloupes have been recommmended in cases of fever, high blood pressure, obesity, rheumatism, arthritis, skin diseases, and blood deficiencies.

CAROB CHIPS

Carob Chips vary in taste according to the sweetener used during their processing. Brown sugar and fructose are the most popular sugars used. Unsweetened chips are also sold. I recommend the unsweetened kind, since carob has a natural sweetness of its own. Because it is a relatively new food product, I was unable to find specific nutritional information.

Chips can be added to cakes, cookies, snack mixes, and candies. They also can be sprinkled on top of a cake batter before baking: the chips melt and provide a self-iced cake.

CAROB POWDER

Carob powder is a flour made from the dried pods of the Carob or Locust tree. These pods are known as St. John's Bread because it is said that St. John lived on the carob pod while meditating in the desert.

Carob contains pectin which makes it beneficial to stomach disorders and diarrhea. It is a well-balanced food, rich in vitamins A and B complex, and a good source of protein, carbohydrates, and minerals (including copper and magnesium).

One of the main objections to chocolate is that it contains theobromine, a substance which produces effects similar to caffeine, and its bitter taste requires sweetening with sugar. The cocoa beans also contain high amounts of oxalic acid which "lock" in calcium, making it unavailable to the body. Carob is an excellent substitute for people allergic to chocolate, or those on low-sugar, low-caffeine diets. Naturally the flavor is not the same, but carob's natural sweetness makes it an ideal food for children. The powder can be mixed into a baby formula, or milk to make nutritious milk shakes. It can be used in cakes, icings, cookies, and candies.

NUTRITIONAL INFORMATION

1 T. carob

Calories	14	Pantothenic	
Carbohydrate g	6.5	acid mg	—
Protein g	.4	Vitamin C mg	—
Fiber g	.64	Vitamin E iu	—
Saturated fat g	—	Sodium mg	—
Unsaturated fat g	—	Phosphorus mg	6
Vitamin A iu	—	Potassium mg	—
Vitamin B_1 mg	—	Calcium mg	28
Vitamin B_2 mg	—	Iron mg	.33
Vitamin B_3 mg	—	Magnesium mg	—
Vitamin B_6 mg	—	Copper mg	—
Vitamin B_{12} mcg	—	Manganese mg	—
Biotin mcg	—	Selenium mg	—
Folic acid mg	—	Zinc mg	—

CARROTS

Different types of carrots are grown around the world. In Egypt, a purple variety is grown. In sixteenth century Holland, carrots were purple and yellow. The orange variety became known a hundred years later. Carrots came to America before the "Mayflower" and became an important staple food of the Colonists.

The carrots in our markets today are the Mediterranean varieties, most likely the Imperator or Nantes. We occasionally get a shorter, stout variety called the Chantenay, which is excellent for baking. Carrots are primarily grown in California, Texas, and Arizona and are shipped fresh to markets year round.

Buy small, well-shaped, fresh-looking carrots. Avoid shriveled, limp, rubbery, or cracked ones. If the stems are black or deeply discolored, the carrot is old.

Carrots were used by ancient Greek physicians as a medicinal herb tonic. Today, they are helpful in relieving cases of obesity, toxemia, constipation, asthma, poor complexion, poor teeth, and high blood pressure. One carrot provides more than the recommended daily allowance of Vitamin A. Carrot sticks are a good snack: they provide fiber, bulk, and nutrition.

NUTRITIONAL INFORMATION

1 lg. carrot, raw

Calories	42	Pantothenic	
Carbohydrate g	9.7	acid mg	—
Protein g	1.1	Vitamin C mg	—
Fiber g	1	Vitamin E iu	—
Saturated fat g	—	Sodium mg	—
Unsaturated fat g	—	Phosphorus mg	—
Vitamin A iu	11,000	Potassium mg	—
Vitamin B_1 mg	.06	Calcium mg	—
Vitamin B_2 mg	.05	Iron mg	—
Vitamin B_3 mg	—	Magnesium mg	—
Vitamin B_6 mg	.15	Copper mg	—
Vitamin B_{12} mcg	—	Manganese mg	—
Biotin mcg	—	Selenium mg	—
Folic acid mg	—	Zinc mg	—

CASHEWS

The nut or fruit of a tropical American tree, cashew nuts are good body builders, helpful in cases of emaciation and problems with teeth and gums. They are best eaten raw or slightly roasted. The nuts are a delicious snack and the nut butter offers a nice change from peanut butter.

NUTRITIONAL INFORMATION

1 c. cashews, roasted

Calories	785	Pantothenic	
Carbohydrate g	41	acid mg	1.82
Protein g	24.1	Vitamin C mg	—
Fiber g	1.96	Vitamin E iu	—
Saturated fat g	10.9	Sodium mg	21
Unsaturated fat g	49.3	Phosphorus mg	522
Vitamin A iu	140	Potassium mg	650
Vitamin B_1 mg	.6	Calcium mg	53
Vitamin B_2 mg	.35	Iron mg	5.3
Vitamin B_3 mg	2.5	Magnesium mg	374
Vitamin B_6 mg	—	Copper mg	—
Vitamin B_{12} mcg	0	Manganese mg	—
Biotin mcg	—	Selenium mg	—
Folic acid mg	.095	Zinc mg	6.1

CHEESE

The first cheeses were probably made by nomadic tribes in eastern Europe and western Asia. Milk would be stored in pouches made from the stomachs of goats, sheep, or cows. The pouches contained rennin, a substance that makes milk coagulate.

Cheese is a complete protein, containing all the essential amino acids that must be supplied in the diet. Not only an inexpensive protein, it can also be used in many ways. Generally, the harder

NUTRITIONAL INFORMATION

1 oz.

	Blue	Brick	Brie	Camembert, domestic	Cheddar, American	Cream	Edam	Gruyere
Calories	103	103	95	84	112	105	101	115
Carbohydrate g	.66	.79	.13	.5	.36	.6	.4	15
Protein g	6	6.59	5.88	5.6	7	2.2	7.7	8.45
Fiber g	0	0	0	0	0	0	0	0
Saturated fat g	5.3	5.32	—	4.33	5.98	5.88	4.98	5.36
Unsaturated fat g	2.44	2.66	—	2.19	2.93	3.64	2.49	3.34
Vitamin A iu	204	307	189	262	300	430	260	346
Vitamin B_1 mg	.008	.004	.02	.01	.008	.006	.01	.017
Vitamin B_2 mg	.108	.1	.147	.21	.106	.06	.11	.079
Vitamin B_3 mg	.288	.033	.108	.2	.023	+	.023	.03
Vitamin B_6 mg	.047	.018	.067	.064	.021	.013	.022	.023
Vitamin B_{12} mcg	.345	.28	.468	0	.234	.12	.435	.454
Biotin mcg	—	—	—	1	1	—	—	—
Folic acid mg	.01	.006	.018	.018	.005	.004	.005	.003
Pantothenic acid mg	.490	.081	.196	.387	.117	.077	.08	.159
Vitamin C mg	0	0	0	0	0	0	0	0
Vitamin E iu	—	—	—	—	—	—	—	—
Sodium mg	396	159	178	239	176	70	274	95
Phosphorus mg	110	127	53	98	145	23	136	172
Potassium mg	73	38	43	53	28	21	53	23
Calcium mg	150	191	52	110	211	17	225	287
Iron mg	.09	.1	.14	.1	.19	.1	.12	.3
Magnesium mg	7	7	—	6	8	2	8	12
Copper mg	.011	.007	—	.022	.031	.011	.008	—
Manganese mg	.003	.003	—	.011	.003	.011	.003	—
Selenium mg	—	—	—	—	—	—	—	—
Zinc mg	.75	.74	—	.68	.88	.15	1.06	1.11

cheeses, such as Cheddar, have a higher nutritional content because they have less moisture. Most natural cheeses are made at temperatures much lower than 130°F. Processed cheeses are cooked at well over 150°F to stop bacterial action and give longer shelf life. Cheese spreads lose substantial amounts of protein, calcium, iron, vitamin A, and in some cases, B vitamins. The main objection to their use lies in the additives they contain. Pasteurized process cheese loses few nutrients and compares favorably with Cheddar cheese (from which it is made). See *Dessert Cheeses, Fruits & Nuts* for information on individual cheese varieties.

NUTRITIONAL INFORMATION

	Monterey Jack	Muenster	Port du Salut	Provolone	1 cup Ricotta, part-skim	Roquefort	Swiss
	1 oz.						
Calories	106	104	100	100	340	105	107
Carbohydrate g	.19	.32	.16	.61	12.6	.57	.96
Protein g	6.94	6.64	6.74	7.25	28	6.1	8.06
Fiber g	0	0	0	0	0	0	0
Saturated fat g	—	5.42	4.73	4.84	12.1	5.46	5.04
Unsaturated fat g	—	2.66	2.86	2.32	6	2.77	2.34
Vitamin A iu	269	318	378	231	1063	297	240
Vitamin B_1 mg	—	.004	—	.005	.052	.011	.006
Vitamin B_2 mg	.11	.091	.068	.091	.455	.166	.103
Vitamin B_3 mg	—	.029	.017	.044	.192	.208	.026
Vitamin B_6 mg	—	.016	.015	.021	.049	.035	.024
Vitamin B_{12} mcg	—	.418	.425	.415	.716	.182	.475
Biotin mcg	—	—	—	—	—	.8	—
Folic acid mg	—	.003	.005	.003	—	.014	.002
Pantothenic acid mg	—	.054	.06	.135	—	.491	.122
Vitamin C mg	0	0	0	0	0	0	0
Vitamin E iu	—	—	—	—	—	—	.098
Sodium mg	152	178	151	248	307	513	74
Phosphorus mg	126	133	102	141	449	111	171
Potassium mg	23	38	—	39	308	26	31
Calcium mg	212	203	184	214	669	188	272
Iron mg	.2	.12	—	.15	1.08	.16	.3
Magnesium mg	8	8	—	8	36	8	10
Copper mg	.009	.009	—	.007	—	.01	.036
Manganese mg	.003	.002	—	.003	—	.009	.004
Selenium mg	—	—	—	—	—	—	2.83
Zinc mg	.85	.8	—	.92	3.3	.59	1.11

CHERRIES

Cherry pits found in Stone Age caves and prehistoric cliff dwellings in America testify to the cherry's early beginnings. Cherries were probably cultivated first in Asia Minor, but now they are grown in a temperate belt from the Arctic Circle to the Tropic of Cancer. All commercially grown cherries come from European stock. They are divided into the sweet and sour types.

The sour varieties are canned for pies and rarely sold in the markets.

Bing. This is by far the most popular sweet cherry. It is an extra large, heart-shaped fruit with smooth glossy skin ranging in color from maroon to black when ripe. The firm, meaty flesh and delicious sweet flavor make Bing cherries ideal for fresh fruit salads, gelatins, cakes, and pies where little other sweetening is necessary.

The Royal Ann. A light-colored sweet cherry, it is large, heart-shaped and yellowish in color. This variety bruises easily, but is good eaten fresh.

Cherries are fresh from late April through August, though June is the peak of the season with the lowest prices. Buy firm, plump cherries with green stems. The darker the color, the better the flavor.

NUTRITIONAL INFORMATION

	1 c. sour, raw	1 c. sweet, raw		1 c. sour, raw	1 c. sweet, raw
Calories	90	82	Pantothenic		
Carbohydrate g	22.2	20.4	acid mg	.213	.339
Protein g	1.9	1.5	Vitamin C mg	16	12
Fiber g	.4	.52	Vitamin E iu	—	—
Saturated fat g	—	—	Sodium mg	3	2
Unsaturated fat g	—	—	Phosphorus mg	29	22
Vitamin A iu	1550	130	Potassium mg	296	223
Vitamin B_1 mg	.08	.06	Calcium mg	34	26
Vitamin B_2 mg	.09	.07	Iron mg	.6	.5
Vitamin B_3 mg	.6	.5	Magnesium mg	21	18
Vitamin B_6 mg	.095	.041	Copper mg	.18	.156
Vitamin B_{12} mcg	0	0	Manganese mg	.045	.039
Biotin mcg	.6	.52	Selenium mg	—	—
Folic acid mg	.012	.01	Zinc mg	—	—

Ripe, raw cherries are excellent blood purifiers due to the large quantity of magnesium, iron, and silicon in them. They are a valuable aid in relieving anemia, poor complexion, bad blood, constipation, cramps, obesity, high blood pressure, rheumatism, and asthma. Eating large quantities of cherries (up to half a pound daily) has been effective in relieving gout, which is caused by excess uric acid in the blood.

CHIA SEEDS

A longtime staple of Mexican and American Indians, who used them to increase their endurance on long hunts and migrations. Chia seeds are a member of the mint family. They have a mild flaxlike taste and are among the mucilaginous seeds. This means they become sticky when soaked in water. They can be chewed raw; sprinkled into hot or cold cereals; baked in bread, cookies, and candies; or sprouted.

CHOCOLATE

Chocolate comes from the bean of the cacao tree, grown in Mexico and the West Indies. The beans are enclosed in a fleshy mass inside pods. When freshly harvested, the beans are bitter in flavor and a light, purplish or pale-green color. Roasting gives the beans the desirable flavor. Next, shells are cracked and kernels are broken into small pieces. A grinder reduces the chocolate into a thick oily liquid which is then cooled and poured into molds for plain, bitter, or baking chocolate. Sugar and cocoa-butter are added to make sweet chocolate.

The main objection to using chocolate is the large amount of sugar necessary to counteract its bitterness. In addition, the bean contains theobromine, which produces effects similar to the stimulating properties of caffeine.

NUTRITIONAL INFORMATION

	1 oz. bitter or baking	1 oz. semisweet		1 oz. bitter or baking	1 oz. semisweet
Calories	143	144	Pantothenic		
Carbohydrate g	8.2	16.2	acid mg	—	—
Protein g	3	1.2	Vitamin C mg	0	+
Fiber g	.7	.28	Vitamin E iu	3.12	—
Saturated fat g	8	5.6	Sodium mg	1	1
Unsaturated fat g	6	3.79	Phosphorus mg	109	43
Vitamin A iu	20	10	Potassium mg	235	92
Vitamin B_1 mg	.01	+	Calcium mg	22	9
Vitamin B_2 mg	.07	.02	Iron mg	1.9	.7
Vitamin B_3 mg	.4	.1	Magnesium mg	81.8	—
Vitamin B_6 mg	—	—	Copper mg	.748	—
Vitamin B_{12} mcg	—	—	Manganese mg	—	—
Biotin mcg	—	—	Selenium mg	—	—
Folic acid mg	—	—	Zinc mg	—	—

CINNAMON

The inner bark of a small evergreen tree grown primarily in Ceylon, sold in sticks or ground powder. One of the oldest spices known to man, used in temples as incense or as an ingredient in holy anointing oils. "Cassia" comes from the same family and is sold in the

NUTRITIONAL INFORMATION

	1 t. ground cinnamon		
Calories	6	Pantothenic	
Carbohydrate g	1.84	acid mg	—
Protein g	.09	Vitamin C mg	.65
Fiber g	.56	Vitamin E iu	—
Saturated fat g	.01	Sodium mg	1
Unsaturated fat g	.02	Phosphorus mg	1
Vitamin A iu	6	Potassium mg	11
Vitamin B_1 mg	.002	Calcium mg	28
Vitamin B_2 mg	.003	Iron mg	.88
Vitamin B_3 mg	.03	Magnesium mg	1
Vitamin B_6 mg	—	Copper mg	*
Vitamin B_{12} mcg	0	Manganese mg	*
Biotin mcg	—	Selenium mg	.5
Folic acid mg	—	Zinc mg	.05

*Present but value in mg unavailable

United States as cinnamon. Cinnamon is lighter and has a more deli-cate flavor than cassia. Cinnamon sticks add flavor to hot drinks, the powder is used in baking. The powerful antiseptic oil, phenol, has preserving qualities.

CLOVES

The dried, nail-shaped flower bud of the clove tree grown in the Moluccas, or Spice Islands. The clove tree is very rich in essential oils, whose pungent, sweet flavor and odor are useful in perfumes, soaps, toothpastes, and mouthwashes. Clove oil also aids digestion and relieves toothaches. The essential oil, phenol, prevents pu-trification of meats. In cooking, cloves are an important curry ingre-dient, as well as being used in many baked foods.

NUTRITIONAL INFORMATION

1 t. ground cloves

Calories	7	Pantothenic	
Carbohydrate g	1.29	acid mg	—
Protein g	.13	Vitamin C mg	1.7
Fiber g	.2	Vitamin E iu	—
Saturated fat g	.09	Sodium mg	5
Unsaturated fat g	—	Phosphorus mg	2
Vitamin A iu	11	Potassium mg	23
Vitamin B_1 mg	.002	Calcium mg	14
Vitamin B_2 mg	.006	Iron mg	.18
Vitamin B_3 mg	.031	Magnesium mg	6
Vitamin B_6 mg	—	Copper mg	*
Vitamin B_{12} mcg	0	Manganese mg	*
Biotin mcg	—	Selenium mg	—
Folic acid mg	—	Zinc mg	.02

COCONUTS

The fruit or nut of the coconut palm. The seed is enclosed in a hard shell protected by a thick fibrous husk.

Coconut is a good protein food and also provides minerals.

Coconuts contain organic iodine, which prevents thyroid gland problems. The milk relieves stomach ulcers while the meat is recommended for relieving constipation and gas in the stomach and intestinal tract and for destroying tapeworms acquired by eating infected meat. Coconut oil heals cuts, scratches, and burns, including sunburns. It is beneficial to the hair, scalp, and skin.

NUTRITIONAL INFORMATION

1 c. fresh shedded coconut

Calories	277	Pantothenic	
Carbohydrate g	7.5	acid mg	.16
Protein g	2.8	Vitamin C mg	2
Fiber g	2.7	Vitamin E iu	.8
Saturated fat g	24.3	Sodium mg	18
Unsaturated fat g	2	Phosphorus mg	76
Vitamin A iu	0	Potassium mg	205
Vitamin B_1 mg	.04	Calcium mg	10
Vitamin B_2 mg	.02	Iron mg	1.4
Vitamin B_3 mg	.4	Magnesium mg	37
Vitamin B_6 mg	.035	Copper mg	.368
Vitamin B_{12} mcg	0	Manganese mg	1.05
Biotin mcg	—	Selenium mg	—
Folic acid mg	.031	Zinc mg	—

COFFEE

There are two types of coffees. Robusta, grown in Africa, has a harsh flavor. The second kind, Arabica, originally from the Middle East, is now grown in the Americas. It is mild, aromatic, and more expensive than Robusta and has less caffeine. The two are generally mixed for instant coffee.

Instant coffees are made by percolating ground coffee, then spray-drying or freeze-drying the liquid. Freeze-drying is more expensive and results in a better flavor, because it doesn't use the high temperatures of the spray-drying process. Instant coffee has half the caffeine of regular coffee.

Although coffee begins as a nutritious product, the temperatures of 500°F used during processing destroy all the nutrients except for a little niacin.

Decaffeinated coffee is approximately 97 percent caffeine-free, but the chemical residue left from chemicals used during the processing may cause health problems. The solvent trichlorethylene, which was used in Sanka and Brim, was banned in 1975 as a possible cause of liver cancer. Now methylene chloride is used, but it is also questionable, since it is related to other known cancer-causing chemicals.

NUTRITIONAL INFORMATION

1 c. coffee, clear

Calories	5	Pantothenic	
Carbohydrate g	.8	acid mg	.008
Protein g	.3	Vitamin C mg	0
Fiber g	0	Vitamin E iu	—
Saturated fat g	—	Sodium mg	2.3
Unsaturated fat g	—	Phosphorus mg	5
Vitamin A iu	0	Potassium mg	83
Vitamin B_1 mg	.02	Calcium mg	4.6
Vitamin B_2 mg	.02	Iron mg	.23
Vitamin B_3 mg	.9	Magnesium mg	21.8
Vitamin B_6 mg	+	Copper mg	.05
Vitamin B_{12} mcg	0	Manganese mg	.22
Biotin mcg	—	Selenium mg	.3
Folic acid mg	—	Zinc mg	.05

COFFEE SUBSTITUTES

Coffee substitutes are roasted cereals, ground and brewed in water to make a caffeine-free drink. Although popular in the first part of this century, their use declined with the introduction of decaffeinated coffee. Postum and Pero are still fairly popular and readily available in most markets. Postum is made from roasted wheat, roasted bran, and molasses which are ground and mixed together.

CORIANDER

Coriander is an annual herb of the parsley family indigenous to southern Europe and the Mediterranean region. The dried ripe fruits are the spice known as coriander seed. An ancient flavoring used for both medicinal and culinary purposes, it is still used in some countries as a tonic, cough medicine, stomachic, and a flavoring in disagreeable medicines.

Coriander is one of the ingredients in curry powder and is also used for flavoring candy, cocoa, chocolate, tobacco, meat products, baked goods, and liqueurs. It has a distinctive fragrant odor and mild, sweet yet slightly pungent taste. The whole seed is used as a pickling spice, while the ground powder is used in spice mixtures and baking.

NUTRITIONAL INFORMATION

1 t. coriander seeds

Calories	5	Pantothenic	
Carbohydrate g	.99	acid mg	—
Protein g	.22	Vitamin C mg	—
Fiber g	.52	Vitamin E iu	—
Saturated fat g	.02	Sodium mg	1
Unsaturated fat g	.27	Phosphorus mg	7
Vitamin A iu	—	Potassium mg	23
Vitamin B$_1$ mg	.004	Calcium mg	13
Vitamin B$_2$ mg	.005	Iron mg	.29
Vitamin B$_3$ mg	.038	Magnesium mg	6
Vitamin B$_6$ mg	—	Copper mg	*
Vitamin B$_{12}$ mcg	0	Manganese mg	*
Biotin mcg	—	Selenium mg	—
Folic acid mg	—	Zinc mg	.08

CORNSTARCH

Cornstarch is a refined starch obtained from the endosperm of corn. It's chief value in cooking is its thickening power. It contains traces of sodium and potassium. One tablespoon of cornstarch can be substituted for 2 tablespoons flour or arrowroot powder.

NUTRITIONAL INFORMATION

1 t. cornstarch

Calories	29	Pantothenic	
Carbohydrate g	7	acid mg	—
Protein g	+	Vitamin C mg	0
Fiber g	+	Vitamin E iu	—
Saturated fat g	+	Sodium mg	.32
Unsaturated fat g	—	Phosphorus mg	2.4
Vitamin A iu	0	Potassium mg	.32
Vitamin B_1 mg	0	Calcium mg	0
Vitamin B_2 mg	.006	Iron mg	.04
Vitamin B_3 mg	.002	Magnesium mg	.16
Vitamin B_6 mg	+	Copper mg	.004
Vitamin B_{12} mcg	0	Manganese mg	—
Biotin mcg	—	Selenium mg	—
Folic acid mg	—	Zinc mg	.3

COTTAGE CHEESE

Sometimes called pot cheese, cottage cheese is a fresh, unripened cheese. It is lower in calories than most cheeses, and provides the most protein for the money. Cottage cheese can be served with fresh fruits and gelatins to make healthy protein snacks and desserts with fewer calories than other desserts.

NUTRITIONAL INFORMATION

	1 c. creamed	*1 c. 2% fat*		*1 c. creamed*	*1 c. 2% fat*
Calories	217	203	Pantothenic		
Carbohydrate g	5.6	8.2	acid mg	.447	.547
Protein g	26.2	31	Vitamin C mg	+	+
Fiber g	0	0	Vitamin E iu	—	—
Saturated fat g	5.99	2.76	Sodium mg	850	918
Unsaturated fat g	3	1.37	Phosphorus mg	277	340
Vitamin A iu	342	158	Potassium mg	177	217
Vitamin B_1 mg	.044	.054	Calcium mg	126	155
Vitamin B_2 mg	.342	.418	Iron mg	.29	.36
Vitamin B_3 mg	.265	.325	Magnesium mg	11	14
Vitamin B_6 mg	.141	.172	Copper mg	.04	—
Vitamin B_{12} mcg	1.31	1.61	Manganese mg	.007	—
Biotin mcg	—	—	Selenium mg	11.3	—
Folic acid mg	.026	.03	Zinc mg	.78	.95

CRANBERRIES

Cranberries are a native fruit used by the North American Indians long before the Pilgrims arrived. They crushed the berries and added them to their meat as a preservative, made poultices from them to draw poisons from wounds, and made red dye from them.

Cranberries grow on bogs (swampland) in New Jersey and Cape Cod. Their commercial cultivation began in 1830 and spread west to Wisconsin, Washington, and Oregon.

There is a very high tannic and oxalic acid content in cranberries, and they are beneficial in treating problem skin, for high blood pressure, constipation, and fevers. Cranberry juice is also used to treat cystitis.

NUTRITIONAL INFORMATION

1 c. cranberries, raw

Calories	46	Pantothenic	
Carbohydrate g	10.8	acid mg	—
Protein g	.4	Vitamin C mg	8
Fiber g	1.4	Vitamin E iu	—
Saturated fat g	—	Sodium mg	1
Unsaturated fat g	—	Phosphorus mg	13
Vitamin A iu	40	Potassium mg	110
Vitamin B_1 mg	.03	Calcium mg	6
Vitamin B_2 mg	.02	Iron mg	.3
Vitamin B_3 mg	.1	Magnesium mg	—
Vitamin B_6 mg	.035	Copper mg	—
Vitamin B_{12} mcg	—	Manganese mg	—
Biotin mcg	—	Selenium mg	—
Folic acid mg	—	Zinc mg	—

CREAM

Half and half cream is a mixture of milk and cream, usually homogenized. It contains 10½ percent to 18 percent milk fat. It is used in our ice cream recipes.

Whipping cream comes in light or heavy cream. This is made by skimming the cream from milk that has been standing 24 hours or longer. Light whipping cream contains 30 to 36 percent milkfat.

Heavy whipping cream contains 36 to 40 percent milkfat. Either kind is fine to use in recipes calling for whipping cream.

NUTRITIONAL INFORMATION

	1 c. half and half	1 c. whip- ping, light	1 c. whip- ping, heavy		1 c. half and half	1 c. whip- ping, light	1 c. whip- ping, heavy
Calories	315	699	821	Pantothenic			
Carbohydrate g	10.4	7.07	6.64	acid mg	.699	.619	.607
Protein g	7.16	5.19	4.88	Vitamin C mg	2.08	1.46	1.38
Fiber g	0	0	0	Vitamin E iu	—	1.4	3
Saturated fat g	17.3	46.2	54.8	Sodium mg	98	82	89
Unsaturated fat g	9.07	23.8	28.7	Phosphorus mg	230	146	149
Vitamin A iu	1050	2694	3499	Potassium mg	314	231	179
Vitamin B_1 mg	.085	.057	.052	Calcium mg	254	166	154
Vitamin B_2 mg	.361	.299	.262	Iron mg	.17	.07	.07
Vitamin B_3 mg	.189	.1	.093	Magnesium mg	25	17	17
Vitamin B_6 mg	.094	.067	.062	Copper mg	—	—	—
Vitamin B_{12} mcg	.796	.466	.428	Manganese mg	—	—	—
Biotin mcg	—	.119	.071	Selenium mg	—	—	—
Folic acid mg	.006	.009	.009	Zinc mg	1.23	.6	.55

CREAM CHEESE

Cream cheese is unripened, meaning it is ready to eat as soon as it is made. The slightly acid flavor is due to lactic acid which is not entirely fermented out of the cheese. It has a high moisture content and is very perishable. For fat-restricted diets, try yogurt cheese for a substitute.

NUTRITIONAL INFORMATION

1 oz. cream cheese			
Calories	105	Pantothenic	
Carbohydrate g	.6	acid mg	.007
Protein g	2.2	Vitamin C mg	0
Fiber g	0	Vitamin E iu	—
Saturated fat g	5.88	Sodium mg	70
Unsaturated fat g	3.64	Phosphorus mg	23
Vitamin A iu	430	Potassium mg	21
Vitamin B_1 mg	.006	Calcium mg	17
Vitamin B_2 mg	.06	Iron mg	.1
Vitamin B_3 mg	+	Magnesium mg	2
Vitamin B_6 mg	.013	Copper mg	.011
Vitamin B_{12} mcg	.12	Manganese mg	.001
Biotin mcg	—	Selenium mg	—
Folic acid mg	.004	Zinc mg	.15

CRENSHAW MELONS

A cross between Persian and Casaba melons, Crenshaw melons are large and smooth skinned with lengthwise ribbing. They are a golden color when ripe. The stem end is rounded or flat rather than pointed. The flesh is golden-salmon in color, with a rich, juicy, spicy flavor. In season from July through October with the peak in August and September, Crenshaw melons are grown in California, Arizona, and Texas.

DATES

Dates are the fruit of the date palm, which grows in desert conditions where other fruit trees cannot live. Dates have been cultivated between the Tigres and Euphrates for over 7000 years.

Dates are a concentrated carbohydrate—approximately 75 percent sugar—and are an excellent substitute for candy. They are a good source of calcium and supply smaller amounts of B vitamins and essential minerals.

Deglet Noor, Halawy, Khadrawy, and Tahidi are the varieties of dates most frequently sold in the markets. The dates are usually cleaned, pasteurized, and inspected before being packaged. Fresh

NUTRITIONAL INFORMATION

10 med. dates			
Calories	274	Pantothenic	
Carbohydrate g	72.9	acid mg	.78
Protein g	2.2	Vitamin C mg	0
Fiber g	2.3	Vitamin E iu	—
Saturated fat g	—	Sodium mg	1
Unsaturated fat g	—	Phosphorus mg	63
Vitamin A iu	50	Potassium mg	648
Vitamin B_1 mg	.09	Calcium mg	59
Vitamin B_2 mg	.1	Iron mg	3
Vitamin B_3 mg	2.2	Magnesium mg	58
Vitamin B_6 mg	.153	Copper mg	.22
Vitamin B_{12} mcg	0	Manganese mg	.15
Biotin mcg	—	Selenium mg	—
Folic acid mg	.021	Zinc mg	—

dates are available from September through May; the season's peak is in November. Fresh dates should be moist and plump with a smooth glossy skin. Since they are perishable, refrigerate them in sealed containers. Dried dates store well and are available year round.

DATE SUGAR

A granulated date sugar is available in most health food stores. It is a rich brown color and has the distinctive flavor of dry dates. It can be used to substitute for granulated white and brown sugars, using the same proportions. Try using it in cooked candy recipes to get a firmer texture. I do not recommend using it in recipes that don't require cooking, because it adds a gritty texture to the food.

DRIED MILK POWDER

I recommend the noninstant skim milk powder, since the instant variety is a little more processed. Spray-dried skim milk powder is the

NUTRITIONAL INFORMATION

	1 c. whole, dried	1 c. nonfat, dried		1 c. whole, dried	1 c. nonfat, dried
Calories	635	435	Pantothenic		
Carbohydrate g	49.2	62.4	acid mg	2.91	4.28
Protein g	33.7	43.4	Vitamin C mg	11.1	8.1
Fiber g	0	0	Vitamin E iu	—	—
Saturated fat g	21.4	.6	Sodium mg	475	642
Unsaturated fat g	11	.28	Phosphorus mg	993	1162
Vitamin A iu	1180	43*	Potassium mg	1702	2153
Vitamin B_1 mg	.362	.498	Calcium mg	1168	1508
Vitamin B_2 mg	1.54	1.86	Iron mg	.6	.38
Vitamin B_3 mg	.827	1.14	Magnesium mg	108	132
Vitamin B_6 mg	.387	.433	Copper mg	.4	—
Vitamin B_{12} mcg	4.16	4.84	Manganese mg	—	—
Biotin mcg	17	19	Selenium mg	—	—
Folic acid mg	.047	.06	Zinc mg	4.28	4.9

*Value based on data without added vitamin A. If vitamin A is added, each cup of reconstituted milk contains 500 iu.

best, because the temperatures used in processing are lower than those used in roller-drying. Skim milk has more of the water-soluble vitamins, including B_{12}, than whole milk powder and it has less fat, making it a good choice if you wish to reduce the amount of fat in your diet.

EGGS

A valuable and inexpensive source of protein. The balance of the amino acids make 95 percent of the egg's protein available to the body. They are also the easiest animal protein to digest. For additional information about eggs, cholesterol, and health, see *Dessert Foods & Health*.

Eggs should be refrigerated in the carton wide end up, until ready to use.

Eggs are 73 percent water, 13 percent protein, 11 percent fat, 1 percent carbohydrate. In addition to the nutrients below, the yolk also contains vitamins E and K.

NUTRITIONAL INFORMATION

1 lg. egg, raw

Calories	82	Pantothenic acid mg	.986
Carbohydrate g	.5	Vitamin C mg	0
Protein g	6.5	Vitamin E iu	.57
Fiber g	0	Sodium mg	61
Saturated fat g	1.94	Phosphorus mg	103
Unsaturated fat g	2.37	Potassium mg	65
Vitamin A iu	590	Calcium mg	27
Vitamin B_1 mg	.05	Iron mg	1.2
Vitamin B_2 mg	.15	Magnesium mg	6
Vitamin B_3 mg	.035	Copper mg	.1
Vitamin B_6 mg	.068	Manganese mg	.029
Vitamin B_{12} mcg	.88	Selenium mg	13.2
Biotin mcg	11	Zinc mg	84
Folic acid mg	.036		

FIGS

Originating from western Asia and the Mediterranean area, the fig is one of the most ancient fruits known to man. The following are some of the varieties you find in the markets.

Mission. This purple-black fig with small seeds is delicious fresh, but also popular in dried form. Buy them when color is black to insure ripeness.

Calimyrna. Originating in Turkey, this large fig has a smooth thick yellow skin, and is usually sold in dried form.

Adriatic. This is an Italian fig with light green skin and dark pink flesh.

Fig season is June through October, but figs are sold dried year-round. Figs are best eaten very ripe, even a little overripe. The fruit should be soft, and a slightly wrinkled skin means the fig will be very ripe and sweet. Since figs bruise easily and are very perishable, eat right away or refrigerate immediately.

Figs are helpful in relieving constipation, low blood pressure, anemia, colitis, gout, and skin diseases.

NUTRITIONAL INFORMATION

2 lg. figs, raw

Calories	80	Pantothenic	
Carbohydrate g	20.3	acid mg	.3
Protein g	1.2	Vitamin C mg	2
Fiber g	1.2	Vitamin E iu	—
Saturated fat g	—	Sodium mg	2
Unsaturated fat g	—	Phosphorus mg	22
Vitamin A iu	80	Potassium mg	194
Vitamin B_1 mg	.06	Calcium mg	35
Vitamin B_2 mg	.05	Iron mg	.6
Vitamin B_3 mg	.4	Magnesium mg	20
Vitamin B_6 mg	.113	Copper mg	.07
Vitamin B_{12} mcg	0	Manganese mg	.128
Biotin mcg	—	Selenium mg	—
Folic acid mg	.04	Zinc mg	—

GELATIN

Gelatin has the ability to soak up liquids and to gel. Pure, dry gelatin is 85.5 percent protein, but since it lacks the amino acids tryptophan and tyrosine, the protein cannot sustain life. Gelatin does prevent cracking and splitting nails, and colloidal-gelling action helps relieve constipation.

Buy the pure, unflavored dry gelatin for use in fruit gelatins made with natural unsweetened fruit juices and freshly dried fruits. These gelatins make light desserts, snacks, lunches, or salads.

GINGER

The root of a tropical plant now grown in many hot countries, gingerroot looks like a swollen fist and is called a "hand" of ginger. Fresh ginger may be peeled and minced or crushed and added to curries. The dried root should be bruised before chopping or it may be ground in a coffee mill. The ground ginger packaged for stores unfortunately loses most of its delicate aroma.

NUTRITIONAL INFORMATION

1 t. ground ginger

Calories	6	Pantothenic	
Carbohydrate g	1.27	acid mg	—
Protein g	.16	Vitamin C mg	—
Fiber g	.11	Vitamin E iu	—
Saturated fat g	.03	Sodium mg	1
Unsaturated fat g	.04	Phosphorus mg	3
Vitamin A iu	3	Potassium mg	24
Vitamin B_1 mg	.001	Calcium mg	2
Vitamin B_2 mg	.003	Iron mg	.21
Vitamin B_3 mg	.093	Magnesium mg	3
Vitamin B_6 mg	—	Copper mg	.01
Vitamin B_{12} mcg	0	Manganese mg	*
Biotin mcg	—	Selenium mg	—
Folic acid mg	—	Zinc mg	.08

Ginger has a warming effect on the stomach and helps digestion. It was used by ancient Greek physicians as an antidote to poisons. Makes an excellent flavoring for gingerbread, pies, cookies, pickles, puddings, and syrups.

GRANOLA

A combination of lightly processed grain, usually rolled oats, wheat germ, dried fruits, nuts, oil, nonfat dry milk and a sweetener such as honey, molasses, sugar, or maple syrup. Most of the commercially prepared brands are not healthful, due to the large amount of sugar used in the processing. Look for granola made with honey or molasses.

Since the ingredients vary with the type of granola, it was not possible to give nutritional information. For a homemade granola recipe, see *Toppings & Fillings*.

GRAPES

Grapes are fruit grown since ancient times in Europe and Asia Minor. They also grew wild in North America hundreds of years before the Vikings arrived on these shores. There are many varieties of grapes. Some are specifically eating grapes, others are cultivated for wine, grape juice, raisins, and jelly.

Grapes are a source of quick energy and are good blood and body builders. They are an alkaline fruit and can help decrease the acidity of uric acid and the entire system.

Thompson Seedless. A medium-sized, greenish-yellow oval grape, it is an excellent eating grape and is also used to make raisins. They are in season early June through November.

Perlette. Another seedless variety quite similar in appearance to the Thompson Seedless, the grapes are a waxy white color and are round.

Tokay. These grapes are large and red. Their beautiful color make them an excellent choice for a fruit and cheese plate. Their season is from September through November.

Ribier. This is a large sweet grape with a deep purple-black color. These rich grapes also make a beautiful fruit bowl. Season from July into February.

Buy grapes that are plump and fresh. If the grapes are fresh and haven't been handled too much, they should have a nice bloom (the velvet powdery appearance of the skin).

NUTRITIONAL INFORMATION

	1 c. Thompson, raw	1 c. Concord juice, unsweetened		1 c. Thompson, raw	1 c. Concord juice, unsweetened
Calories	107	167	Pantothenic		
Carbohydrate g	27.7	42	acid mg	.119	.175
Protein g	1	.5	Vitamin C mg	6	+
Fiber g	.8	+	Vitamin E iu	—	—
Saturated fat g	—	—	Sodium mg	5	5
Unsaturated fat g	—	—	Phosphorus mg	32	30
Vitamin A iu	160	—	Potassium mg	278	293
Vitamin B$_1$ mg	.08	.1	Calcium mg	19	28
Vitamin B$_2$ mg	.05	.05	Iron mg	.6	.8
Vitamin B$_3$ mg	.5	.5	Magnesium mg	9.6	32.5
Vitamin B$_6$ mg	.13	.1	Copper mg	.15	.22
Vitamin B$_{12}$ mcg	0	0	Manganese mg	.13	—
Biotin mcg	3.2	.9	Selenium mg	—	10
Folic acid mg	.011	.005	Zinc mg	—	—

HONEY

A natural, unrefined sweetener. Generally speaking, the lighter the color, the milder the flavor. Suggested dessert honeys include: clover, thistle, safflower, and tupelo. Others to try that have a more distinct flavor: avocado, orange, sage, and wildflower. Eucalyptus and buckwheat honey are both medicinal in taste. See *Honey & Other Sweeteners* for specific information.

NUTRITIONAL INFORMATION

1 t. honey

Calories	64	Pantothenic	
Carbohydrate g	17.3	acid mg	.04
Protein g	.1	Vitamin C mg	+
Fiber g	0	Vitamin E iu	—
Saturated fat g	—	Sodium mg	1
Unsaturated fat g	—	Phosphorus mg	1
Vitamin A iu	0	Potassium mg	11
Vitamin B$_1$ mg	.002	Calcium mg	1
Vitamin B$_2$ mg	.014	Iron mg	.1
Vitamin B$_3$ mg	.1	Magnesium mg	.6
Vitamin B$_6$ mg	.004	Copper mg	.008
Vitamin B$_{12}$ mcg	0	Manganese mg	.006
Biotin mcg	—	Selenium mg	—
Folic acid mg	.001	Zinc mg	.016

LECITHIN GRANULES

Lecithin is manufactured by the body and is also found naturally in certain foods. Research indicates it has a cholesterol-lowering function when added to the diet. Granular lecithin sold in health food stores comes primarily from soybeans. The granules can be added to food or beverages to supplement the diet with lecithin. Unrefined vegetable oils, particularly sunflower, safflower, wheat germ, olive, and corn are excellent sources of lecithin.

LEMONS

Lemons originated in Asia and made their way west to Africa with Arab traders to southern Europe with returning Crusaders and then to North America with Columbus. Now California and Arizona grow half the world's lemons.

Eureka. This variety is the most common in the markets. It is a bright yellow when ripe and has few seeds. The skin is pitted with a flat nipple at the stem end. It is at its peak during the summer.

Lisbon. This variety is smoother skinned than the Eureka and has a longer nipple at the stem end. It also produces more fruit than the Eureka during the winter.

Lemons are a natural antiseptic. Applied directly to infected cuts, their juice will destroy disease bacteria. Lemon juice will also help heal problem skin, wrinkles, tan spots, or freckles when applied directy and left to dry. Lemon juice will also relieve the itch of insect bites or poison oak or ivy. Lemon juice mixed with equal amounts of honey and taken every two hours is an effective cough medicine. The juice of half a lemon diluted with water and taken before the first meal of the day helps prevent indigestion and the accumulation of fatty deposits.

Lemons contain bioflavonoids, which increase the effectiveness of the vitamin C they contain.

NUTRITIONAL INFORMATION

1 med. lemon, raw			
Calories	20	Pantothenic	
Carbohydrate g	6	acid mg	.19
Protein g	.8	Vitamin C mg	39
Fiber g	.4	Vitamin E iu	—
Saturated fat g	—	Sodium mg	1
Unsaturated fat g	—	Phosphorus mg	12
Vitamin A iu	10	Potassium mg	102
Vitamin B_1 mg	.03	Calcium mg	19
Vitamin B_2 mg	.01	Iron mg	—
Vitamin B_3 mg	.1	Magnesium mg	9
Vitamin B_6 mg	.08	Copper mg	.15
Vitamin B_{12} mcg	0	Manganese mg	.04
Biotin mcg	—	Selenium mg	—
Folic acid mg	.012	Zinc mg	—

LIMES

Lower in vitamin C than the other citrus fruits, limes are nevertheless valuable for their high vitamin content. Limes have an antiseptic quality similar to that of lemons, and they are also helpful in healing arthritis and scurvy.

The ascorbic acid in lemons and limes will prevent some fruits from darkening after they are cut, such as peaches, bananas, and pears.

NUTRITIONAL INFORMATION

1 sm. lime, raw			
Calories	19	Pantothenic	
Carbohydrate g	6.4	acid mg	217
Protein g	.5	Vitamin C mg	25
Fiber g	.5	Vitamin E iu	—
Saturated fat g	—	Sodium mg	1
Unsaturated fat g	—	Phosphorus mg	12
Vitamin A iu	10	Potassium mg	69
Vitamin B_1 mg	.02	Calcium mg	22
Vitamin B_2 mg	.01	Iron mg	.4
Vitamin B_3 mg	.1	Magnesium mg	—
Vitamin B_6 mg	—	Copper mg	—
Vitamin B_{12} mcg	0	Manganese mg	—
Biotin mcg	—	Selenium mg	—
Folic acid mg	.003	Zinc mg	—

MACE

The fleshy fruit of the nutmeg tree, when ripe, splits in half to reveal the brilliant scarlet, netlike membrane or aril, known as mace. This membrane is wrapped around a brittle shell inside of which is the oily nutmeg seed. When dried, mace is yellowish-brown in color.

NUTRITIONAL INFORMATION

1 t. ground mace			
Calories	8	Pantothenic	
Carbohydrate g	.86	acid mg	—
Protein g	.11	Vitamin C mg	—
Fiber g	.08	Vitamin E iu	—
Saturated fat g	.16	Sodium mg	1
Unsaturated fat g	.26	Phosphorus mg	2
Vitamin A iu	14	Potassium mg	8
Vitamin B_1 mg	.005	Calcium mg	4
Vitamin B_2 mg	.008	Iron mg	.24
Vitamin B_3 mg	.023	Magnesium mg	3
Vitamin B_6 mg	—	Copper mg	*
Vitamin B_{12} mcg	0	Manganese mg	*
Biotin mcg	—	Selenium mg	—
Folic acid mg	—	Zinc mg	.04

Whole mace is called "blades of mace" but is not usually found in retail stores, whereas ground mace is easy to find. The flavor is sweet, warm, and more delicate (and more expensive) than nutmeg.

Mace is an excellent mild baking spice suitable for cakes, cookies, and donuts.

MALT SYRUP

Malt syrup is made from barley malt and contains the sugar maltose. It is made by combining the cooked grain with fresh barley sprouts. It is allowed to stand for several hours until a sweet stage is reached. Then the liquid is pressed through cheesecloth, lightly salted and cooked to the desired consistency.

Malt syrup has a lovely pale-amber color and is the same consistency as honey, although not as sweet. Malt syrup can be thinned with fruit juices to make a nice pancake syrup.

MANGOES

A tropical spicy fruit with orange skin and flesh, mangoes probably originated in the Himalayan region of India and Burma. They are

NUTRITIONAL INFORMATION

1 mango, raw			
Calories	152	Pantothenic	
Carbohydrate g	38.8	acid mg	.48
Protein g	1.6	Vitamin C mg	81
Fiber g	2.7	Vitamin E iu	3
Saturated fat g	—	Sodium mg	16
Unsaturated fat g	—	Phosphorus mg	30
Vitamin A iu	11.090	Potassium mg	437
Vitamin B_1 mg	.12	Calcium mg	23
Vitamin B_2 mg	.12	Iron mg	.9
Vitamin B_3 mg	2.5	Magnesium mg	54
Vitamin B_6 mg	—	Copper mg	.36
Vitamin B_{12} mcg	0	Manganese mg	.078
Biotin mcg	—	Selenium mg	—
Folic acid mg	—	Zinc mg	1.41

high in vitamin A and C, which are helpful in combating acidity and poor digestion. Also beneficial in reducing kidney inflammation, fevers, and respiratory problems.

MAPLE SYRUP

Pure maple syrup comes in three grades. Grade A is the first run. It has a mild, sweet taste but has few minerals and is more expensive than the other grades. Grade B is the second run, with more minerals and a stronger maple flavor. It is less expensive. Grade C is the third run and has the highest mineral content and strongest taste and is the least expensive. Maple sugar contains sodium, potassium, calcium, magnesium, manganese, iron, copper, phosphorus, sulfur, chlorine, and silicon. Vitamins A, B_1, B_2, B_6, C, nicotinic acid, and pantothenic acid are also present.

NUTRITIONAL INFORMATION

1 T. maple syrup			
Calories	50	Pantothenic	
Carbohydrate g	12.8	acid mg	—
Protein g	0	Vitamin C mg	0
Fiber g	0	Vitamin E iu	—
Saturated fat g	—	Sodium mg	3
Unsaturated fat g	—	Phosphorus mg	3
Vitamin A iu	0	Potassium mg	26
Vitamin B_1 mg	—	Calcium mg	33
Vitamin B_2 mg	—	Iron mg	.2
Vitamin B_3 mg	—	Magnesium mg	—
Vitamin B_6 mg	—	Copper mg	.09
Vitamin B_{12} mcg	—	Manganese mg	—
Biotin mcg	—	Selenium mg	—
Folic acid mg	—	Zinc mg	—

MILK

Recently milk has become a very controversial subject. There are perhaps more people allergic or intolerant to milk than any other food.

For instance, while only 5 to 10 percent of Caucasian adults are intolerant to large amounts of milk, more than 70 percent of the adults among other racial groups show milk intolerance.

The Dairy Industry claims milk is needed by everyone and can be consumed in unlimited quantity. Other sources argue that cow's milk is for cows, and not a good food for people. Milk is also controversial because of its saturated fat content. Many authorities (including the American Heart Association) recommend only moderate consumption of whole milk by adults.

Cow's milk is a relatively new staple food in the human diet. The earliest evidence of its use as a human food has been dated about 9000 B.C. Today, a large portion of the world's people still do not drink milk, and yet they maintain adequate calcium because of the body's ability to utilize low levels of calcium more efficiently.

Since every body is different, diet is a personal, individual matter, and each person must decide for themselves whether they need milk. For those concerned about the saturated fat content of whole milk, skim milk and low-fat milk are good alternatives. Those with milk (lactose) intolerance can replace fluid milk with fermented milk products, such as cheese, yogurt, and buttermilk, which are all very low in lactose. Many of the recipes can be adapted to use yogurt (thinned with a little water) instead of milk.

NUTRITIONAL INFORMATION

	1 c. whole	1 c. lowfat	1 c. skim		1 c. whole	1 c. lowfat	1 c. skim
Calories	159	121	86	Pantothenic acid mg	.766	.78	.806
Carbohydrate g	11.4	11.7	11.8	Vitamin C mg	2.29	2.32	2.4
Protein g	8.5	8.12	8.35	Vitamin E iu	.293	—	+
Fiber g	0	0	0	Sodium mg	120	122	126
Saturated fat g	5.07	2.92	.287	Phosphorus mg	228	232	247
Unsaturated fat g	2.65	1.52	.132	Potassium mg	351	377	406
Vitamin A iu	350	500*	500	Calcium mg	291	297	302
Vitamin B$_1$ mg	.093	.095	.088	Iron mg	.12	.12	.1
Vitamin B$_2$ mg	.395	.403	.343	Magnesium mg	33	33	28
Vitamin B$_3$ mg	.205	.21	.216	Copper mg	.5	—	.1
Vitamin B$_6$ mg	.102	.105	.098	Manganese mg	.005	—	—
Vitamin B$_{12}$ mcg	.871	.888	.926	Selenium mg	3.17	—	11
Biotin mcg	5	—	5	Zinc mg	.93	.95	.98
Folic acid mg	.012	.012	.013				

*Value if vitamin A is added.

MILLET FLOUR

The seed of a grass cultivated for use as a cereal, millet was a staple food in China more than 12,000 years ago, and is still an important staple in Africa. Millet is also a staple food of the Hunza tribe living in the Himalayan foothills, who are noted for their health and longevity. It is easily digested and low in starch and helps relieve constipation.

Millet is well balanced in essential amino acids and has more iron than any other cereal. The flour is slightly more nutritious than the whole grain. The flour adds flavor to gravies, soups, and casseroles, but because it lacks gluten, bread made with millet flour will not rise very high. I was unable to find nutritional information for the flour, so I will give it for the whole grain.

NUTRITIONAL INFORMATION

1 c. millet flour			
Calories	660	Pantothenic	
Carbohydrate g	150	acid mg	—
Protein g	20	Vitamin C mg	—
Fiber g	6.5	Vitamin E iu	—
Saturated fat g	—	Sodium mg	—
Unsaturated fat g	—	Phosphorus mg	630
Vitamin A iu	—	Potassium mg	870
Vitamin B_1 mg	1.5	Calcium mg	40
Vitamin B_2 mg	.77	Iron mg	14
Vitamin B_3 mg	4.6	Magnesium mg	—
Vitamin B_6 mg	—	Copper mg	—
Vitamin B_{12} mcg	—	Manganese mg	—
Biotin mcg	—	Selenium mg	—
Folic acid mg	—	Zinc mg	—

MOLASSES

A by-product of the sugar-refining process, light molasses is the result of the first run or extraction. It has a light brown color and pleasant flavor and is the most popular. The second run produces a medium brown molasses. The third and final run yields a very dark, almost medicinal tasting molasses, called blackstrap. Blackstrap contains the most vitamins and minerals and was commonly used in folk medicine to make spring tonics. The recipes in this book were tested using light, or Barbados, molasses.

NUTRITIONAL INFORMATION

	1 T. blackstrap	1 T. light		1 T. blackstrap	1 T. light
Calories	43	50	Pantothenic		
Carbohydrate g	11	13	acid mg	.1	—
Protein g	0	0	Vitamin C mg	—	—
Fiber g	—	—	Vitamin E iu	—	—
Saturated fat g	—	—	Sodium mg	19	3
Unsaturated fat g	—	—	Phosphorus mg	17	9
Vitamin A iu	—	—	Potassium mg	585	183
Vitamin B_1 mg	.02	.01	Calcium mg	137	33
Vitamin B_2 mg	.04	.01	Iron mg	3.2	.9
Vitamin B_3 mg	.4	+	Magnesium mg	51.6	9.2
Vitamin B_6 mg	.054	—	Copper mg	.284	.2
Vitamin B_{12} mcg	0	—	Manganese mg	—	—
Biotin mcg	1.8	—	Selenium mg	—	5.2
Folic acid mg	.002	—	Zinc mg	—	—

NUTMEG

Nutmeg is the inner seed of the fleshy apricotlike fruit of the nutmeg tree. Frequently referred to in the sacred Vedic literature, nutmeg was used by early Hindu physicians to cure headaches, fevers, and intestinal disorders.

Arabian medical writings from the ninth century recommend the spice as a carminative and aphrodisiac and to treat various kidney and stomach problems. During the sixteenth and seventeenth centuries, European physicians and herbalists used nutmeg as a cure-all. Today it is used primarily to flavor food.

Nutmeg can be bought whole or ground and adds a delicate spicy flavor to cakes, custards, spiced wine and eggnog, and Middle

Eastern dishes. It is important to remember, however, that it has a powerful narcotic effect in large doses.

NUTRITIONAL INFORMATION

1 t. ground nutmeg

Calories	12	Pantothenic	
Carbohydrate g	1.08	acid mg	—
Protein g	.13	Vitamin C mg	—
Fiber g	.09	Vitamin E iu	—
Saturated fat g	.57	Sodium mg	+
Unsaturated fat g	.08	Phosphorus mg	5
Vitamin A iu	2	Potassium mg	8
Vitamin B_1 mg	.008	Calcium mg	4
Vitamin B_2 mg	.001	Iron mg	.07
Vitamin B_3 mg	.029	Magnesium mg	4
Vitamin B_6 mg	—	Copper mg	*
Vitamin B_{12} mcg	0	Manganese mg	*
Biotin mcg	—	Selenium mg	.4
Folic acid mg	—	Zinc mg	.05

*Present but value in mg unavailable.

OAT FLOUR

The oat groats are ground into a finer consistency to make a flour. It is an excellent addition to breads, muffins, or cookies when used with whole wheat flour. Use equal portions of oat flour with whole wheat flour.

NUTRITIONAL INFORMATION

1 c. oat flour

Calories	312	Pantothenic	
Carbohydrate g	55	acid mg	—
Protein g	11	Vitamin C mg	—
Fiber g	1.0	Vitamin E iu	—
Saturated fat g	—	Sodium mg	2
Unsaturated fat g	—	Phosphorus mg	320
Vitamin A iu	—	Potassium mg	280
Vitamin B_1 mg	.48	Calcium mg	42
Vitamin B_2 mg	.11	Iron mg	3.6
Vitamin B_3 mg	.8	Magnesium mg	—
Vitamin B_6 mg	.11	Copper mg	—
Vitamin B_{12} mcg	—	Manganese mg	—
Biotin mcg	—	Selenium mg	—
Folic acid mg	—	Zinc mg	—

ORANGES

Oranges probably originated in China and Southeast Asia. The orange was introduced to Europe by the Arabs, and Columbus brought orange seeds to be planted in America. A Jesuit priest started the California orange industry in 1804 by planting a grove of 400 trees at the San Gabriel Mission.

Oranges have been used to relieve asthma, bronchitis, tuberculosis, pneumonia, rheumatism, and high blood pressure. Eating large quantities of oranges will decrease mucus secretions from nose and head. In some cases, however, this may cause skin eruptions due to toxins being eliminated by the effect of the oranges. The orange peel and white membrane contain pectin, which is a digestive aid. The pectin also reduces the cholesterol level in the blood (see the chapter, *Eggs*). The sweet eating oranges familiar to us are the Navels and Valencias.

The Washington Navel. This variety accounts for 10 percent of the total orange crop and is an excellent eating orange, easy to peel and

NUTRITIONAL INFORMATION

	1 med., fresh	1 c. unsweetened juice	1 c. unsweetened, diluted frozen concentrate		1 med., fresh	1 c. unsweetened juice	1 c. unsweetened, diluted frozen concentrate
Calories	64	112	122	Pantothenic			
Carbohydrate g	16	25.8	28.9	acid mg	.45	.47	.41
Protein g	1.3	1.7	1.7	Vitamin C mg	66	124	120
Fiber g	.9	.3	+	Vitamin E iu	.43	—	—
Saturated fat g	—	—	—	Sodium mg	1	2	2
Unsaturated fat g	—	—	—	Phosphorus mg	26	42	42
Vitamin A iu	260	.500	.540	Potassium mg	263	496	503
Vitamin B$_1$ mg	.13	.22	.23	Calcium mg	54	27	25
Vitamin B$_2$ mg	.05	.07	.03	Iron mg	.5	.5	.2
Vitamin B$_3$ mg	.5	1	.9	Magnesium mg	19.8	49	25
Vitamin B$_6$ mg	.108	1	.07	Copper mg	.11	.2	.025
Vitamin B$_{12}$ mcg	0	0	0	Manganese mg	.045	—	—
Biotin mcg	1.8	.8	—	Selenium mg	2.5	14.9	—
Folic acid mg	.083	.136	.136	Zinc mg	.26	.09	.09

separate into sections. Navel oranges are large and seedless and generally have an excellent flavor. California Navels are available from mid-November through mid-May. Arizona harvests from November through February.

Valencia. This round or slightly oval, medium-sized orange makes up about half the orange crop in this country. The skin of Valencias is thin and smooth, and their juice is sweet and plentiful, which makes them popular as juicing oranges. Valencias are produced in Florida, California, Arizona, and Texas. They have a late season and are available throughout the year, from one area or another, except in December and January.

PAPAYAS

Papaya, also known as papaw fruit, is a tree melon of elongated shape, yellow or orange skin, and juicy orange flesh. The black seeds in the center of the fruit resemble large-size caviar. The papaya originated either in Mexico or the West Indies. They were brought to Hawaii by the same Spanish settler who introduced the pineapple, in the late eighteenth century.

Hawaii is the biggest supplier of papaya, with Florida and Puerto Rico also supplying some to the East Coast. May and June are the heaviest months of availability, with a smaller, even rate of distribution throughout the rest of the year. The papaya ripens at the blossom end first, so choose fruit that have started to color and have speckled yellow over 35 percent of the skin. This means the papaya will ripen in two to three days at room temperature. A ripe papaya will have a fruity aroma and will yield to slight pressure. Avoid shriveled or overly soft fruit. Dark spots on the skin are a bad sign: as with avocados, these spots usually get worse and penetrate to the flesh, causing bad flavor.

Papaya contains the protein-digesting enzyme papain, which aids digestion. Taken alone for two or three days the fruit has a tonic effect on the stomach and intestines. Papaya juice helps relieve infections in the colon and can break down pus and mucus. The fruit also contains vitamins D, E, and K.

NUTRITIONAL INFORMATION

½ med. papaya, raw

Calories	58	Pantothenic	
Carbohydrate g	15	acid mg	.327
Protein g	.9	Vitamin C mg	84
Fiber g	1.8	Vitamin E iu	—
Saturated fat g	—	Sodium mg	4.5
Unsaturated fat g	—	Phosphorus mg	24
Vitamin A iu	2625	Potassium mg	351
Vitamin B$_1$ mg	.06	Calcium mg	30
Vitamin B$_2$ mg	.06	Iron mg	.45
Vitamin B$_3$ mg	.45	Magnesium mg	11.4
Vitamin B$_6$ mg	—	Copper mg	.015
Vitamin B$_{12}$ mcg	0	Manganese mg	.013
Biotin mcg	—	Selenium mg	—
Folic acid mg	—	Zinc mg	—

PEACHES

Peaches grew wild in China where their cultivation began as early as the tenth century B.C. They were carried via caravan to Persia where they were a symbol of long life and named "Persica" by the Romans. Known as "Persian Apples," they were a luxury item in Rome and later in Europe. Columbus brought peach seeds to America and other Europeans planted them wherever they landed.

Peaches spread so fast that they were considered native to North America by botanists. Peaches are grown commercially in 35 states and are the third most important fruit crop in the United States, outranked only by apples and oranges. Peach season extends from early May through mid-September. July and August are the peak months. When buying peaches, select fruit with a yellowish or creamy background color: the pink or red color is not a good indication of ripeness. Ripe peaches are firm with a slight give and a lovely aroma.

Peaches improve the health of the skin and add color to the complexion. Peaches are helpful in relieving anemia, constipation, high blood pressure, gastritis, bronchitis, asthma, difficult digestion, bladder and kidney stones, and inflammation of the kidney.

NUTRITIONAL INFORMATION

	1 med., fresh	1 c., dried		1 med., fresh	1 c., dried
Calories	38	419	Pantothenic		
Carbohydrate g	9.7	109	acid mg	.177	—
Protein g	.6	5	Vitamin C mg	7	29
Fiber g	.69	5	Vitamin E iu	—	—
Saturated fat g	—	—	Sodium mg	1	26
Unsaturated fat g	—	—	Phosphorus mg	19	187
Vitamin A iu	1330	6240	Potassium mg	202	1520
Vitamin B_1 mg	.02	.02	Calcium mg	9	77
Vitamin B_2 mg	.05	.3	Iron mg	.5	—
Vitamin B_3 mg	1	8.5	Magnesium mg	11.5	76.7
Vitamin B_6 mg	.026	.16	Copper mg	.09	.48
Vitamin B_{12} mcg	0	0	Manganese mg	.11	1.07
Biotin mcg	2	—	Selenium mg	.46	—
Folic acid mg	.004	—	Zinc mg	.2	—

PEANUTS

Although often considered a nut, the peanut is actually a member of the legume family. Peanuts originated in South America, where peanuts have been found in Peruvian tombs dating from 950 B.C. They have an unusual way of growing on long tendrils underground, which has given them the name "ground nut."

Peanuts are rich in all eight essential amino acids. Some nutritionists consider peanuts an incomplete protein because tryptophan and methionine are present in low amounts. Peanuts are rich in the essential fatty acid, linoleic acid, which has been shown to reduce the risk of cholesterol deposits. They also supply a higher proportion of pantothenic acid than any other food except liver.

Peanut flour is an excellent substitute for wheat flour. It contains four times as much protein as wheat flour and nine times as many minerals. Substitute peanut flour for 15 to 20 percent of the wheat flour called for in recipes.

NUTRITIONAL INFORMATION

1 c. peanuts, roasted

Calories	838	Pantothenic	
Carbohydrate g	29.7	acid mg	3
Protein g	37.7	Vitamin C mg	—
Fiber g	3.89	Vitamin E iu	9.36
Saturated fat g	15.4	Sodium mg	7
Unsaturated fat g	50.5	Phosphorus mg	586
Vitamin A iu	+	Potassium mg	1009
Vitamin B_1 mg	.46	Calcium mg	104
Vitamin B_2 mg	.19	Iron mg	3.2
Vitamin B_3 mg	24.6	Magnesium mg	252
Vitamin B_6 mg	.576	Copper mg	.62
Vitamin B_{12} mcg	0	Manganese mg	2.17
Biotin mcg	49	Selenium mg	—
Folic acid mg	.153	Zinc mg	—

PEANUT BUTTER

I recommend buying 100 percent peanut butter. This kind of peanut butter is ground under pressure and extracts enough oil from the nut meal to give the peanut butter the desirable creamy texture. Peanut butter is an excellent food for children: not only is it filling and full of vitamins and minerals, but also 2 tablespoons of it provides more protein than an egg.

NUTRITIONAL INFORMATION

1 T. peanut butter

Calories	86	Pantothenic	
Carbohydrate g	3.2	acid mg	—
Protein g	3.9	Vitamin C mg	0
Fiber g	.33	Vitamin E iu	—
Saturated fat g	1.5	Sodium mg	18
Unsaturated fat g	6.1	Phosphorus mg	59
Vitamin A iu	0	Potassium mg	123
Vitamin B_1 mg	.018	Calcium mg	11
Vitamin B_2 mg	.02	Iron mg	.3
Vitamin B_3 mg	2.4	Magnesium mg	26
Vitamin B_6 mg	.05	Copper mg	.085
Vitamin B_{12} mcg	0	Manganese mg	—
Biotin mcg	5.8	Selenium mg	—
Folic acid mg	.013	Zinc mg	—

To make your own peanut butter: put one cupful of shelled peanuts, raw or roasted, into a grinder. Grind until crunchy or smooth according to your taste. A little vegetable oil and salt may be added if you prefer.

PEARS

Pears originated in central Asia many centuries before Christ. Marco Polo reported that the Chinese had perfected the cultivation of pears and produced fruit that were white on the inside, melted in the mouth, and weighed 10 pounds each. The Romans brought pears to England where the monks cultivated many varieties. Pears became very popular in France in the middle of the nineteenth century as an elegant dessert item. Pears were introduced into California by the Franciscan monks who planted them into their mission gardens.

Pears are divided into two groups: European, which are soft and include the Bartlett and Anjou; and Chinese or Asian, which are hard and gritty and are sometimes called sand pears. These are preferred for preserves, while the European varieties are excellent eating and canning pears.

Anjou. This winter pear, similar in size to the Bartlett with a shorter neck, has a yellowish-green skin and a yellowish-white flesh. It has a sweet flavor and stores well. Available from October through May.

Bartlett. This is a summer pear, medium to large in size and bell shaped. The bright yellow skin sometimes has a red blush when ripe. The skin is very tender and bruises easily. An excellent eating pear, it is juicy, sweet, and very smooth. Available from mid-July through early November.

Bosc. This pear has a long tapering neck with a dark yellow to tannish brown skin. The flesh is yellowish-white and not too juicy, but very sweet.

Comice. The Comice is a delicate, sweet, smooth, and juicy pear. It is a large neckless pear, oval in shape. These pears are excellent for both eating and juicing. Available from October through March.

Pears are recommended for constipation and poor digestion. They improve skin condition and relieve inflammation of the kidneys and colon.

NUTRITIONAL INFORMATION

	1 med., fresh	1 c., dried		1 med., fresh	1 c., dried
Calories	122	482	Pantothenic		
Carbohydrate g	30.6	121	acid mg	.14	—
Protein g	1.4	5.6	Vitamin C mg	8	13
Fiber g	2.8	6.2	Vitamin E iu	—	—
Saturated fat g	—	—	Sodium mg	4	13
Unsaturated fat g	—	—	Phosphorus mg	22	86
Vitamin A iu	40	130	Potassium mg	260	1031
Vitamin B_1 mg	.04	.02	Calcium mg	16	63
Vitamin B_2 mg	.08	.32	Iron mg	.6	2.3
Vitamin B_3 mg	.2	1.1	Magnesium mg	14	55.8
Vitamin B_6 mg	.034	—	Copper mg	.3	—
Vitamin B_{12} mcg	0	—	Manganese mg	.12	—
Biotin mcg	.2	—	Selenium mg	1.2	—
Folic acid mg	.028	—	Zinc mg	—	—

PECANS

Pecans are native to North America. Some North American Indians believed the pecan tree to be a manifestation of the Great Spirit and valued them highly enough to trade hides and mats for nuts from the early Spaniards. The Mariames, an Indian tribe living in Texas, ate only pecans for two months of the year. Meal was made from the ground dried nuts and mashed, and chewed nut meats were often force-fed to starving infants.

Pecans grow wild throughout the Mississippi valley region and in the river valleys of Texas. They were first cultivated in Texas in the seventeenth century. Pecans are now the first in economic importance of the native North American nut trees.

Pecans are delicious eaten raw; ground into meal; and baked into pies, breads, cakes, and cookies. They are very rich and are recommended in cases of low blood pressure, general weakness, and emaciation and for the nourishment of the teeth.

NUTRITIONAL INFORMATION

1 c. pecan halves, raw

Calories	742	Pantothenic	
Carbohydrate g	15.8	acid mg	1.7
Protein g	9.9	Vitamin C mg	2
Fiber g	2.3	Vitamin E iu	1.5
Saturated fat g	5.4	Sodium mg	+
Unsaturated fat g	63.8	Phosphorus mg	312
Vitamin A iu	140	Potassium mg	651
Vitamin B$_1$ mg	.93	Calcium mg	79
Vitamin B$_2$ mg	.14	Iron mg	2.6
Vitamin B$_3$ mg	1	Magnesium mg	142
Vitamin B$_6$ mg	.183	Copper mg	1.14
Vitamin B$_{12}$ mcg	0	Manganese mg	1.54
Biotin mcg	—	Selenium mg	3.24
Folic acid mg	.026	Zinc mg	—

PERSIMMONS

The persimmon is the national fruit of Japan, its cultivation there dating back 1000 years. The persimmon originated in China and requires a warm temperate climate. There are two varieties of persimmon; the Hachiya, which is the most commercially produced variety, and the Fuyu. The Hachiya is acorn shaped with a glossy bright

NUTRITIONAL INFORMATION

	1 med. Japanese, raw	1 med. Native, raw		1 med. Japanese, raw	1 med. Native, raw
Calories	77	127	Pantothenic		
Carbohydrate g	19.7	33.5	acid mg	—	—
Protein g	.7	.8	Vitamin C mg	11	66
Fiber g	1.6	1.5	Vitamin E iu	—	—
Saturated fat g	—	—	Sodium mg	6	1
Unsaturated fat g	—	—	Phosphorus mg	26	26
Vitamin A iu	2710	—	Potassium mg	174	310
Vitamin B$_1$ mg	.03	—	Calcium mg	6	27
Vitamin B$_2$ mg	.02	—	Iron mg	.3	2.5
Vitamin B$_3$ mg	.1	—	Magnesium mg	8	—
Vitamin B$_6$ mg	—	—	Copper mg	—	—
Vitamin B$_{12}$ mcg	—	—	Manganese mg	—	—
Biotin mcg	—	—	Selenium mg	—	—
Folic acid mg	—	—	Zinc mg	—	—

orange-red color. The Fuyu is rounder and orange. Both are very astringent and cause puckering of the mouth if eaten unripe. Persimmons are available from late September through mid-December. The peak is mid-October through late November. Choose fruit that is really soft—perhaps even a little shriveled—and plump and has the green stem cap attached. They will ripen at room temperature in a couple of days inside a closed plastic bag.

Persimmons are rich in pepsin, making them excellent aids to digestion. They are soothing on the intestinal tract and are an excellent food for energy. They are also recommended for pleurisy and sore throat conditions.

PINEAPPLES

First cultivated by the pre-Incas and Incas of Peru, the fruit was introduced to the North American Indians who then offered it to Columbus and his men. The pineapple is an old symbol of hospitality: a West Indian custom was to put pineapples near the huts to show strangers they were welcome. Explorers and traders spread the pineapple throughout the tropical areas of the world.

NUTRITIONAL INFORMATION

1 c. diced pineapple, raw			
Calories	81	Pantothenic	
Carbohydrate g	21.2	acid mg	.24
Protein g	.6	Vitamin C mg	26
Fiber g	.5	Vitamin E iu	—
Saturated fat g	—	Sodium mg	2
Unsaturated fat g	—	Phosphorus mg	12
Vitamin A iu	110	Potassium mg	226
Vitamin B_1 mg	.14	Calcium mg	26
Vitamin B_2 mg	.05	Iron mg	.8
Vitamin B_3 mg		Magnesium mg	20
Vitamin B_6 mg	.132	Copper mg	.09
Vitamin B_{12} mcg	0	Manganese mg	1.57
Biotin mcg	—	Selenium mg	.93
Folic acid mg	.017	Zinc mg	—

Today pineapples are grown commercially in Hawaii, Australia, the Philippines, South Africa, Puerto Rico, Florida, Cuba, and Mexico. They are available year-round, but the greatest supply is from March through June. Select pineapples with a yellow-to-golden-orange outer color to ensure sweet flavor inside.

Pineapples contain papain and bromelin, enzymes that aid the digestion of proteins. It is excellent to cure constipation and help rid the body of excess weight. Pineapple also regulates glands and is helpful in cases of goiter, bronchitis, high blood pressure, arthritis, and tumors.

PLUMS

The plum tree is associated with great age and wisdom in Chinese mythology. (Lao-tse, the founder of Taoism, was supposedly born white-haired under a plum tree in 604 B.C.) Plums also go back to the Stone Age tribes in Europe and are a native tree of the Northern hemisphere. They have been cultivated for over 2000 years. Three hundred years ago, the Japanese began cultivating plums, while only 100 years ago the famous horticulturist Luther Burbank brought them to California, where they are called Japanese plums. There are hundreds of varieties of plums, so I'll just mention a few of the best known.

Santa Rosa. This important early variety is cone shaped with purplish-crimson skin and yellow flesh that tends to redden toward the skin. This is a very juicy, excellent eating plum with a pleasant tart flavor. This is the plum developed by Mr. Burbank and is named after the town he lived in. These are available in mid-May. The Late Santa Rosa is harvested in early July.

El Dorado. A mid-season variety, available in June, it is heart-shaped with black-red skin and light amber flesh.

Laroda. A late-season plum, it is large and roundish, and the skin is reddish-yellow with firm yellow flesh.

Queen Ann. This is a fairly new plum with mahogany-colored skin, amber flesh, and a rich flavor. Queen Ann and Laroda are late-season plums, available in early July.

Plums are recommended for liver disorders, constipation, poor digestion, stomach gas, bronchitis, and skin eruptions.

NUTRITIONAL INFORMATION

2 med. plums (Damson variety), raw			
Calories	66	Pantothenic	
Carbohydrate g	17.8	acid mg	.186
Protein g	.5	Vitamin C mg	6
Fiber g	.4	Vitamin E iu	—
Saturated fat g	—	Sodium mg	2
Unsaturated fat g	—	Phosphorus mg	17
Vitamin A iu	300	Potassium mg	299
Vitamin B_1 mg	.08	Calcium mg	18
Vitamin B_2 mg	.03	Iron mg	.5
Vitamin B_3 mg	.5	Magnesium mg	9
Vitamin B_6 mg	.052	Copper mg	.1
Vitamin B_{12} mcg	0	Manganese mg	.1
Biotin mcg	+	Selenium mg	—
Folic acid mg	.006	Zinc mg	—

POPPY SEEDS

Used in small quantities, poppy seeds enhance the appearance and flavor of breads, cakes, and cookies. The most desirable seeds come from Holland and are slate-blue in color. Roasting, steaming, or crushing the seed before cooking releases its full flavor.

Opium is not made from the seeds, but from the unopened pods of the poppy. However, poppy seeds *are* soporific. They can be chewed raw or boiled in water to the thickness of honey and mixed with milk or honey to induce sleep for adults and children.

NUTRITIONAL INFORMATION

1 t. poppy seeds

Calories	15	Pantothenic	
Carbohydrate g	.66	acid mg	—
Protein g	.5	Vitamin C mg	—
Fiber g	.18	Vitamin E iu	—
Saturated fat g	.14	Sodium mg	1
Unsaturated fat g	1.04	Phosphorus mg	24
Vitamin A iu	—	Potassium mg	20
Vitamin B_1 mg	.024	Calcium mg	41
Vitamin B_2 mg	.005	Iron mg	.26
Vitamin B_3 mg	.027	Magnesium mg	9
Vitamin B_6 mg	.012	Copper mg	*
Vitamin B_{12} mcg	0	Manganese mg	*
Biotin mcg	—	Selenium mg	
Folic acid mg	—	Zinc mg	.29

*Present but value in mg unavailable.

PRUNES

Not all plums can be dried into prunes without fermenting if the pit is intact. Special plum trees produce deep blue to almost black fruit when ripe and can be dried without removing the pit. The Huns, Turks, Mongols, and Tartars used prunes as a staple in their diets.

NUTRITIONAL INFORMATION

1 c. dried prunes, hydrated

Calories	411	Pantothenic	
Carbohydrate g	108	acid mg	.85
Protein g	3.4	Vitamin C mg	5
Fiber g	1.96	Vitamin E iu	—
Saturated fat g	—	Sodium mg	13
Unsaturated fat g	—	Phosphorus mg	127
Vitamin A iu	2580	Potassium mg	1117
Vitamin B_1 mg	.14	Calcium mg	82
Vitamin B_2 mg	.27	Iron mg	6.3
Vitamin B_3 mg	26	Magnesium mg	74
Vitamin B_6 mg	.44	Copper mg	.52
Vitamin B_{12} mcg	0	Manganese mg	—
Biotin mcg	—	Selenium mg	—
Folic acid mg	.007	Zinc mg	—

Today the best known prune is the D'Agen, a French prune, which is grown mainly in California, where 98 percent of the United States prune supply is grown.

Prunes increase vitality and improve blood circulation. The fruit is also an excellent remedy for constipation, as most people know, and also benefits cases of anemia. Prune juice is a good remedy for sore throat.

Because of their oxalic acid content, it is best to soak prunes overnight to soften, rather than cooking them. Boiling foods with oxalic acid causes them to remove the calcium content of the body. Prunes, like cranberries, produce an acid reaction in the body, rather than the usual alkaline one produced by most other fruits.

PUMPKINS AND PUMPKIN SEEDS

Pumpkins are a member of the gourd family and are a native of China. In China, the pumpkin is called "the Emperor of the Garden" and is a symbol of fruitfulness and health. Pumpkin helps relieve infected or inflamed intestines, stomach ulcers, and hemorrhoids. It also raises blood pressure, enabling the blood to carry nourishment throughout the body.

Seeds from pumpkins and all kinds of squash are a good food. For example, for centuries the seed of the pepitoria squash was the main source of protein and fats for the Maya Indians in Guatamala. Combined with corn, beans, fresh vegetables, and fruits, the squash seeds account in part for the good health, fertility, and excellent teeth of these people.

Pumpkin seeds have been mentioned in old herbals for the treatment of prostate disorders. They are also effective in treating bladder and urinary disorders and tapeworms.

The seeds are 30 percent protein and 40 percent fat, which is rich in unsaturated fatty acids. Pumpkin seeds are richer in iron than other seeds and very high in phosphorus. They are also a good source of many B vitamins.

NUTRITIONAL INFORMATION

	1 c. pump-kin, canned	1 c. pumpkin seeds, dried and hulled		1 c. pump-kin, canned	1 c. pumpkin seeds, dried and hulled
Calories	81	774	Pantothenic		
Carbohydrate g	19.4	21	acid mg	1	—
Protein g	2.5	40.6	Vitamin C mg	12	—
Fiber g	3	2.66	Vitamin E iu	1095	—
Saturated fat g	—	11.8	Sodium mg	299	—
Unsaturated fat g	—	51	Phosphorus mg	750	1602
Vitamin A iu	15,860	100	Potassium mg	311	—
Vitamin B_1 mg	.07	.34	Calcium mg	1.2	71
Vitamin B_2 mg	.12	.27	Iron mg	—	15.7
Vitamin B_3 mg	1.5	3.4	Magnesium mg	—	—
Vitamin B_6 mg	.139	—	Copper mg	—	—
Vitamin B_{12} mcg	0	—	Manganese mg	—	—
Biotin mcg	—	—	Selenium mg	—	—
Folic acid mg	.047	.144	Zinc mg	—	—

RAISINS

Raisins have been used at least 4000 years. In 1000 B.C., the Israelites used raisins to pay their taxes to King David, and 600 years later Armenia was the center of a large raisin industry. Today most of the

NUTRITIONAL INFORMATION

	1 c. raisins		
Calories	477	Pantothenic	
Carbohydrate g	128	acid mg	.074
Protein g	4.1	Vitamin C mg	2
Fiber g	1.4	Vitamin E iu	—
Saturated fat g	—	Sodium mg	45
Unsaturated fat g	—	Phosphorus mg	167
Vitamin A iu	30	Potassium mg	1259
Vitamin B_1 mg	.18	Calcium mg	102
Vitamin B_2 mg	.13	Iron mg	5.8
Vitamin B_3 mg	.8	Magnesium mg	57.7
Vitamin B_6 mg	.396	Copper mg	.41
Vitamin B_{12} mcg	0	Manganese mg	.47
Biotin mcg	7	Selenium mg	—
Folic acid mg	.007	Zinc mg	.3

world's raisins are produced in California's San Joaquin Valley and are of Armenian descent.

Raisins are dried grapes that contain a high amount of natural sugar. They are either sun-dried or oven-dried. The most common varieties are large, ordinary raisins, sultanas or seedless raisins, and currants or corinth raisins.

Raisins are a strength-building food and are beneficial to those who are weak or anemic. They help in cases of tuberculosis, low blood pressure, and constipation.

RASPBERRIES

Raspberries are native to Asia, Europe, and North America. They have begun to be cultivated only recently, since they grow abundantly in the wild, their seeds being distributed by birds. There are two commercial types: the red and the black raspberry. Raspberry season starts in May with June and July being the peak times. When selecting berries, look for plump, fully colored ones. The berries are ripe when they drop their cores, leaving little hollow cups. They will

NUTRITIONAL INFORMATION

	1 c. black, raw	1 c. red, raw		1 c. black, raw	1 c. red, raw
Calories	98	70	Pantothenic		
Carbohydrate g	21	16.7	acid mg	.324	.288
Protein g	2	1.5	Vitamin C mg	24	31
Fiber g	7.65	4	Vitamin E iu	—	—
Saturated fat g	—	—	Sodium mg	1	1
Unsaturated fat g	—	—	Phosphorus mg	29	27
Vitamin A iu	+	100	Potassium mg	267	207
Vitamin B$_1$ mg	.04	.04	Calcium mg	40	27
Vitamin B$_2$ mg	.12	.11	Iron mg	1.2	1.1
Vitamin B$_3$ mg	1.2	1.1	Magnesium mg	40.5	24
Vitamin B$_6$ mg	.08	.072	Copper mg	.24	.22
Vitamin B$_{12}$ mcg	0	0	Manganese mg	68	.61
Biotin mcg	2.5	2.28	Selenium mg	—	—
Folic acid mg	.007	.006	Zinc mg	—	—

last a few days in the refrigerator, but it is best to use them as quickly as possible.

Raspberries are recommended for cases of constipation, high blood pressure, and congested liver. They are reputedly good for destroying body worms, removing excess fat from the body, and relieving menstrual cramps. A tea made from the leaves is an old remedy for miscarriage and labor pains.

RICE FLOUR AND POLISHINGS

Rice flour is made from the by-products of the milling process, including some bran, and ground into a fine powder. The flour is rich in B vitamins. One cup rice flour minus 2 tablespoons can substitute for 1 cup all-purpose flour to make close but delicately textured cakes.

Rice polishings consist of the bran that is removed during milling. They are an excellent source of B vitamins and can be incorporated into cookies, muffins, and pancakes.

NUTRITIONAL INFORMATION

1 c. rice polishings

Calories	278	Pantothenic	
Carbohydrate g	60.6	acid mg	—
Protein g	12.7	Vitamin C mg	0
Fiber g	2.4	Vitamin E iu	—
Saturated fat g	2.44	Sodium mg	+
Unsaturated fat g	9.34	Phosphorus mg	1161
Vitamin A iu	0	Potassium mg	750
Vitamin B_1 mg	1.93	Calcium mg	72
Vitamin B_2 mg	.19	Iron mg	16.9
Vitamin B_3 mg	29.6	Magnesium mg	—
Vitamin B_6 mg	—	Copper mg	—
Vitamin B_{12} mcg	—	Manganese mg	—
Biotin mcg	—	Selenium mg	—
Folic acid mg	.039	Zinc mg	—

ROLLED OATS

Oats are hulled and cracked or rolled into the familiar form. Rolled oats are shot with steam for a few seconds and then passed through rollers. Rolled oats are faster cooking than whole oat groats and are recommended for cookie recipes. When cooking oatmeal, I recommend the whole oat groats, also known as Irish oatmeal, Scotch oats, or steel-cut oats. These oats have more nutrients and should be soaked overnight before cooking into a porridge. Oatmeal is 16.7 percent protein, is rich in inositol, and has more thiamin than any other breakfast cereal. It is rich in iron and phosphorus and has traces of copper, manganese, zinc, and potassium. It forms a good protein when mixed with milk. Much of the fiber-rich bran has also been retained.

NUTRITIONAL INFORMATION

1 c. rolled oats, fortified			
Calories	147	Pantothenic	
Carbohydrate g	26.7	acid mg	—
Protein g	6.67	Vitamin C mg	—
Fiber g	.5	Vitamin E iu	.09
Saturated fat g	—	Sodium mg	420
Unsaturated fat g	—	Phosphorus mg	133
Vitamin A iu	—	Potassium mg	133
Vitamin B_1 mg	.5	Calcium mg	53
Vitamin B_2 mg	.57	Iron mg	3.1
Vitamin B_3 mg	32	Magnesium mg	53.7
Vitamin B_6 mg	.67	Copper mg	.274
Vitamin B_{12} mcg	2	Manganese mg	1.81
Biotin mcg	—	Selenium mg	—
Folic acid mg	.13	Zinc mg	—

SASSAFRAS BARK

Sassafras was used as a medicine and tea as early as 1569 by Monardes, a Spanish doctor. American Indians used the roots of the small tree to make a tonic.

The dried inner bark of the sassafras root makes a delicious tea with the flavor of root beer. In fact, it is one of the ingredients used to give root beer its characteristic flavor.

Sassafras bark has many medicinal uses. It is used as a spring tonic to purify the blood and cleanse the entire system. It has a stimulating tonic effect on the stomach and bowels and will help relieve gas. Sassafras bark is valuable in treating colic, skin diseases and eruptions, chest and throat troubles, and kidney and bladder problems. It also makes a good wash for inflammed eyes.

SEA SALT

I recommend using sea salt in our recipes. Buy the natural sun- or kiln-dried varieties. The advantage of sea salt over common table salt is its high percentage of trace minerals. Sea salt is 75 percent sodium chloride (table salt is 99.9 percent sodium chloride) and 25 percent minerals. All salt was at one time sea salt, however the minerals in salt from inland rock deposits have been leached out by water over time.

SESAME SEEDS

Sesame seeds have been used for centuries in the East, where it is a symbol of immortality. The seeds we get in the United States come mostly from Mexico. You may get them hulled or unhulled; the latter are nutritionally superior due to the high mineral content of the hull.

Sesame seeds are an excellent source of protein, unsaturated fatty acids, calcium, magnesium, niacin, and vitamins A and E. The protein in sesame seeds perfectly complements the protein of legumes, since each contain large quantities of the other's deficient amino acids. Therefore, use sesame seeds in combination with soy-beans and peanuts. In addition to the following nutrients, sesame seeds also supply us with good amounts of lecithin, inositol, and choline.

NUTRITIONAL INFORMATION

1 c. sesame seeds, dried and hulled			
Calories	873	Pantothenic	
Carbohydrate g	26.4	acid mg	—
Protein g	27.3	Vitamin C mg	0
Fiber g	3.6	Vitamin E iu	—
Saturated fat g	11.2	Sodium mg	—
Unsaturated fat g	64	Phosphorus mg	888
Vitamin A iu	—	Potassium mg	—
Vitamin B$_1$ mg	.27	Calcium mg	165
Vitamin B$_2$ mg	.2	Iron mg	3.6
Vitamin B$_3$ mg	8.1	Magnesium mg	270
Vitamin B$_6$ mg	.126	Copper mg	2.39
Vitamin B$_{12}$ mcg	0	Manganese mg	—
Biotin mcg	—	Selenium mg	—
Folic acid mg	—	Zinc mg	—

SORGHUM SYRUP

Sorghum is a grain grown in much the same way as corn. In Africa and Asia sorghum is a staple food for both humans and animals, but in our country it is used only as feed for stock. We do, however,

NUTRITIONAL INFORMATION

1 c. Sorghum Syrup			
Calories	330	Pantothenic	
Carbohydrate g	220	acid mg	—
Protein g	—	Vitamin C mg	—
Fiber g	—	Vitamin E iu	—
Saturated fat g	—	Sodium mg	—
Unsaturated fat g	—	Phosphorus mg	83
Vitamin A iu	—	Potassium mg	—
Vitamin B$_1$ mg	—	Calcium mg	570
Vitamin B$_2$ mg	.33	Iron mg	41
Vitamin B$_3$ mg	.3	Magnesium mg	—
Vitamin B$_6$ mg	—	Copper mg	—
Vitamin B$_{12}$ mcg	—	Manganese mg	—
Biotin mcg	—	Selenium mg	—
Folic acid mg	—	Zinc mg	—

make a syrup from sorghum that can be used instead of honey or molasses. It is a light amber color and thinner and more sour in flavor than cane molasses. Thin it a little with fruit juice and use as a pancake syrup.

SOUR CREAM

The addition of acid or a culture of acid-producing bacteria changes fresh cream to sour cream. Cultured sour cream contains 18 percent milk fat. Stabilizers are sometimes added to give it its characteristic smooth texture.

NUTRITIONAL INFORMATION

1 c. sour cream, cultured

Calories	493	Pantothenic	
Carbohydrate g	9.8	acid mg	.828
Protein g	7.27	Vitamin C mg	1.98
Fiber g	0	Vitamin E iu	—
Saturated fat g	30	Sodium mg	123
Unsaturated fat g	15.7	Phosphorus mg	195
Vitamin A iu	1817	Potassium mg	331
Vitamin B_1 mg	.081	Calcium mg	268
Vitamin B_2 mg	.343	Iron mg	.14
Vitamin B_3 mg	.154	Magnesium mg	26
Vitamin B_6 mg	.037	Copper mg	—
Vitamin B_{12} mcg	.690	Manganese mg	—
Biotin mcg	—	Selenium mg	—
Folic acid mg	.025	Zinc mg	.62

SOY MILK POWDER

Soy milk powder is a spray-dried product made from fresh soy milk. It is a valuable "milk" for those who are allergic to cow's milk. The powder can be used in bread, cakes, cookies, muffins, and pastry.

To make your own soy milk: Soak 100g (about ¼ pound) of good yellow soybeans 8 hours or overnight. Thoroughly wash away skins and cover the beans with ¾ liter (about ¾ quart) of water.

Blend into a milky solution. Put this mixture into a linen bag and press out the liquid. Heat the soy milk in a large pot for 5 to 10 minutes. Strain off the lecithin in the milk, which floats to the top. In China, where cow's milk is rarely used, soy milk is used in the nourishment of the children. The Chinese also use the residue, adding it to baked goods, puddings, and casseroles. Use the soy milk for blended drinks, or substitute it for cow's milk in the recipes.

NUTRITIONAL INFORMATION

¼ c. soy milk powder

Calories	98	Pantothenic	
Carbohydrate g	6	acid mg	–
Protein g	12	Vitamin C mg	–
Fiber g	–	Vitamin E iu	–
Saturated fat g	–	Sodium mg	1
Unsaturated fat g	–	Phosphorus mg	27
Vitamin A iu	–	Potassium mg	–
Vitamin B$_1$ mg	.22	Calcium mg	51
Vitamin B$_2$ mg	.08	Iron mg	2.6
Vitamin B$_3$ mg	1.2	Magnesium mg	–
Vitamin B$_6$ mg	–	Copper mg	–
Vitamin B$_{12}$ mcg	–	Manganese mg	–
Biotin mcg	–	Selenium mg	–
Folic acid mg	–	Zinc mg	–

STRAWBERRIES

Strawberries are perennial herbs. The seeds are embedded on the surface of the large fleshy fruits. Wild strawberries grow abundantly almost anywhere the climate is temperate. In fifteenth century France, *fraises de bois* were a delicacy, since the fruits gathered in the woods were exquisitely flavored but sparse. The early American colonists were surprised to see wild strawberries growing so abundantly that it was difficult to avoid stepping on them. However, the strawberries we buy today have been developed for their size from a Chilean variety. May is the time of heaviest supply of strawberries to market. In California, however, strawberry season may last from February through November.

Select solid-colored, bright, well-shaped berries. They can be refrigerated for about three days, but don't wash them until you are ready to use them.

Some people are allergic to strawberries, but for those who are not, strawberries have many therapeutic qualities. For example, they are a good skin-cleanser and a very effective blood purifier. They are recommended for a sluggish liver, gout, rheumatism, constipation, high blood pressure, and skin cancer. Crushed strawberries can be made into a poultice and applied to sore eyes and ringworm eruptions. To remove tartar from teeth and gums, apply strawberry juice, allow it to remain on teeth as long as possible, and rinse with warm water. Strawberry leaves can be steeped to make a tea that is useful in treating diarrhea and some urinary infections and in relieving aches in hips and thighs.

NUTRITIONAL INFORMATION

1 c. strawberries, raw

Calories	56	Pantothenic	
Carbohydrate g	12.6	acid mg	.51
Protein g	1	Vitamin C mg	88
Fiber g	2	Vitamin E iu	—
Saturated fat g	—	Sodium mg	2
Unsaturated fat g	—	Phosphorus mg	32
Vitamin A iu	90	Potassium mg	246
Vitamin B_1 mg	.04	Calcium mg	32
Vitamin B_2 mg	.1	Iron mg	1.5
Vitamin B_3 mg	.9	Magnesium mg	18
Vitamin B_6 mg	.082	Copper mg	.11
Vitamin B_{12} mcg	0	Manganese mg	.09
Biotin mcg	1.6	Selenium mg	—
Folic acid mg	.024	Zinc mg	.12

SUNFLOWER SEEDS

Because of the sunflower's peculiar habit of turning its head across the sky to follow the sun through all hours of the day, it was a mystic symbol to many ancient people, notably the Incas, who worshipped the sun. American Indians had a more practical attitude, using the seeds to make bread, thicken soups, and make oil.

Sunflower seeds are rich in protein, unsaturated fatty acids, phosphorus, calcium, iron, fluorine, iodine, potassium, magnesium, zinc, several B vitamins, and vitamins E and D. The sunflower plant's large root system enables it to penetrate deep into the soil and get nutrients. The flower head which faces the sun stores vitamin D and is one of the few vegetable sources of this vitamin.

NUTRITIONAL INFORMATION

1 c. sunflower seeds, dried and hulled			
Calories	812	Pantothenic	
Carbohydrate g	28.9	acid mg	2
Protein g	34.8	Vitamin C mg	—
Fiber g	5.5	Vitamin E iu	—
Saturated fat g	8.2	Sodium mg	—
Unsaturated fat g	56.9	Phosphorus mg	1214
Vitamin A iu	70	Potassium mg	1334
Vitamin B_1 mg	2.84	Calcium mg	174
Vitamin B_2 mg	.33	Iron mg	10.3
Vitamin B_3 mg	7.8	Magnesium mg	57
Vitamin B_6 mg	1.8	Copper mg	2.57
Vitamin B_{12} mcg	0	Manganese mg	—
Biotin mcg	—	Selenium mg	—
Folic acid mg	—	Zinc mg	—

TOFU

Tofu, or soy bean curd, is made by grinding soybeans and then curdling them with powdered gypsum, which has the same coagulating effect as rennin. Tofu's soft texture lends itself well to slicing, chopping, or mashing. When blended, it has a creamy consistency ideal for sauces, dressings, and blended protein shakes. Its pale color makes it a good substitute in recipes calling for cottage cheese. For people allergic to dairy products, tofu can be used in place of an egg, milk, or cheese. For those wishing to eat less meat, 4 ounces of tofu provides 8.8 grams of high quality protein comparable to chicken or steak. Tofu is a very versatile food, low in fat and calories, with no cholesterol, and very easy to digest. Tofu comes packed in water to keep it moist and fresh. Refrigerate until ready to use, then drain off the water, rinse under clear water, and let drain for a minute or two. Tofu is best when fresh, so check the container for the expiration date.

Often when standing in the check-out line at the market, I am asked what I do with tofu. I am always enthusiastic and my answer is tofu can be prepared in many ways: plain, baked, marinated, fried, whipped, blended, or barbequed.

NUTRITIONAL INFORMATION

3.5 oz. (or ¼ block) tofu			
Calories	72	Pantothenic	
Carbohydrate g	2.4	acid mg	—
Protein g	7.8	Vitamin C mg	0
Fiber g	.1	Vitamin E iu	—
Saturated fat g	—	Sodium mg	7
Unsaturated fat g	—	Phosphorus mg	126
Vitamin A iu	0	Potassium mg	42
Vitamin B_1 mg	.06	Calcium mg	128
Vitamin B_2 mg	.03	Iron mg	1.9
Vitamin B_3 mg	.1	Magnesium mg	111
Vitamin B_6 mg	—	Copper mg	—
Vitamin B_{12} mcg	—	Manganese mg	—
Biotin mcg	—	Selenium mg	—
Folic acid mg	—	Zinc mg	—

VANILLA

Vanilla is made from the pod of an exotic climbing orchid native to Central America. The pods are picked before fully-ripe and are dried and cured to bring out the characteristic vanilla aroma.

Long before the discovery of America, Aztec Indians in Mexico used vanilla as a flavoring, a medium of exchange, a source of perfume, and an herbal medicinal tonic. During the sixteenth and seventeenth centuries vanilla was used by European physicians as a stimulant, stomachic, aphrodisiac, and antidote to poison. It was listed in the British and German pharmacopoeias for many years, and was official in the U.S. Pharmacopoeia from 1860 to 1910. Today its medicinal use has declined and it is more highly regarded as a flavoring for sweet foods than as a drug.

Gourmet chefs and serious cooks buy vanilla pods, generally called "beans," instead of the extract because the taste is much better and the bean can be used over again if it is rinsed in cool water, patted dry, and stored in an airtight jar. Those wishing to make their own essence should purchase well-cured beans that are dark brown, leathery, and oily and shaped like a long thin cigar. The bean should also be highly aromatic and free of mildew and insect infestation.

WALNUTS

Walnuts are native to Iran. The Greeks called it the Persian tree and associated it with Diana and Jove. Roman tradition links the walnut to Jupiter and Juno, and walnuts were used during wedding ceremonies and feasts to symbolize fertility.

The two most important species of walnuts are the English (or Persian) and the Black walnut. The English walnut tree flourishes in European countries and on the West Coast of the United States. The

NUTRITIONAL INFORMATION

	1 c. chopped, black, raw	1 c. chopped, English, raw		1 c. chopped, black, raw	1 c. chopped, English, raw
Calories	785	651	Pantothenic		
Carbohydrate g	18.5	15.8	acid mg	—	.9
Protein g	25.6	14.8	Vitamin C mg	—	2
Fiber g	2.13	2.1	Vitamin E iu	—	1.5
Saturated fat g	4.5	4.5	Sodium mg	4	2
Unsaturated fat g	61.6	49.5	Phosphorus mg	713	380
Vitamin A iu	380	30	Potassium mg	575	450
Vitamin B_1 mg	.28	.33	Calcium mg	+	99
Vitamin B_2 mg	.14	.13	Iron mg	7.5	3.1
Vitamin B_3 mg	.9	.9	Magnesium mg	238	131
Vitamin B_6 mg	—	.73	Copper mg	1.74	1.39
Vitamin B_{12} mcg	—	0	Manganese mg	—	1.8
Biotin mcg	—	37	Selenium mg	—	—
Folic acid mg	—	.066	Zinc mg	2.82	2.26

Black walnut is a native of North America and grows best in New England, Florida, Nebraska, and eastern Texas.

Walnuts have a definite laxative effect. They are excellent for building muscles and strong healthy teeth and gums. They improve the body's metabolism and are recommended to people with liver ailments.

WHEAT GERM

The wheat germ is the embryo of the wheat kernel and contains all the nutrients necessary to sprout and sustain a new plant. In our recipes I recommend raw wheat germ, which has more nutrients than toasted germ. Wheat germ can be introduced to the diet through breads, muffins, pastry, cakes, and cookies. A good proportion to use is 50g (2 oz.) wheat germ to 400g (14 oz.) flour.

Wheat germ is a good way to get the vitamin B complex and amino acids for building a good protein in combination with legumes and seeds.

NUTRITIONAL INFORMATION

1 c. wheat germ, raw

Calories	363	Pantothenic	
Carbohydrate g	46.7	acid mg	2.2
Protein g	26.6	Vitamin C mg	0
Fiber g	2.5	Vitamin E iu	15
Saturated fat g	1.88	Sodium mg	3
Unsaturated fat g	8.18	Phosphorus mg	1118
Vitamin A iu	0	Potassium mg	827
Vitamin B_1 mg	2	Calcium mg	72
Vitamin B_2 mg	.68	Iron mg	9.4
Vitamin B_3 mg	4.2	Magnesium mg	336
Vitamin B_6 mg	.92	Copper mg	1.3
Vitamin B_{12} mcg	—	Manganese mg	—
Biotin mcg	—	Selenium mg	83.3
Folic acid mg	.328	Zinc mg	14.3

WHOLE WHEAT FLOUR

Wholemeal wheat flour contains all the grain including the bran and the germ. It has a coarse texture and a higher nutritional content than other flours (except soy flour). It is sold as *whole wheat flour*, 100 percent extraction. It is best to buy stone-ground whole wheat flour, since stone grinding distributes the germ oil more evenly and smoothly, using slower speeds and lower temperatures than the steel or roller plate mills.

Whole wheat pastry flour is 81 percent or 85 percent extraction flour and is a finer flour due to the fact that the bran and some of the protein aleurone layer is removed by sieving 19 percent of the ground grain. Whole wheat pastry flour will produce lighter textured cakes and breads, but either may be used successfully.

NUTRITIONAL INFORMATION

	1 c. whole wheat flour, stirred	1 c. whole wheat pastry flour, sifted		1 c. whole wheat flour, stirred	1 c. whole wheat pastry flour, sifted
Calories	400	364	Pantothenic		
Carbohydrate g	852	79.4	acid mg	—	.32
Protein g	16	7.5	Vitamin C mg	0	0
Fiber g	2.8	.2	Vitamin E iu	—	—
Saturated fat g	+	—	Sodium mg	1^3	2
Unsaturated fat g	2	—	Phosphorus mg	70	73
Vitamin A iu	0	0	Potassium mg	85	95
Vitamin B_1 mg	.66	.03	Calcium mg	11	17
Vitamin B_2 mg	.14	.03	Iron mg	1.2	.5
Vitamin B_3 mg	1.5	.7	Magnesium mg	25	26
Vitamin B_6 mg	.41	.045	Copper mg	.028	—
Vitamin B_{12} mcg	0	0	Manganese mg	—	—
Biotin mcg	—	—	Selenium mg	—	—
Folic acid mg	—	—	Zinc mg	.7	.3

YOGURT

According to ancient folklore, an angel appeared to the prophet Abraham and revealed to him the method of making yogurt. Even to this day, kefir, a similar cultured milk drink is known as "the drink of the Prophet" in Islamic countries. Yogurt has been made for thousands of years by the Mongolian, Armenian, Persian, and Arabian people. It has also been used since the Roman times as a medicine for gaseous, burning stomachs.

Yogurt is made from homogenized, low-fat, or skim milk with nonfat dry milk added to give it additional body. A bacteria culture ferments the milk sugar, turning it into lactic acid, which gives yogurt its characteristic tartness and makes it more readily digestible. Yogurt is a nice addition to many desserts and can replace ice cream and sour cream if desired. When added to cakes in place of milk, it produces a more tender texture.

NUTRITIONAL INFORMATION

	8 oz. whole milk, plain	8 oz. lowfat milk, plain	8 oz. skim milk, plain		8 oz. whole milk, plain	8 oz. lowfat milk, plain	8 oz. skim milk, plain
Calories	139	144	127	Pantothenic			
Carbohydrate g	10.6	16	17.4	acid mg	.883	1.34	1.46
Protein g	7.88	11.9	13	Vitamin C mg	1.2	1.82	1.98
Fiber g	0	0	0	Vitamin E iu	—	—	—
Saturated fat g	4.76	2.27	.264	Sodium mg	105	159	174
Unsaturated fat g	2.24	1.07	.124	Phosphorus mg	215	326	355
Vitamin A iu	279	150	16	Potassium mg	351	531	579
Vitamin B_1 mg	.066	.1	.109	Calcium mg	274	415	452
Vitamin B_2 mg	.322	.486	.531	Iron mg	.11	.18	.2
Vitamin B_3 mg	.17	.259	.281	Magnesium mg	26	40	43
Vitamin B_6 mg	.073	.11	.12	Copper mg	—	—	—
Vitamin B_{12} mcg	.844	1.28	1.39	Manganese mg	—	—	—
Biotin mcg	—	—	—	Selenium mg	—	—	—
Folic acid mg	.017	.025	.028	Zinc mg	1.34	2.02	2.2

NOTES

1. Vicki Peterson, *The Natural Food Catalog*, New York: Arco Publishing Company Inc., 1978, p. 105.

The tables in this section have been compiled from information in the following reference materials.

Composition of Foods, Agricultural Handbook no. 8, Department of Agriculture.

Food Values, Bowes and Curch, J.B. Lippincott, New York.

The Composition of Foods, McCance and Widdowson, Medical Research Council Special Report Series no. 297, Her Majesty's Stationery Office, London, England.

Bloom,
Wherever
you are
planted.
　　—*Ella Grasso*
　　　late governor of Connecticut

Recipes

*H*ere you are in the kitchen, with your bowls and spoons. The flour is sifted, and the eggs and honey are being whipped into the milk with a gentle sprinkling of raisins and nuts. The oven is warming, and the cake pan is oiled. All is in readiness. Now you, with all your thoughts and feelings, and all these earthy ingredients are brought together in a mandala of energy, and magically transform quite ordinary things into something much more.

Your cake is more than just a cake. It is both a result and a symbol of your dance with life's energies. This awareness of pure nature is nothing you could express in words, but the feeling generated by this kind of spiritual discovery is unity with all things.

Dessert Cheeses, Fruits & Nuts

THE DESSERT OF CHEESE, FRUIT, AND BREAD is a classic originating at European tables. Simple and elegant, the cheese and bread board is a natural, healthful way to end a meal. Most fruits and wines go with most cheeses and you need not be a connoisseur to present a nice spread. Personal taste is always the deciding factor.

During the winter holiday season it was always a custom in our home to put out bowls of fresh fruits and nuts. Brazil nuts, almonds, walnuts, pecans, and hickory nuts were offered, along with nutcrackers and picks, to family guests and relatives who came to call during the season. What a wonderful way to extend hospitality and good cheer to visitors, I used to think, yet I never understood why these simple, no-fuss elegant delicacies were not served during the rest of the year at party times.

Later, when my family moved to Europe, it was standard procedure to complete the dinner meal with an assortment of fruit and cheeses. This ancient ritual I found relaxing and truly a taste of "the good life." Beautiful fruits glistening in a fine glass bowl were served onto glass dessert plates and eaten with fork and knife. The skin was carefully and slowly cut away as close to the skin as possible. The fruit was then pitted or pared, if necessary, and eaten a slice at a time. A ripe Camembert, served at room temperature, was always my favorite accompaniment. Crackers or french bread completed the spread.

Nuts are a natural companion to fruit, in combination with dried fruits, or they may be served alone. Nuts in the shell ensure freshness of flavor, and allow family or friends to enjoy one another's company while lingering longer around the dinner table.

Some people believe nuts are hard to digest, and so they do not include them in their diet. I think most people could easily eliminate this problem by chewing the nuts sufficiently, and eating only a moderate amount at a time. The truth is that nuts have a high fat content, which means they take longer to digest than proteins or carbohydrates. If the nuts are not chewed enough, digestive juices can't penetrate their dense structure. These are good reasons to serve nuts with fruits. Fruits, which are low in fats, balance the richness of nuts. Also, serving nuts with fresh or dried fruits reduces the temptation to eat too many nuts.

If you are concerned about the way many sweet desserts cause a quick rise in blood sugar, this section offers you an alternative. Cheeses, fruits, and nuts are very satisfying and curb the desire for sweets after a meal. Not only do these desserts provide a feast of vitamins, minerals, and protein, but also their natural complex sugars are released slowly into the bloodstream, giving you hours of sustained energy.

The following section will explore an assortment of cheeses especially suitable for dessert, along with compatible fruit, bread, and wine combinations to complete their flavors. This should be helpful to those who have never considered this traditional dessert, those who wish to expand their knowledge of the many dessert cheese possibilities, and those who wish to create an atmosphere of Old World conviviality.

BRICK CHEESE ✖

A semisoft American cheese. Softer than Cheddar and firmer than Limburger, this cheese has a creamy yellow color and numerous, small round holes. The young cheese is mild and firm, the aged brick is earthy in flavor.

Fruit and Wine Suggestions:

Serve with fresh peaches, apricots, cherries, melons, apples, or pears.

Serve with light, fruity, and dry whites, rosés, and reds. Try Clarets, Beaujolais, and Chablis.

BRIE CHEESE ✦

A soft-ripening French cheese, similar to but slightly firmer than Camembert. It is creamy gold inside with a thin, edible, brown and white crust. Its mild-to-pungent flavor is at its height when served at room temperature.

Fruit and Wine Suggestions:

Serve with fresh peaches or pears, sesame and rye crackers, and dark whole grain breads.

Robust red wines are recommended, but also try lighter reds, such as Beaujolais and Clarets, and light, dry Sherries.

CAMEMBERT CHEESE ✦

Another soft-ripening French cheese that is creamy yellow inside and ripens to the consistency of heavy cream. The whitish gray crust is also edible. To maximize the strength of its flavor, this cheese is best served at room temperature.

Fruit and Wine Suggestions:

Serve with fresh peaches, apples, pears, fresh plums, and walnuts.

All full-bodied red wines go best, but also try Beaujolais and light, dry Sherries.

CHEDDAR CHEESE ✦

A major English cheese made in most English-speaking countries. Color may range from white to orange, texture from firm to crumbly, and flavor from mild to sharp, depending on the amount of aging.

Fruit and Wine Suggestions:

Serve with fresh pears, apples, or cherries.

Wine suggestions include light Clarets, Tawny Port, red Burgundies and Elderberry.

CREAM CHEESE ✍

A soft, unripened cheese popular in England, France, and the United States. It is white and creamy with a rich, mild flavor. Its soft, buttery consistency lends itself well to cheese blintzes and crepes, or it may be thinned with cream to make a spreadable dip for crackers and dessert breads with jam.

Fruit and Wine Suggestions:

Delicious when served with fresh apricots, grapes, peaches, pears, sectioned oranges, and nuts.

Try dry white wines such as Alsace, Muscadet, Chablis, and White Graves. Also try the sweet rosés, average-bodied reds, and dessert fruit wines.

EDAM, GOUDA CHEESE ✍

A hard, Dutch cheese made from whole or partially skimmed milk. Distinctively spherical in shape and coated in bright red wax, this cheese will liven up any dessert spread. It is yellowish gold inside, and has a firm, smooth texture and a mild, sweet, nutlike flavor.

Fruit and Wine Suggestions:

Serve with fresh grapes, sectioned oranges, and black bread with butter.

I recommend full-bodied reds, dry whites, or rosés.

GORGONZOLA CHEESE ✍

A major Italian cheese in the bleu cheese family. The inside is a creamy, soft white with a blue-green mold. It is packaged in a reddish rind wrapped in tin foil. The flavor is spicy.

Fruit and Wine Suggestions:

Serve with fresh apples, pears, melons, crackers, and French or Italian bread.

Best with medium to full-bodied red wines such as Burgundies and Bordeaux.

GRUYÈRE CHEESE ✍

A cooked, hard, whole-milk cheese made in both France and Switzerland. It is pale yellow in color, with many holes throughout and has a nutlike, salty flavor.

Fruit and Wine Suggestions:

Good with most fruits and crackers.

Serve with dry white or light red wines.

LIEDERKRANZ CHEESE ✍

A soft-ripened, native American cheese invented in the 1890s by a young New York delicatessen keeper named Emil Frey. Trying to imitate the German Bismark Schlosskäse cheese, he came up with something even better and called it "wreath of song." Liederkranz has a light, orange-colored rind and a golden-yellow inside. The texture is soft and creamy and the flavor is tangy yet mellow, much like a mild Limburger but without having the characteristic odor.

Fruit and Wine Suggestions:

Good with fresh apples, pears, and Tokay grapes. Spread on toast, crackers, rye, or pumpernickel breads.

Try dry or semidry white wines, such as Pinot Chardonnay, Pinot Blanc, and Moselle. Also good with full-bodied red wines.

MONTEREY JACK CHEESE ✌

A semisoft, American cheese originating in California. It is made from either whole milk or partially skimmed milk. No coloring is added and the cheese is white to light cream in color. The flavor ranges from mild to sharp depending on the amount of aging.

Fruit and Wine Suggestions:

Serve with fresh peaches, apricots, apples, and pears. Spear cheese cubes on toothpicks, alternating with chunks of fruit. Also good with crackers.

Best with fruity, dry white wines, rosés, or Clarets.

MUENSTER CHEESE ✌

Originally made in the valley of Müenster in Alsace, France, this smooth-tasting cheese is now also made in the United States, where its flavor is milder due to a shorter curing time. Made from whole milk, it is a fermented, medium-hard cheese. White and creamy with tiny holes, it has a mild to mellow flavor.

Fruit and Wine Suggestions:

Serve with fresh dark cherries, wedges of cantaloupe or honeydew melon, apples, pears, grapes, and sectioned oranges.

Generally good with dry aromatic white or rosé wines. Try white wines of Alsace or warm, robust reds.

PORT DU SALUT CHEESE ﻌ

A French, semihard, pressed cheese made from whole milk, this favorite of restaurants is made in many cheese-making countries. Creamy and yellow inside, its flavor lies between Cheddar and Limburger.

Fruit and Wine Suggestions:

Serve with fresh cherries, pears, apples, grapes, and crackers.

Good with dry white or light dry red wines. Also try the fruity reds.

PROVOLONE CHEESE ﻌ

A major Italian cheese made from whole milk, with a thin, shiny, golden rind outside and a creamy white to yellow inside. The texture is smooth and hard, while the taste ranges from sweet to sharp depending on the aging process and the type of rennet used.

Fruit and Wine Suggestions:

Serve with crackers, dark whole grain breads, fresh apples, sectioned oranges, tangerines, and all kinds of melon.

Generally, dry white or red wines are recommended. Dry Sherries, Tawny Port, and Barolo, an Italian wine, are also compatible.

RICOTTA CHEESE ✎

A soft, unripened cheese made from whole milk or whole milk and whey. It is a fresh, soft cheese, somewhat sweet and mild in flavor.

Use in cooking to make cheese blintzes, or thin to a dipping consistency. See Cream Cheese for further suggestions.

Fruit and Wine Suggestions:

Serve with red and white wines of average body, or sweet rosés. Also try the sweet dessert wines. Light and fragrant wines of the Rhine and Moselle are suitable companions for cheese blintzes.

ROQUEFORT CHEESE ✎

A major French, blue-veined cheese, and the only one made from ewe's milk. This makes it a finer, richer cheese with a well-aged, piquant, and salty flavor.

Fruit and Wine Suggestions:

Serve with fresh apples, pears, and crusty French or Italian bread.

Best with robust, strong red wines, or dry Champagne. Also try Barolo, Clarets, dry Sherries, and Madeiras.

STILTON CHEESE ✃

A major English cheese, white with a blue mold. When left to mature for eight months, it is moist, soft, and crumbly with a spicy flavor.

Fruit and Wine Suggestions:

See Roquefort for serving ideas.

I recommend Elderberry wine, Tawny or Vintage Port, red Burgundies, Barolo, and Clarets. Also try the bigger dry Sherries and Madeiras.

SWISS CHEESE ✃

Called "Emmenthal" in Switzerland, this cheese only represents one of many varieties that fall into the major category of "Swiss" cheese. Made in many cheese-making countries, it is generally pale cream to tan in color, and sweet, nutty, and zesty in flavor. All types have holes of varying sizes.

Fruit and Wine Suggestions:

Serve with fruit juices, fresh apricots, melons, grapes, peaches, sectioned oranges, tangerines, and dark and rye breads.

Good with most dry white or light red wines.

TILSIT CHEESE ✃

Originally from Germany, but now widely made in cheese-making countries. This is a medium-firm, cream-colored cheese with small, round holes. Fully cured at six months, it is yellow-streaked inside and has a medium-to-sharp flavor.

Fruit and Wine Suggestions:

Good with fresh apples, pears, grapes, sectioned oranges, crackers, toast, and light rye bread.

Serve with aromatic white or rosé wines. Also try dry white Sherries or Ports.

BLANCHED ALMONDS ✌

Soak the almonds in boiling water for 10 minutes and then remove the skins. Dry on paper towels.

1 c. raw shelled almonds

MARZIPAN ✌

Marzipan is a European delicacy sold in gourmet shops, but it is easily made at home.

Blanch almonds and grind the nuts to a paste. A food processor or blender will do the job easily. You may have to add a little almond or safflower oil to the ground nuts. The paste can be rolled into balls and flattened with a cookie press (the kind with a pretty pattern on the bottom) or pressed into small candy molds. Often a little vegetable dye is added to the marzipan, which is then formed into fruit shapes.

2 c. raw almonds

SWEET MARZIPAN ✌

If you have a "sweet tooth," you'll enjoy this variation.

Follow the directions for marzipan, and add the maple syrup. Add a little at a time, and sweeten to taste. Other sweeteners to use are sorghum, malt syrup, or rice syrup. If you use honey, try one teaspoon at a time because it is sweeter than the above syrups, and its flavor can dominate the marzipan if too much is used.

2 c. raw shelled almonds
1 T. maple syrup

PERSIAN ALMONDS ✌

The anise seeds, served after a meal, freshen the breath and aid in digestion.

Toss the dates and anise seeds together in a bowl so that the seeds adhere to the sticky dates. Add the almonds, and toss well. Serve in a decorative dessert bowl.

2 c. raw almonds, sliced into large slivers
2 c. pitted dates, sliced into thin slivers
1 T. anise seeds

CASABLANCA CASHEWS ✌

In Middle Eastern countries the cardamon seeds are traditionally chewed after meals to sweeten the breath.

Mix the cashews, raisins, and seeds together and serve them in a decorative dessert bowl.

2 c. raw cashews
2 c. raisins
1 t. cardamom seeds

BRAZIL SUNRISES ✌

The tartness of the apricots is a nice balance for the rich nuts.

Grind fresh coriander on the insides of the whole dried apricots. Spoon the Brazil nuts on top and fold the apricot around them. Spear the apricots together with party toothpicks.

5 Brazil nuts, sliced into slivers
10 dried apricots
Fresh ground coriander

TURKISH SNOW ✌

You can prepare the components of this dish ahead of time and assemble it just before serving.

Slit the dates lengthwise to remove the pits. Stuff the centers of each date with a walnut. Arrange the dessert plates with a piece of fresh, crisp iceburg lettuce. Place a mound of shredded coconut on top, and sprinkle on some fresh ground cardamom. Top with the stuffed dates. Serves 6.

6 Bahri dates, pitted
6 shelled walnuts
1 fresh coconut, shredded
Fresh ground cardamom
6 iceburg lettuce leaves

TUTTI FRUTTI WINTER MIX ✌

Excellent movie, hiking, or camping treats. Children enjoy mixing these up into small snack bags. The following two recipes are given in proportions so that you can make any quantity you wish.

Mix all ingredients together in a bowl and bag into small snack sacks with twist tops, or larger bags for pantry storage.

1 part Black Mission figs, de-stemmed and quartered
1 part dates, pitted and halved
1 part dried apricots, quartered or halved
1 part dried pears, quartered
1 part dried apples, halved
2 parts roasted peanuts
2 parts roasted sunflower seeds
4 parts coconut ribbons

TUTTI-FRUTTI SUMMER MIX ✌

This variation is super for picnics and vacation celebrations.

Mix and bag as for Winter Mix in previous recipe. These mixes also make nice TV munchies or informal desserts for family and friends.

1 part dried papaya strips, cut into chunks
1 part dried pineapple, cut into chunks
1 part dried peaches, cut into chunks
1 part pumpkin seeds
2 parts raisins
2 parts raw cashews
4 parts coconut ribbons

CALICO NUT BARS ✌

The trick is not to overmix the fruits and thereby keep the marbled effect. If the mix is too dry, knead in a little water to moisten.

Put the dried fruits through a food mill. Next, grind the cashews, mix together with the cardamom, and set them aside. Chop the Brazil nuts and mix them with the ground fruits. Hand mix the different fruits together until they become marbled. Press mixture into a ball and then roll out into a long, thick rectangle. Square the sides by pressing down firmly on a counter. Press in the ground cashews and wrap in wax paper. Place in the freezer for 2 hours and then cut into bars.

2 c. prunes, pitted
1 c. dates, pitted
1 c. dried apricots
¼ c. ground Brazil nuts
1 c. chopped cashews
1 t. ground cardamom

CASHEW MARBLE BARS ✌

Creamy fruits with contrasting crunchy texture of cashews makes this an unusual confection.

Run ½ cup of the cashews through a food mill and set aside. Next, put the dried fruits through a food mill or processor. Press the ground fruits together with the chopped cashews and spice, using your hands to mix the nuts well. Don't overly mix and check carefully for a marbled color. When you achieve this effect, press the mixture into a long roll and square the edges by pressing down firmly on the counter.

Spread out the ground cashews on a piece of wax paper that is large enough to fit the roll you just made. Press roll into the nuts to cover sides and then wrap the roll in wax paper. Chill for 2 hours in the freezer. Slice roll as the occasion arises, but continue to store it in the freezer. This will keep the candy from being sticky and enhances the flavor.

1 c. dates, pitted.
2 c. dried pears
1 c. dried peaches
1½ c. chopped cashews
1 t. ground coriander

Fruit Desserts

FRUITS ARE NATURE'S PERFECT DESSERT. Eaten fresh and raw, they are one of the simplest ways to offer your family a feast of vitamins and minerals. Fully ripened fruits require no sweetening and can be made into sumptuous fruit salads, which can be dressed elegantly with yogurt, cottage cheese, or sour cream. Prepared in this way, there are no nutritional losses, plus the simplicity of preparation will please those who like to spend less time in the kitchen.

In addition to these raw fruit recipes, this section includes many fruit gelatins using both gelatin and agar-agar. Agar-agar, or *kanten*, is made from seaweed and is a gelling agent used in Japanese cooking. It has a soothing action on the intestines, and is beneficial in cases of constipation. It is tasteless, easy to use, and obtainable at most health food stores. The recipes call for natural juices—no preservatives, sweeteners, colorings, or flavorings. Unfiltered juices are best as many of the nutrients are in the sediment.

The remaining fruit desserts in this section require cooking or baking. Baked fruits are very easy to make and are excellent cold weather desserts. Those who wish to cut down on rich, heavy desserts will find this section appealing.

YOGURT MELON RINGS ✌

For the weight-watcher. A light, tasty treat that takes minutes to prepare and serves a crowd.

Slice the melons into 1-inch-thick rings. Remove the rinds and place the rings on dessert plates. Fill the center of each ring with a scoop of yogurt and drizzle honey on top.

Cantaloupe
Low-fat yogurt
Honey or date sugar to taste

BANANA SPLITS ✌

Here's a simple, uncooked dessert you can whip together in minutes to satisfy the late-night munchies. Let your imagination run wild with the fruits, seeds, nuts, and sweeteners on hand in your pantry.

On a platter or in a large bowl, place the banana halves on either side and place the scoops of ice cream or yogurt in the center. Sprinkle all the ingredients with seeds or nuts, dried fruits or one of the suggested toppings. For a quick sauce, drizzle honey, molasses, or maple syrup on top.

VARIATION: You can spread peanut or other nut butters on the bananas for added protein and flavor.

1 banana, split lengthwise
Honey ice cream or yogurt scoops
Seeds or nuts: sesame and sunflower seeds, or cashews, peanuts, walnuts, almonds
Dried fruits: raisins, dates, pineapple, apricots
Toppings: Jiffy Carob Sauce, Fruit Topping, Coconut Caramel (see Toppings and Fillings, pp. 295-300)

ORANGE RAISIN DESSERT SALAD ✌

This salad makes a lovely ending to a rich, full meal. Sweet and colorful, it can be served with lettuce, cottage cheese, yogurt, or whipped cream.

Toss fruit in a salad bowl. Mix together lemon juice, honey, and spice in a small bowl and toss into the fruit salad. Chill and serve. Serves 4.

5 oranges, peeled and sliced
3 bananas, peeled and sliced
1 c. raisins
½ c. lemon juice
1 T. honey or date sugar
1 t. ground coriander

SUNRISE FRUIT DELIGHTS ❧

Delicious and elegant looking, this dessert is so easy that my children love to prepare it for the family.

Rinse the fruits and set aside to drain. Whip the cream with the honey and vanilla until stiff peaks form. Spoon it out onto four dessert plates or small bowls. Arrange the peach slices at the edge of the bowl, like petals of a flower. Next, make two circles of black raspberries inside the peaches, leaving space between fruits. Working toward the middle, repeat a single row of red raspberries and top it off with a large strawberry. Chill and serve. Serves 4–6.

2 fresh peaches, thinly sliced
1½–2 c. fresh black raspberries
1 c. fresh red raspberries
4 large ripe strawberries, destemmed
1 pt. whipping cream
1 T. honey
1 t. vanilla

CANTALOUPE FRUIT SALAD ❧

A delightful summer brunch. Fresh, cooling, and very satisfying.

Cut the cantaloupes into small chunks and mix with all the other fruit and the walnuts in a large salad bowl. Scoop yogurt into the bottoms of individual bowls and cover it with a generous serving of fruit salad. Serves 6.

2 cantaloupes, with rind and seeds removed
1 large pineapple, cut into small chunks
1 c. raisins
1 c. fresh shredded coconut
1 c. finely chopped walnuts
1 apple, cored and cut into small chunks
Low-fat yogurt

FRUIT CUPS AU VIN ❧

An easy-to-make light dessert.

Blend the wine and honey, pour it over the pineapple and chill. Sprinkle with fresh coconut and serve in small fruit cups. Serves 4.

VARIATION: Oranges (1 per person), peeled, then sliced into rounds are an excellent alternative to pineapple.

UNSWEETENED VARIATION: Instead of honey, use 1 tablespoon frozen orange juice concentrate, and mix with the wine before pouring over the fruit.

4 c. diced fresh pineapple
2 c. fresh shredded coconut
6 t. Sauterne
4 t. honey

FRUIT SUNDAE ❧

A fruit salad with yogurt. Any fruit combination will work—plain or with your choice of our natural toppings.

Peel the skin from the mangoes, and slice fruit away from the stone. Wash and remove stems from the berries and cut large ones in half. Mix the fruits, honey, and lemon juice together in a bowl. Using 4-oz. glasses, layer with yogurt, fruit, yogurt, and fruit. Serves 4.

2 mangoes, 2 peaches, or 2 c. chopped pineapple
1 box strawberries, destemmed
2 T. honey, optional
2 T. lemon juice
2 c. low-fat yogurt

PINEAPPLE STRAWBERRY BOAT ✌

A delicious tropical treat for hot summer weather.

Cut the pineapple in half lengthwise and carefully remove the fruit while keeping shells intact. Cut out the core and slice the pineapple into chunks. Cut the strawberries into halves or quarters.

Combine pineapple and strawberries in a bowl, and then add the sliced bananas. Pour lemon juice on top, plus any extra juice from the pineapple. Mix in the coconut ribbons and toss gently but thoroughly. Spoon the fruit salad back into the pineapple boat shells and chill. Serves 6.

1 large pineapple
2 boxes strawberries, destemmed
2 bananas, sliced
Juice of 1 lemon
1 c. coconut ribbons

DRIED FRUIT COMPOTE ✌

A very rich mixture. Delicious when used as a jam, a topping for ice cream, or to flavor cereals.

Combine the fruits and water in a medium saucepan and bring to a boil. Simmer, with the lid off, until most of the water has cooked off. Add the orange juice and continue cooking until a thick sauce forms. Serve warm with milk or a scoop of yogurt. Serves 6.

½ c. dried pears, chopped
½ c. dried peaches, chopped
1 c. raisins
½ c. dates, pitted and chopped
3 c. water
2 c. orange juice
¼ t. ground cinnamon

AMBROSIA JELL ✌

The fresh orange juice makes this jello special. However, if oranges are unavailable, use frozen concentrate instead.

Dissolve the gelatin in cold water in a saucepan and stir over low heat for about 3 minutes. Add the honey and stir until dissolved. Remove the saucepan and cool while you juice the oranges.

Mix the liquids together and pour the mixture into a lightly oiled mold. When it begins to jell a bit, add the grapes gently and evenly around the mold. Chill until set, and then unmold and fill the center with cottage cheese or yogurt. Serves 6.

2 pkgs. plain gelatin
1 c. cold water
3 c. fresh orange juice (about 9 sweet oranges)
1 T. honey, optional
2 c. green grapes

GOLDEN TROPICAL SUNRISE ✌

Full of golden sunshine and freshness.

Mix the gelatin, cold water, pineapple juice, and honey in a saucepan and dissolve over low heat for 3 to 5 minutes. Stir in the mango and coconut and most of the papaya.

Decorate the bottom of a lightly oiled mold with the remaining papaya slices and then gently pour in the fruit gelatin mixture. Refrigerate until set. Unmold onto a decorative platter. Serves 8.

2 pkgs. plain gelatin
1 c. cold water
3 c. unsweetened pineapple juice
1 T. honey, optional
1 mango, cut into chunks
1 small papaya, sliced
½ c. fresh shredded coconut

APPLE FRUIT JELLO ❧

A favorite with children and folks who have never tasted a "natural" jello. Excellent with sour cream.

Mix the gelatin, water, and honey together in a pan and heat until dissolved, for 3 to 5 minutes. Set aside to cool.

Add the juice to the gelatin mixture, pour into a lightly oiled mold, and chill in the freezer for 15 minutes to hasten setting. Then stir in the assorted fruit and pineapple and return to the refrigerator to finish setting. Serves 6.

VARIATION: If using fresh pineapple, heat the gelatin mixture with the apple juice and pineapple, bring to a boil, and simmer 5 minutes. When cooled, remove the pineapple with a slotted spoon and proceed with the preliminary chilling.

2 pkgs. plain gelatin
1 c. cold water
1 T. honey, optional
2½ c. unfiltered apple juice
½ c. pineapple chunks
1 c. assorted fruit in season

PEAR BERRY MOLD ❧

A surprising mixture of flavors, textures, and colors—but unusually delicious.

Dissolve the gelatin in cold water and stir over low heat for about 3 minutes. Stir in the honey and remove from heat. Add the pear juice and pour the mixture into a lightly oiled mold.

Prepare the strawberries, banana, and figs and toss with the coconut. Carefully stir the fruit into the liquid and chill until set. Serves 6.

2 pkgs. plain gelatin
1 c. cold water
2½ c. unsweetened pear juice
1 c. strawberries, destemmed
1 banana, sliced into rounds
5 dried figs, chopped
3 T. shredded coconut
1 T. honey, optional

BOYSENBERRY MELLOW JELL ✌

This is great for cooling down on a hot summer's day.

Dissolve the gelatin in cold water and heat for 3 minutes in a small saucepan. Stir in the honey and then add the juice. Cut the banana in half and slice ½ of it into lengthwise strips. Use the strips to decorate the bottom of a lightly oiled mold. Slice the remaining ½ banana into rounds and add to the juice, along with the cantaloupe chunks or balls. Gently pour the mixture into the mold, taking care not to disturb the banana strips. Chill for several hours until set. Serves 8.

2 pkgs. plain gelatin
1 c. cold water
1 T. honey, optional
3 c. boysenberry-apple juice
 (or plain boysenberry)
1 cantaloupe (cut into chunks
 or scoop out melon balls)
1 banana

JELLED HOLIDAY SALAD ✌

I like to serve this at holiday meals where there is a lot of food being served. This jelled salad adds lightness and contrast to the rich casseroles, gravies, and roasts generally served at these meals.

Dissolve the gelatin in 1 cup of the apple juice in a small saucepan, by heating it over a low flame. When the crystals are dissolved, remove from heat.

In a large bowl, combine the grated carrot, pineapple and juice, apples, and remaining apple juice. Stir in the gelatin mixture, and pour all this into a lightly oiled decorative gelatin mold. Refrigerate until set. Serve with cottage cheese or yogurt.

4 pkgs. plain gelatin
1 large carrot, grated
1-15¼ oz. can of crushed pine-
 apple plus the juice
2 apples, cut into bite-size pieces
6 c. apple juice, unsweetened

CHERRY KANTEN ❧

This pudding is more like a gelatin in texture.

In a saucepan, combine the juice, blended pineapple, honey, and agar flakes. Bring the mixture to a boil and simmer for 15 minutes. Cool for about 5 to 10 minutes, then add the fruit. Pour the kanten into individual dessert cups and set in the refrigerator to cool for several hours. Serves 6 to 8.

UNSWEETENED VARIATION: Replace the honey with an equal measure of frozen apple juice concentrate.

3 c. black cherry juice
3 c. blended fresh pineapple
2 T. honey
6 T. agar flakes
2 c. pitted cherry halves or other fruit in season

ISLAND KANTEN ❧

Kanten, or agar-agar, does not set as firmly as gelatin does but makes a soft-textured, puddinglike dessert.

Combine the papaya juice, orange juice, agar flakes, and honey in a saucepan and bring to a boil. Simmer gently for 15 minutes, and then remove pan from heat and cool for 10 minutes.

Prepare the fruits and add them to the juices. Gently pour the mixture into individual dessert cups and refrigerate until set. Serves 6.

4 c. papaya juice
1 c. orange juice
1 T. honey, optional
6 T. agar flakes
1 banana, sliced into rounds
1 mango, sliced

STRAWBERRY KANTEN

Light, refreshing, and soothing to the stomach.

Soak the agar-agar in the juice for 5 minutes. Cook the juice and agar-agar for 15 to 20 minutes, allowing it to simmer. Arrange the berry slices in individual bowls and pour the juice on top. Chill to set.

4 c. apple juice
1 stick (or ¾ c.) agar-agar
1 basket fresh strawberries, sliced

APRICOT SURPRISE MOUSSE

Although not like a traditional "mousse," this has the same texture and is quite rich.

Put apricots, and water, into a blender and whir until puréed. Transfer the mixture to a medium saucepan and bring to a boil. Add the agar flakes and simmer for 15 minutes. Remove from heat and cool for 10 minutes.

In a bowl, mix together the sour cream, honey, cashew pieces, and carob chips. Pour the apricot nectar into the bowl, mix gently and pour into a lightly oiled mold. Refrigerate until set. Unmold onto a decorative platter. Serves 8 to 12.

UNSWEETENED VARIATION: Replace the honey with ¾ cup frozen apple juice concentrate, and add to the cooled apricot mixture after it has cooled about 10 minutes. Proceed with rest of recipe.

3 c. sliced apricots (about 14 medium-sized, fresh apricots)
2 c. water
4 T. agar flakes
1 c. sour cream
¾ c. honey
½ c. raw cashew pieces
½ c. carob chips

RASPBERRY MADNESS

A very special, colorful dessert. Takes time to prepare, but it is well worth it.

Combine the gelatin, water, and honey in a saucepan and heat until gelatin is clear and dissolved. Remove pan from heat and stir in the juice and fruit. Sprinkle ½ the walnuts on the bottom of a lightly oiled gelatin mold and pour Layer 1 on top. Chill in the freezer for about 15 minutes to hasten setting.

Meanwhile, prepare Layer 2 by heating the gelatin, water, and honey as before. In a blender, whir together the gelatin mix, juice, and cream cheese until creamy.

When Layer 1 has thickened a little, sprinkle the remaining walnuts on top. Next, pour Layer 2 mixture on top of this. Chill in the refrigerator until set. Loosen mold by running cold water quickly over the bottom of the mold, and then turn upside down over a serving plate and gently tap the bottom with a knife to loosen. Serves 8.

UNSWEETENED VARIATION: To replace the honey in Layer 1, use 2 teaspoons of frozen orange juice concentrate. In Layer 2, use 1 tablespoon frozen orange juice concentrate.

Layer 1:

1 pkg. plain gelatin
½ c. cold water
½ T. honey
1½ c. raspberry juice
1 c. raspberries (or blackberrries)
1 c. chopped walnuts

Layer 2:

1 pkg. plain gelatin
½ c. cold water
2 T. honey
1½ c. papaya juice
8 oz. cream cheese or yogurt
    cheese

SPICED BRANDIED PEACHES ❧

An elegant dessert to end an intimate dinner for two, yet easy enough to make for a crowd.

Preheat oven to 350° F. Arrange the peach halves center up in an 8x8-inch baking pan. Melt the butter in a saucepan and stir in the honey and cloves. Add the brandy, mix thoroughly, and pour over the peaches. Bake covered for 30 minutes, and serve warm in dessert bowls—over ice cream if you like. Serves 6.

UNSWEETENED VARIATION: Replace the honey with an equal measure of frozen apple juice concenrtrate.

6 peaches, peeled, halved,
    and pitted
2 T. butter, melted
4 T. honey
¼ t. ground cloves
½ c. brandy

CRUNCHY PEACH COMPOTE ❧

Delicious and very filling. The orange juice makes an unexpected and delightful flavor combination with peaches.

Preheat oven to 350° F. Thoroughly mix the orange juice and cornstarch together, and combine with the sliced peaches and dates in a deep baking dish.

To make the topping, melt the butter in a saucepan and stir in the honey until dissolved. In a bowl, mix together the dry ingredients. Add the butter and honey and blend with a fork until the mixture forms crumbs the size of peas. Spread the topping over the peach mixture and bake for about 35 minutes, or until topping is golden brown. Serve warm. Makes 8 servings.

1 c. orange juice
2 T. cornstarch
6 c. fresh peaches, sliced (about
    3 large peaches)
1 c. dates, pitted and chopped

Topping:

2 T. butter
1 T. honey or date sugar
½ c. chopped cashews
½ c. whole wheat pastry flour
¼ t. cinnamon

ORANGE GLAZED PEARS ✌

A delicately spiced orange sauce coupled with fresh pears make this dessert very elegant, especially when served over a bed of whipped cream.

Preheat oven to 400° F. You should have about ¾ cup of orange juice after, juicing the oranges. Save one orange half and scrape out the excess white membrane. Slice the peel into very thin strips. Combine the juices, peel, honey, and stick cinnamon in a small saucepan and bring to a boil. Cover and simmer for 5 minutes. Remove from heat.

Place the sliced pears cut side down in a baking dish and pour the syrup on top. Arrange the cooked orange peel and cinnamon over the pears, then cover and bake for 30 minutes. Baste with the juice 2 or 3 times during baking.

Meanwhile, prepare the whipped cream and chill until the pears are baked.

When pears are done, remove the cinnamon and peel and spoon the pears carefully onto beds of whipped cream in small dessert cups. Top with orange sauce and serve warm. Serves 4 to 8.

UNSWEETENED VARIATION: Replace the honey with ¼ cup more orange juice (fresh or frozen) and 1 teaspoon arrowroot powder. Heat in saucepan with peel and spice, and proceed with recipe.

2 oranges, juiced
1½ T. lemon juice
¼ c. honey
2 inches stick cinnamon
4 medium pears, halved and cored
½ pt. whipping cream

BAKED APPLE SURPRISES ✍

My children like to make this for the family, because it's easy to put together and fun to eat. Delicious as is, this is absolutely "sinful" with whipped cream.

Preheat oven to 350° F. Core the apples to remove all seeds. Pit the dates by slitting one side open, and stuff 1 teaspoon of peanut butter into each date. Fill the apples with the stuffed dates and place in a baking dish.

Mix up the remaining ingredients for the cinnamon glaze and pour 1 tablespoon of glaze over each apple, saving the rest for later. Cover the apples and bake for 1 hour. Pour the remaining glaze over the apples and cool for 5 minutes before serving. Serves 4.

UNSWEETENED VARIATION: Replace the honey with ¼ cup frozen orange juice concentrate, 2 tablespoons water, and 1 teaspoon arrowroot powder, mixed together.

4 large Delicious apples
4 dates
4 T. crunchy peanut butter

Glaze:

4 T. pure maple syrup
2 T. honey
2 T. lemon juice
1 T. ground cinnamon

FRESH FRUIT DESSERT CREPES ❧

Instead of fresh fruit, you can fill the crepes with cooked fruit compotes and serve with a topping that strikes your fancy.

Blend the eggs, oil, salt, and milk together. Add the sifted flour and whip until mixture is creamy. Refrigerate at least 2 hours, preferably overnight.

To prepare the crepes, heat a small or medium fry pan and butter it lightly. When the butter begins bubbling, add 3 to 5 tablespoons of batter (depending on the size of your pan). Tip the pan from side to side to coat the entire bottom of the pan. Cook the crepes over a medium heat until golden, and then turn and cook the other side for another minute. Place the cooked crepes covered in a warm oven while you are making the remaining crepes.

Mix together the cottage cheese and fruit and fill the center of each crepe with the mixture. Then fold each end toward the center and roll. Top with the Honey Syrup. Makes 10 to 20 crepes (depending on the size of the pan).

Batter:

4 eggs, beaten
1 T. oil
¼ t. salt
1⅓ c. low-fat milk
1 c. millet flour, sifted

Filling:

1 pt. low-fat cottage cheese or
    yogurt
4 c. fresh sliced fruit in season
1 t. cinnamon
Honey Syrup or Fruit Juice Syrup
    (see p. 299)

APPLE BETTY ✒

A very filling dessert. The honey and fruit juice make this a sweet one.

Preheat oven to 350°F. Combine the fruits, juice, honey, flour, and spice in a large bowl, and turn the mixture into a deep baking dish. In another bowl, combine the oats, flour, wheat germ, and seeds and mix thoroughly. Melt the butter and honey together and cut them into the dry ingredients with a pastry knife or fork until the mixture has a uniform texture. Spread the topping over the apple mixture and then bake for 45 to 50 minutes. Serves 8.

UNSWEETENED VARIATION: Replace the honey in filling with 1 cup date sugar, and increase the juice to 2 cups. In the topping, use 4 tablespoons of date sugar instead of honey.

Filling:

10 c. pared, cored, and sliced
    apples (10 to 12 apples)
¾ c. apple or orange juice
½ c. dates
⅔ c. honey
3 T. whole wheat pastry flour
1 t. ground cinnamon

Topping:

½ c. quick-cooking rolled oats
½ c. whole wheat pastry flour
½ c. wheat germ
1 t. nutmeg
½ c. sunflower seeds
4 T. honey
4 T. butter, melted

Parfaits &
Puddings

Parfaits, with their swirls of contrasting colors and smooth texture, are best served in lovely tall shapely glasses. Puddings and parfaits are generally easy to assemble, making them a good way to introduce young people to cooking. These recipes are basic formulas. I encourage you to use other fruits and flavorings with them.

The essential ingredient in parfaits and puddings is the thickening agent. Cornstarch is frequently used. It is best to prepare it in a cup or glass, first adding the cornstarch, then stirring in cold water. Add a little at a time until a smooth, pourable paste is made. Add this mixture to the cooking pudding until it thickens to the desired consistency. Arrowroot powder is an unrefined, nutritious, white flour which can be used as a substitute for cornstarch. For every ¼ cup of cornstarch, use ⅓ cup arrowroot.

Gelatin is used in some parfaits to make them light and smooth. The gelatin must first be dissolved in hot water or fruit juice and then added to the parfait ingredients. Fruits, fruit juice, cottage cheese or yogurt can be blended with the prepared gelatin to make quick, inventive desserts.

Agar-agar, or kanten—a gelling agent made from seaweed— produces a soft pudding. It can be bought as flakes or in sticks. The flakes can be added to the pudding liquid immediately, whereas the sticks require soaking for about 10 minutes before cooking. Bring the agar-agar and pudding liquid to a boil, reduce heat and continue to simmer the mixture for 15 to 20 minutes. The agar-agar pudding must then be refrigerated until set. If you prefer using agar-agar instead of gelatin, substitute 1 tablespoon of agar-agar for 1 tablespoon of gelatin for a soft consistency, or 2 tablespoons agar-agar for a firm consistency.

Flour is used primarily in baked or cooked puddings. I have used soy milk powder and whole wheat flour in some of the cooked puddings, but I also recommend trying barley and brown rice flour. Both are excellent thickening agents.

MANGO BERRY PARFAIT ✦

A creamy delight. Peaches are an excellent substitute if mangoes are unavailable.

Prepare the mangoes and strawberries, cutting large berries in half. Mix them together in a bowl and refrigerate. Whir together the sour cream, honey, vanilla, lemon juice, and rind in a blender. Add the cream cheese a little at a time until the mixture becomes creamy. Pour ½ of the parfait cream mix into clear serving glasses, and add a layer of the fruit mix. Repeat, ending with a layer of fruit on top. Makes approximately 4 parfaits.

UNSWEETENED VARIATION: Replace the honey with an equal measure of frozen apple juice concentrate.

2 mangoes, peeled, pitted, and sliced
1 box strawberries, destemmed
8 oz. cream cheese, softened (or ricotta cheese)
16 oz. sour cream
1 T. vanilla
2 T. honey
Juice and grated rind of 2 lemons

PINEAPPLE PUFF PARFAIT ✦

These are easy to make and their light, airy texture and delicate flavor make them fun to eat. They'll be gone in minutes.

Combine gelatin and water over low heat and stir until the mixture is clear. Combine the gelatin, orange juice, pineapple, and yogurt in a blender and whir until smooth. Pour into tall parfait glasses, and place an orange slice on the rim of each glass. Chill in the refrigerator until set. Serves 6 to 8.

UNSWEETENED VARIATION: Replace the honey with ¾ cup frozen apple juice concentrate.

2 pkgs. plain gelatin
⅓ c. cold water
2½ c. orange juice
2 c. unsweetened crushed pineapple
3 c. low-fat yogurt
¾ c. honey
Orange slices for garnish

PEACH CREAM PARFAIT ❧

Easy to make with no cooking required—this is a great one for children to make.

Blend the ingredients together, except for the fruit. Add the strawberries and blend until the mixture is creamy pink. To arrange the parfaits, pour a little strawberry cream into clear glasses and add a layer of peach slices. Repeat again, and top off with sliced peaches. Chill for 2 hours. Serves 4.

UNSWEETENED VARIATION: Replace honey with 2 tablespoons frozen apple juice concentrate.

1 box tofu, rinsed, drained, and cut into squares
1 T. vanilla
3 T. lemon juice
3 T. skim milk powder
2 T. honey
1 c. strawberries, destemmed
2 c. sliced peaches

BANANA SWIRL PARFAIT ❧

For the banana lover. The tofu adds body and plenty of protein to this deliciously filling dessert. A nice way to end a light meal.

In a blender whir the carob layer ingredients until smooth. Heat the mixture in a saucepan for 5 to 10 minutes until thickened. Meanwhile, blend the banana mixture until creamy. Beginning with the carob mixture, layer in tall glasses. Alternate layers until the mixtures are used up. Then sprinkle the tops of the glasses with the chopped walnuts and chill. Serves 6 to 8.

UNSWEETENED VARIATION: In the carob layer, replace the honey with ½ cup frozen apple juice concentrate. In the banana layer, replace it with an equal measure of frozen apple juice concentrate.

Carob Layer:

1½ c. low-fat milk
¼ c. soy milk powder
4 T. carob powder
2 T. cornstarch or 5 T. arrowroot
½ c. honey

Banana Layer:

½ box tofu, rinsed, drained, and cut into chunks
3 T. honey
1 T. vanilla
2 T. lemon juice
3 ripe bananas
Chopped walnuts for garnish

WHIPPED PRUNE PARFAIT ↝

A delicious way to bring prunes into your diet. Its creamy texture and rich flavor keep everyone coming back for more.

Bring the prunes and water to a boil, then reduce heat and simmer for 5 minutes. Add the gelatin and stir for an additional 3 minutes. Combine the remaining ingredients, except walnuts, in a blender and whir until smooth. If using yogurt instead of cream, fold it into the blended ingredients gently. Pour into tall parfait glasses and sprinkle the walnuts on top of each glass. Chill until firm. Serves 4 to 6.

3 c. prunes
2 c. water
1 pkg. plain gelatin
2 lemons, juiced
1 pt. whipping cream or 2 c. low-fat yogurt
2 T. honey, optional
½ c. orange juice
½ c. chopped walnuts

PINK LADY PARFAIT ↝

This dessert creates a bright pallet of colors and is tops for eye appeal; not to mention its scrumptious and unusual blend of fruit flavors.

Mix the gelatin with the cold water and heat about 3 minutes or until the mixture is clear. In a blender, whir the juices, gelatin mixture, honey, and ricotta cheese until smooth. Stir in the blackberries and ½ the grapes, pour into tall parfait glasses and chill. As the parfaits set, garnish each glass with the remaining grapes. Serves 6 to 8.

UNSWEETENED VARIATION: Replace the honey with ¼ cup unsweetened white grape juice or apple juice.

2 pkgs. plain gelatin
½ c. cold water
1 qt. black cherry juice
¼ c. honey
8 oz. ricotta cheese or cream cheese
1 c. blackberries, washed and drained well
1 c. seedless green grapes

CRANBERRY MARBLE PARFAIT ❧

A colorful party parfait of vanilla coconut pudding swirled with bright-red cranberry sauce.

Whir the cranberries with the water in the blender; pour the mixture into a saucepan; and bring to a boil. Reduce heat to a simmer and cook the berries until soft, about 5 minutes. Add the honey and continue cooking, stirring frequently to prevent sticking or scorching.

Meanwhile, prepare the pudding. When it is done cooking, in a separate bowl mix the cornstarch with enough cold water to form a smooth paste, and whip it into the cranberry sauce. Stir until thickened, and remove from heat.

To assemble the parfaits, spoon a little sauce into clear parfait glasses, and then add a little of the pudding. Repeat until the glasses are ¾ full. Top with the sauce, and sprinkle coconut ribbons or fresh shredded coconut on top. Serves 6.

UNSWEETENED VARIATION: Replace the water with 1½ cups apple juice and the honey with ½ cup frozen apple juice concentrate.

1 pkg. fresh cranberries
1½ c. water
½ c. honey
1 Vanilla Coconut Pudding, (See
*   p. 235)*
3 T. cornstarch or 6 T. arrowroot
Coconut ribbons

LEMON CUSTARD ❧

A light, lemony delight with lots of protein.

Melt the butter in a saucepan. Add the lemon juice, honey, milk, and flour and cook over medium heat until the mixture begins to boil. Remove from heat and add the beaten eggs. Cook another 5 minutes and then pour into dessert cups. Chill for 2 or more hours. Serves 6.

UNSWEETENED VARIATION: Replace the honey with ½ cup frozen apple juice.

3 T. butter
1 c. lemon juice
½ c. honey
1½ c. low-fat milk
½ c. whole wheat pastry flour
3 eggs, beaten

ORANGE PLUM CUSTARD ❧

A warm fruit custard pudding which is also a delicious breakfast treat. The eggs pack this dessert with protein, as well as rich flavor.

Preheat oven to 375° F. In a bowl, mix together the plums, honey, and cinnamon and spoon mixture into an oiled 8 x 8-inch baking pan. Bake covered for 25 minutes, then remove from oven. Reduce heat to 325° F.

Beat the eggs, yogurt, sour cream, juice, orange rind, and vanilla together until well blended. Pour this mixture over the fruit, sprinkle the top with cinnamon and bake for 45 minutes. Cut into squares and serve warm. Serves 8.

4 c. plums, pitted and chopped
2 T. honey or date sugar
2 t. cinnamon
3 eggs
½ c. low-fat yogurt
1 c. sour cream or mock sour cream
¼ c. honey or orange juice
2 T. grated orange rind
1 t. vanilla
Cinnamon

PERSIMMON PUDDING ✌

A mellow autumn dessert, very light and sweet.

In a saucepan, combine the juice, blended persimmons, honey, and agar flakes. Bring to a boil and simmer for 15 minutes. Cool for 5 to 10 minutes, and add the walnuts. Pour into individual dessert cups and set in the refrigerator to cool for several hours. If you like, serve with whipped cream. Serves 6.

3 c. unsweetened apple juice
3 c. blended ripe persimmons
   (about 4 large fruit)
2 T. honey, optional
6 T. agar flakes
1 c. chopped walnuts

PUMPKIN RAISIN PUDDING ✌

Why throw out Halloween pumpkins? They are a very tasty sweet squash, perfect for making puddings and pies.

Combine the pumpkin, milk, and flour and blend until creamy. Pour into a saucepan and add the remaining ingredients, except the sherry. Cook for 30 minutes, then stir in the sherry. Cook for a few more minutes and remove from heat. Serve warm. Makes 6 servings.

UNSWEETENED VARIATION: Replace the honey with ½ cup date sugar and increase the milk to 1½ cups.

2 c. pumpkin, chopped and cooked
1 c. low fat milk
2 T. whole wheat pastry flour
½ c. raisins
¼–½ c. honey (sweeten to your
   taste)
4 T. butter
1 T. vanilla
1 t. ground ginger
1 t. ground cinnamon
¼ t. ground cloves
1 T. sherry, optional

VANILLA COCONUT PUDDING ❧

This is a great basic pudding to which you may add many other ingredients for variety: raisins, dates, nuts, bananas, peaches, wheat germ, vanilla, or other extracts.

Whir in the blender all the ingredients except the coconut. Pour the mixture into a saucepan and cook over medium heat for 15 minutes. Stir in the coconut and cook for 10 more minutes or until the mixture has a thick consistency. If you want a thicker pudding, add more cornstarch by first mixing it in a little cold water until completely dissolved and then stirring it into the hot pudding. Serves 6.

UNSWEETENED VARIATION: Replace the honey with ¾ cup frozen apple juice concentrate or unsweetened white grape juice.

4 c. low-fat milk
¾ c. soy milk powder
¼ c. cornstarch or ⅓ c. arrowroot
½ t. salt
1 T. vanilla
¾ c. honey
¾ c. coconut

APPLE DATE PUDDING ❧

This tastes like an old-fashioned apple pie filling, and can be poured into a graham cracker crust and chilled.

In a large pot or kettle, combine the apples, dates, and hot water and bring to a boil. Lower heat to a simmer. Add the seasonings and orange juice, and cook covered until the apples are tender. Just before serving, mix the cornstarch with just enough cold water to make a smooth paste, and then stir it into the pudding. Continue stirring until thickened, and remove the pot from heat. Serve the pudding warm with ice cream or milk. Serves 6 to 8.

UNSWEETENED VARIATION: Omit the honey and increase the orange juice to 2½ cups.

10 c. pared, cored, and sliced apples
1 c. pitted and chopped dates
1 c. hot water
¼ c. honey
2 T. ground cinnamon
¼ t. salt
2¼ c. orange juice
¼ c. cornstarch

CAROB PUDDING ✄

Our answer to chocolate pudding. Children love it, and so do we!

Mix the coffee substitute with just enough hot water to dissolve it, then combine it with the other ingredients in a blender and whir until smooth. Pour the pudding mixture into a saucepan, bring to a boil and then simmer for 15 minutes, stirring frequently to prevent sticking. Cook for another 5 minutes, pour the pudding into individual dessert cups and chill for several hours. Serves 6.

UNSWEETENED VARIATION: Replace the molasses and honey with 1 cup date sugar mixed with 1 cup hot coffee or coffee substitute.

2 T. coffee substitute or instant coffee
3 c. low-fat milk
½ c. soy milk powder
¼ c. carob powder
¼ c. cornstarch or ⅓ c. arrowroot
¼ c. molasses
¾ c. honey

TOPSY-TURVY DATE PUDDING ✄

A rich baked molded pudding. Delicious with other dried fruit combinations, such as apricots and pineapple.

Preheat oven to 375° F. In a bowl, stir together the dates, butter, and 1 cup of boiling water. Add the remaining ingredients, except the honey and 1½ cup boiling water. Beat the mixture with a fork until thoroughly blended, and pour the batter into a 9-inch baking mold or pan. Smooth batter evenly in the pan, and slowly pour the boiling water evenly over the top. Bake for about 40 minutes. Unmold and serve warm with either ice cream or yogurt. Serves 8 to 10.

UNSWEETENED VARIATION: Replace the honey and molasses with 1 cup date sugar mixed in 1 cup hot water.

1 c. dates, pitted and chopped
2 T. butter
2½ c. boiling water
1 egg, beaten
1½ c. whole wheat pastry flour
¼ c. honey
½ c. molasses
1 t. baking soda
½ t. baking powder
½ t. salt
½ c. coarsely chopped walnuts
½ c. honey

STEAMED HOLIDAY PUDDING ✖

Traditionally, steamed puddings are served with hard sauce, which is mainly made of sugar. Instead, I suggest you try our Cream Cheese Frosting or Brandy Cream Topping.

In a bowl, mix the fruits, walnuts, and flour together and stir well. In another bowl combine the molasses, soda, salt, and boiling water and stir it into the fruit mixture. Spoon and press the mixture evenly into a buttered 7-cup tube mold. Cover it tightly with foil and secure with string. Place mold on a rack in a deep kettle and add boiling water to a depth of 1 inch around the mold. Cover and steam for 1¼ hours, adding water as necessary. Cool in the pan for 10 minutes and unmold. Garnish with one of the toppings suggested above. Serves 8.

UNSWEETENED VARIATION: Replace the molasses with ½ cup date sugar mixed in ½ cup hot water. Increase the flour to 1½ cups.

2 c. cranberries
1 c. golden raisins
½ c. chopped walnuts
½ c. dates, pitted and chopped
1⅓ c. whole wheat pastry flour
½ c. molasses
½ t. ground cardamom seeds
2 t. baking soda
½ t. salt
⅓ c. boiling water

ZEN RICE PUDDING ✖

This wholesome dessert served with milk, is a great way to use leftover brown rice.

In a blender, whir the milk and soy milk powder, and pour mixture into a saucepan. Add the remaining ingredients, cover, and cook for 1 hour over medium heat until most of the liquid is absorbed but the rice is still moist. Stir frequently to prevent sticking. Serves 4.

UNSWEETENED VARIATION: Increase the dried fruit to 1 cup and add more liquid if necessary.

2⅔ c. low-fat milk
¼ c. soy milk powder
1 c. cooked brown rice
⅓ c. honey or molasses
1 t. fennel seeds, crushed
½ c. dried fruit
½ t. salt

Frozen Desserts

FROZEN DESSERTS ARE EXCELLENT WARM-WEATHER COOLERS. Summer is the time when everyone loves to gather outside in the evening and share homemade ice cream. What better accompaniment to the American barbecue tradition?

This is also the time when fresh fruits are in abundance. Bruised or slightly overripe fruits make perfect ice cream: the skins are removed anyway, and the ripeness enhances the flavor.

Another plus for these desserts is that they can be made in minutes. Most require only whirring in the blender and pouring into cups, popsicle molds, or your ice-cream maker.

The Freeze recipes are not meant to be a substitute for ice cream. The texture will vary depending on the fruit being used in the recipe. You can control how hard they become: two hours in the freezer yields a softer freeze, while three hours makes for the hardness of a popsicle. You can also experiment with putting the freeze mixes into an electric ice-cream maker and processing as you would for ice cream. Some of these freezes are made with yogurt, cottage cheese, and tofu, which provide grams of good protein in each serving.

The ice-cream recipes call for an electric ice-cream maker. Once the ice-cream mix is prepared, follow the instructions for your model, as suggested in the recipes. Since some models may differ in this regard, I have omitted repeating the specific directions. The recipes are meant to be "basic" formulas for you to use. Since honey tends to make the ice cream soft, skim milk or whole milk powder is added to some recipes to make the mix thicker. I have also found that honey ice cream is best served the next day. The curing time allows the flavors to blend and mature.

PINEAPPLE COCONUT POPSICLES ↝

Say goodbye to commercial popsicles. These are simple enough for children to make and provide them with a healthy nutritious snack.

Whir all the ingredients in a blender until creamy and pour into popsicle molds or glasses. Freeze for 2 to 3 hours. Makes about 4½ cups.

2 c. chopped fresh pineapple
¾ c. shredded coconut
½ box tofu, rinsed, drained, and
    cut into squares
1 T. oil
2 T. honey or frozen orange juice
    concentrate
1 c. plain low-fat yogurt

PAPAYA POPSICLES ↝

For papaya lovers only!

Blend all the ingredients and pour into popsicle molds or glasses. Freeze for 3 hours, or until hard. Serves 6.

1 ripe papaya
¼ box tofu, rinsed, drained, and
    cut into chunks
8 oz. plain low-fat yogurt
2 T. almond butter
1 T. oil
½ t. vanilla
¼ t. cinnamon
3 T. honey or frozen orange juice
    concentrate

"ROOT BEER" POPSICLES ✒

Sassafras bark, honey, and water make a combination that tastes like root beer. This is a nice natural alternative to the popular commercial flavor.

Combine the water and tea in a pan and bring to a boil. Reduce heat and simmer for about 20 minutes, uncovered. When the mixture turns a dark reddish brown color, stir in honey and adjust the flavor to your taste. Cool, strain, and pour into popsicle molds.

2 c. water
1 T. sassafras bark tea
¼ c. honey or frozen apple juice
   concentrate

MELON FREEZE ✒

Take a breather during a heat wave with this cooler.

Blend all ingredients together and pour the mixture into dessert cups or popsicle molds and freeze for 2 hours. For a smoother texture, blend and freeze again for another hour. Serves 4 to 6.

1 c. low-fat yogurt
¼ Crenshaw melon, seeds and
   rind removed
1 t. vanilla
1 T. honey, optional

PINK BANANA FREEZE ✒

A cool, refreshing summertime snack. Can be made into popsicles, too.

Whir in a blender all the ingredients except the nuts. When the mixture is creamy, stir in the nuts, and pour the mixture into dessert cups or glasses. Freeze for 1½ hours. Serves 6.

5 ripe bananas
1 ripe papaya
¼ c. shredded coconut
2 t. skim milk powder
3 T. lecithin granules
¼ c. cranberry juice
¼ c. water
¼ c. chopped Brazil nuts

WHIPPED CAROB FREEZE ❧

Lots of protein in this frozen dessert!

In a blender, whir the cottage cheese and tofu until creamy. Then add the remaining ingredients and blend until smooth. Pour the mixture into a bowl and freeze for 2 hours. Return mix to the blender, then pour into individual dessert cups or glasses and freeze for another hour or more. Makes 4 cups.

1 c. low-fat cottage cheese
½ box tofu, rinsed, drained, and
　　cut into chunks
2 T. carob powder
3 T. honey or frozen apple juice
　　concentrate
1 t. vanilla

WHIPPED STRAWBERRY FREEZE ❧

A light dessert, both in flavor and calories.

Whir the strawberries, tofu, yogurt, and honey in a blender until creamy and smooth. Pour the mixture into a bowl and freeze for 2 hours. Blend again and return to the freezer in dessert cups or glasses for another hour. Freeze for 1 to 2 hours. Makes about 3½ cups.

VARIATION: If you have an ice-cream maker, pour the mixture into the cream can and process as you would to make ice cream.

1 box strawberries, destemmed
½ box tofu, rinsed, drained, and
　　cut into chunks
½ c. low-fat yogurt
3 T. honey or frozen apple juice
　　concentrate

GRAPE ICE ❧

This is a basic fruit ice recipe that can be varied with other juice combinations. A nice, nondairy dessert.

Mix well and pour into the cream can of your ice-cream machine. Proceed as in making ice cream and then freeze. Makes ½ gallon.

3 c. unsweetened grape
　　puree or juice
3 c. apple or pear juice
½ c. honey

RED RASPBERRY ICE ❧

A cooling, refreshing ice that is perfect at the end of a rich meal. Serve in small dishes with a garnish of mint leaves.

Blend the raspberries in a blender or food processor (using the chopping blade), along with the water, honey, and lemon juice. Process this mixture in your ice-cream maker. Fold in the beaten egg white, pour into a freezing container, and freeze. Makes about ½ gallon.

3 c. very ripe red raspberries
3 c. water
¾ c. honey
2 T. lemon juice
1 egg white, beaten stiff

BLACKBERRY FROZEN YOGURT ❧

This is a basic frozen yogurt recipe. Other fruits will give you countless possibilities.

Put the yogurt in the cream can of your ice-cream maker. Slightly blend the fruit and honey and add to the yogurt. Stir the mixture with a wooden spoon until well blended and proceed as in making ice cream. Freeze for a couple of hours. Makes ½ gallon.

4 c. plain low-fat yogurt
2 c. fresh ripe blackberries, rinsed
    and drained
1¼ c. honey

CITRUS SHERBET ❧

This won't have the color of commercial sherbet, but the flavor is natural and can't be beat!

Blend the skim milk powder and milk together and then combine with all the ingredients in the cream can of the ice-cream maker. Stir with a wooden spoon and process as directed for your ice-cream machine. Freeze at least 2 hours or overnight. Makes ½ gallon.

¼ c. skim milk powder
2 c. low-fat milk
1 T. lemon extract
1 c. fresh lime juice
1 c. honey
⅛ t. salt

HONEY VANILLA ICE CREAM ⤳

A basic ice-cream recipe from which you can invent your own ice cream fantasies. Different extracts can provide a variety of flavors. Try lemon, orange, anise, and almond.

Blend all the ingredients together and pour into the cream can of the ice-cream maker. Stir with a wooden spoon and process as directed for your machine. Makes ½ gallon.

2 c. whipping cream
2 c. half and half
½ c. honey
½ c. skim milk powder
1 T. vanilla

CAROB CHIP ICE CREAM ⤳

The chips can be replaced by peanuts, almonds, or walnuts for a new taste.

Whir in a blender all the ingredients except the chips. Pour the mixture into the cream can and process as directed for your ice-cream machine. When finished, stir in the chips, and freeze for 2 to 4 hours or overnight. Makes ½ gallon.

2 c. whipping cream
2 c. half and half
½ c. honey
½ c. carob powder
¼ c. skim milk powder
1 c. carob chips, optional

BANANA NUT ICE CREAM ⤳

A good way to use overripe bananas.

Blend all the ingredients (except nuts) in a food processor or blender. Stir in nuts. Pour the mixture into the cream can of your ice-cream maker, and process as directed. Freeze. Makes ½ gallon ice cream.

1 c. walnuts, finely chopped
4 ripe bananas
2 c. whipping cream
2 c. low-fat milk
½ c. honey

DATE NUT ICE CREAM ✌

The flavor of this ice cream is subtle and grows on you with each bite.

Mix the first four ingredients well. Pour into the cream can of your ice-cream machine and process according to your directions. At the end of the processing time, stir in the last two ingredients. Freeze for a couple hours or overnight. Makes ½ gallon.

2 c. whipping cream
2 c. half and half
¾ c. honey
1 T. peanut butter
½ c. chopped walnuts
2 c. chopped dates

HONEY PEACH ICE CREAM ✌

This ice cream flavor gets better with age.

Blend the honey and peach chunks together. Mix the remaining ingredients (except the peach slices), in a bowl. Transfer to the cream can of the ice-cream maker and proceed as directed for your machine. Stir in the peach slices at the end and ripen in the freezer overnight. Makes ½ gallon.

2 c. whipping cream
2 c. half and half
½ c. honey
1 t. vanilla
½ t. cinnamon
2 c. peach chunks, peeled
1 c. thinly sliced peaches

PEPPERMINT CHIP ICE CREAM ✌

Great flavor and a crunchy texture make this dessert fun to eat. Tends to be a little soft unless frozen for at least 4 hours, preferably overnight.

Blend all the ingredients together, except the carob chips. Pour into the cream can of the ice-cream maker and process as directed. At the end of processing, stir in the carob chips and freeze overnight. Makes ½ gallon.

2 c. whipping cream
2 c. half and half
½ c. honey
½ c. skim milk powder
2 T. peppermint extract
½ c. carob chips

CAPPUCCINO ICE CREAM ✺

The gelatin makes the texture smoother, but it can be omitted without changing the flavor, and the texture will still be creamy.

Mix the gelatin in the cold water until dissolved and whir with the rest of the ingredients in a blender. Pour mixture into the cream can of the ice-cream maker and process as directed. Freeze for 2 or more hours. Makes ½ gallon.

1 pkg. plain gelatin
¼ c. cold water
2 c. whipping cream
2 c. half and half
½ c. honey
½ c. cold espresso coffee or strong coffee

FUDGE SWIRL ICE CREAM ✺

The carob fudge sauce can be used with vanilla, cappuccino, or peppermint flavored ice creams as well. Make sure it is well ripened, preferably overnight.

Blend all the ingredients together except the carob fudge sauce. Pour into the cream can of the ice-cream maker and process as directed for your machine. At the end of the cycle, pour the sauce through the hole in the lid and let the can rotate 2 or 3 times. If your ice-cream maker doesn't have this feature, pour the sauce into the can and swirl by carefully stirring with a wooden spoon. Be careful not to stir too much. Freeze for 2 to 4 hours or overnight. Makes ½ gallon.

2 c. whipping cream
2 c. half and half
½ c. honey
½ c. carob powder
¼ c. skim milk powder
½ c. Jiffy Carob Sauce (see p. 296)

Cookies & Candies

COOKIES ARE A WONDERFUL WAY to incorporate nuts and seeds into the diet of young children. Making these recipes is an ideal way for children to begin learning to cook. Children bored after school, during holidays, or over weekends can be turned into busy helpers, mixing ingredients, oiling pans, and shaping cookies.

Most cookie recipes use eggs. There is, however, an egg substitute that acts as a binder but does not leaven. For each egg called for in the recipe, mix 1 tablespoon of soy milk powder with enough water to form a paste. Add this to the other wet ingredients. The soy milk powder is a healthy addition of protein and lecithin.

Baking powder contains 40 milligrams of sodium per teaspoon, while baking soda (sodium bicarbonate) contains 1232 milligrams of sodium per teaspoon. For those interested in cutting back on salt, the following recipes for homemade baking powder and baking soda contain no salt.

Homemade baking powder. This recipe makes a baking powder that can be used in the same proportions as its commercial counterpart.

½ c. arrowroot powder
½ c. cream of tartar
¼ c. potassium bicarbonate

Sift all the ingredients together and store in an air-tight jar. Keep it cool and dry, and then sift again before using it. The potassium bicarbonate can be purchased at a drugstore pharmacy. Arrowroot powder is obtainable at a health food store.

Homemade baking soda. Potassium bicarbonate is a salt-free substitute for regular baking soda. Use half as much potassium bicarbonate as you would baking soda. (Using the same proportions will leave an unpleasant aftertaste.) This proportion will give you the desired result in texture, without aftertaste.

The most natural uncooked candies are simply chopped dried fruits, nuts or seeds, and sweetener. Children also enjoy chopping and mixing these for snacks or lunches. Some of the candy recipes require a food processor or a meat grinder. If you use a food processor, the metal chopping blade is the most effective.

Cooked candies with honey will not harden to the brittle stage, but will remain in the soft-ball stage. To make them harder and easier to handle, I suggest an hour or more in the refrigerator. Some of the candies are even better when placed in the freezer. In this case, the candies should be eaten in a few days, or removed from the freezer to the refrigerator, to prevent them from freezing completely.

MAPLE CASHEW COOKIES ✌

These cookies have a delicate flavor and a crunchy texture.

Preheat oven to 350° F. Melt butter in a small saucepan and stir in the honey and maple syrup. Remove from heat and slowly stir in the beaten egg, vanilla extract, and cashews. Sift in the salt, baking powder, and flour. Mix well and drop by teaspoonfuls onto an oiled cookie sheet. Bake for 8 minutes, and remove from the cookie sheet by spatula to a board to cool. Makes about 3½ dozen cookies.

½ c. butter or oil
¼ c. honey
½ c. pure maple syrup
1 egg
1 t. vanilla extract
1 c. cashew pieces
½ t. salt
1 t. baking powder
1 c. whole wheat pastry flour

GRANOLA COOKIES ✌

This is a nice basic recipe. I sometimes add chocolate or carob chips for extra taste.

Preheat oven to 350° F. Cream the butter and honey together in a bowl. Add the peanut butter and vanilla, and beat until well blended. Stir in the granola, flour, baking powder, and nuts. Mix well, and spoon 1 tablespoon of cookie batter at a time onto a cookie sheet. Bake for 12 to 15 minutes, or until golden.

½ c. butter
½ c. honey
3 T. peanut butter
1 t. vanilla
1 c. granola
2 c. whole wheat flour
1 t. baking powder
½ c. whole roasted peanuts

COCONUT PUFFS ❧

Fluffy and macaroonlike, these can be made in a jiffy.

Preheat oven to 350° F. In a mixing bowl, beat the eggs, oil, honey, and vanilla together until creamed. Mix in the coconut, flour, and baking powder until well blended. Drop by tablespoonfuls onto an oiled cookie sheet and bake for 10 to 12 minutes. Makes 2 dozen.

UNSWEETENED VARIATION: Replace the honey with ½ cup frozen apple juice concentrate.

3 eggs
¼ c. oil
½ c. honey
2 t. vanilla
3 c. shredded coconut
¼ c. whole wheat pastry flour
½ t. baking powder

CAROB CLOUDS ❧

Beautiful cloudlike shapes and a light texture inspired the name of these cookies.

Preheat oven to 350° F. Cream the oil, honey, and vanilla together. Add the milk. Sift the carob powder, baking powder, and barley flour together into the creamed mixture. Stir in the remaining ingredients and beat until well mixed. Drop heaping teaspoonfuls onto an oiled cookie sheet and bake for 8 minutes. Cool on a rack. Makes about 2 dozen.

UNSWEETENED VARIATION: Replace the honey with ½ cup date sugar and increase milk to ½ cup.

¼ c. oil
¼ c. honey
½ t. vanilla
¼ c. low-fat milk
¼ c. carob powder, sifted
½ t. baking powder
¾ c. barley flour
¼ c. carob chips
¼ c. chopped walnuts

BROWNIES ✺

Don't expect a chocolate brownie here. These carob ones are quite different and must be judged on their own merits. Sweet enough without frosting.

Preheat oven to 350°F. Cream together the butter, oil, carob powder, honey, eggs, vanilla, and salt. Add the flour and nuts and pour into a greased 8x8-inch baking pan. Bake for 25 minutes, remove from oven, allow to cool, and cut them into squares. Makes 12 large brownies.

UNSWEETENED VARIATION: Replace the honey with ¼ cup pitted dates blended with ¼ cup water. Increase flour to 1 cup and add ½ teaspoon baking powder.

¼ c. butter, softened
¼ c. oil
4 T. carob powder
½ c. honey
2 eggs
1 t. vanilla
¼ t. salt
½ c. whole wheat pastry flour
½ c. nuts, optional

CHOCOLATE CHIP COOKIES ✺

These taste just like the traditional Toll House cookies, but with honey and barley flour. The barley flour makes these cookies a must-try for those allergic to wheat products.

Preheat oven to 375°F. Cream the butter, honey, eggs, and vanilla together until smooth. A food processor is ideal for this (use the cutting blade). Stir in the remaining ingredients in the order given, one at a time. Drop by the tablespoon onto cookie sheets and bake 12 minutes, until golden. Makes approximately 8 dozen 2-inch cookies.

2 cubes of butter
1½ c. honey
4 eggs
4 t. vanilla
2 t. baking soda
2 t. salt
4½ c. barley flour
1 12 oz. pkg. real chocolate chips
2 c. coarsely chopped walnuts

NUT BUTTER COOKIES ✨

A basic nutty cookie whose flavor varies with the nut butter used.

Preheat oven to 325°F. Cream the butter, honey, eggs, nut butter, vanilla, and salt together until well blended. Stir in the baking soda and flour and mix well. Drop by tablespoonfuls onto a lightly oiled cookie sheet and press a peanut into the center of each cookie to decorate before baking. You can vary the recipe by chilling the dough for 2 hours and rolling into balls, pressing, and criss-crossing with a fork. Bake for 15 minutes. Makes 3 dozen.

NUT BUTTER SQUARES: Pour the batter into a greased and floured 8 x 8-inch baking pan and bake for 25 minutes or until golden and done. Cool for 15 minutes and cut into squares. Serve as is or frost with *Peanut Butter Glaze, Carob Frosting*, or *Maple Icing*, (see *Toppings & Fillings*, pp. 290–304).

UNSWEETENED VARIATION: Replace the honey with ½ cup pitted dates blended with ½ cup water.

½ c. butter
1 c. honey
2 eggs
1 c. roasted nut butter (peanut, cashew, or almond)
2 T. vanilla
½ t. salt
2 t. baking soda
1½ c. whole wheat pastry flour
Whole peanuts for decoration

CHOCOLATE CHIP CHEWS ❧

These tasty chewies don't last very long around our house.

Preheat oven to 350°F. Cream the butter, honey, and egg together in a bowl until smooth. Stir in the vanilla and salt. Sift in the dry ingredients and blend well. Add more flour if necessary. Stir in chips and drop by the teaspoonfuls onto a lightly oiled cookie sheet. Bake for 8 minutes. Remove from cookie sheet immediately with a spatula and allow to cool on a flat surface. Makes 5 dozen cookies.

UNSWEETENED VARIATION: Replace the honey with 1 cup date sugar, firmly packed.

½ c. butter
½ c. honey
1 egg
1 t. vanilla
½ t. salt
1 t. baking soda
½ t. baking powder
2–2½ c. whole wheat pastry flour
6 oz. semisweet chocolate chips

SESAME CHIA SQUARES ❧

No baking required. These are easy enough for children to assemble and wrap in plastic for their lunches.

Roast sesame seeds in a dry skillet over medium heat, stirring until golden brown. Mix the honey and peanut butter in a small bowl. Add the skim milk powder, coconut, and sesame seeds to the first mixture. Mix and pat into an 8 x 8-inch baking pan and refrigerate until set. Cut into small squares and serve.

UNSWEETENED VARIATION: Replace the honey with ½ cup pitted dates, blended or chopped in a food processor. Mix together with the remaining ingredients.

½ c. honey
½ c. peanut butter
1 c. skim milk powder
½ c. shredded coconut
1 c. sesame seeds, roasted
2 T. chia seeds

MIXED NUT CRUNCHIES ✌

Be careful not to overcook. Let them set in the pan as directed or they will crumble when cut. A fantastic lunch box item, snack, or dessert.

Preheat oven to 375° F. In a bowl, mix together all the nuts and seeds. If you buy the seeds and nuts unroasted, roast each kind of nut separately in a skillet over medium heat. Stir constantly until they are golden in color and have a nutty aroma. Mix them all together with the salt.

Melt the butter in a small pan, and then pour it into another bowl, and add the remaining ingredients. Pour in the nut mixture, and stir well. Smooth the mixture evenly into an 8 x 8-inch oiled baking pan. Bake for 25 to 30 minutes in the center of the oven. (Make sure the bottom of the pan is not too close to the heat element.) Cool for 30 minutes, loosen from sides of the pan, and cut into squares. Completely cool before removing from pan. Makes 16 squares.

1 c. unsalted roasted peanuts
1 c. unsalted roasted cashews
2 c. unsalted roasted sunflower
    seeds
½ t. salt
4 T. melted butter
1 t. apple cider vinegar
½ c. honey
½ c. molasses
4 T. whole wheat pastry flour

LADY FINGERS ✌

Wonderful served with tea.

Preheat oven to 400° F. Warm the butter and honey together. Beat in the eggs and the sifted dry ingredients. Roll out the dough and cut in strips. Roll in fructose or date sugar if you wish. Arrange on a baking sheet and bake until golden, about 15 to 20 minutes.

1 c. honey
2 eggs
½ c. butter
4 c. barley flour
½ t. baking powder
½ t. soda
1 t. salt
Fructose or date sugar, optional

PEANUT BUTTER BALLS ✌

Another easy candy for children to make. Young ones especially love to mix by hand and feel the wonderful textures.

Measure all ingredients into a bowl and mix them together with your hands. Roll a tablespoon of the candy mix between the palms of your hands to form a ball, and then roll in coconut. Store in airtight containers, wrap and freeze, or serve immediately. Makes about 40 candies.

UNSWEETENED VARIATION: Replace the honey with 1 cup raisins blended in ¼ cup water.

2 c. peanut butter
1 c. wheat germ
1 c. dried coconut flakes
½ t. ground cloves
⅔ c. honey
1 c. chopped dates
Coconut for rolling

SNACK COOKIES ✌

My children love these cookies, and I like to serve them after school because they have very little sweetener but lots of nutritious carbohydrates, vitamins, minerals, and protein to sustain that youthful energy until dinnertime.

Preheat oven to 325°F. Add all the above ingredients, except figs, to a food processor, using the chopping blade. Fold in the figs. Spread out extra date sugar on a piece of wax paper, and put the cookie dough on top, with another piece of wax paper to cover. Roll out the dough to one-quarter inch thickness. Sprinkle more date sugar on top and cut the rolled dough into shapes. Arrange shapes on an ungreased cookie sheet and bake about 20 minutes. If you're rushed, these can also be baked at 350°F for 10 to 15 minutes.

½ c. sesame tahini
½ c. date sugar
¾ c. low-fat milk
1 egg
1½ c. rolled oats
1 c. whole wheat flour
1 c. roasted almonds
1 c. figs, chopped

ICED GINGERBREAD MEN ✌

Another great project to do with children.

Sift the first seven dry ingredients onto a piece of wax paper. Beat the remaining five wet ingredients together in a bowl until creamy. Stir in dry ingredients a little at a time, mixing well after each addition. Roll dough into a ball, wrap in wax paper and refrigerate for 4 hours or overnight.

Preheat oven to 350°F. Cut the dough into quarters, and roll out each to a ⅛ inch thickness. Use gingerman cookie cutters to form cookies until the dough is used up. Place gingerbread men 1 inch apart on an ungreased cookie sheet and bake for 8 minutes. Remove to a wire rack and cool completely before icing. Makes 3 dozen small, or 1½ dozen larger men.

In a medium-sized bowl, beat the egg whites and lemon juice together until foamy. Slowly beat in the honey and vanilla until the mixture stands in firm peaks and is stiff enough to hold a sharp line when cut with a knife. Fold in the sifted milk powder until well mixed. Keep the frosting covered with a damp paper towel until ready to use. Ice the cooled gingerbread men and decorate icing with raisins, sunflower seeds, or carob chips. Makes about 1½ cups icing.

Dough:

3 c. whole wheat pastry flour
½ t. baking soda
½ t. salt
1 t. ground cinnamon
½ t. ground ginger
½ t. ground cloves
¼ t. ground nutmeg
½ c. oil
¼ c. honey
½ c. molasses
1 T. water
½ t. vanilla

Icing:

2 egg whites
1 t. lemon juice
½ c. honey
1 t. vanilla
1 c. skim milk powder, sifted

ORANGE RAISIN TEA COOKIES ৵

These are best when served with your favorite tea.

Cream the oil and honey together in a bowl. Blend in the eggs, vanilla, orange juice, and rind. Sift in the salt, baking power, and flour and stir well. Chill for at least 2 hours.

Preheat oven to 350° F. Drop the batter from a teaspoon onto a lightly oiled cookie sheet and decorate the centers of the cookies with one or more raisins. Bake for 10 minutes or until the edges are browned. Makes 3 dozen cookies.

UNSWEETENED VARIATION: Replace the honey with ½ cup date sugar, and increase the orange juice to ⅓ cup.

½ c. oil
¼ c. honey
2 eggs
¼ t. vanilla
6 T. orange juice
1 T. grated orange rind
½ t. ground coriander
½ t. salt
1¼ t. baking powder
½ c. barley flour
1 c. whole wheat pastry flour
Raisins for decorating cookie
centers

JAM-FILLED COOKIES ৵

Without the jam, this becomes a basic cookie recipe to which you can add nuts, dried fruit, carob chips, or coconut to suit your fancy.

Preheat oven to 350° F. Crush the anise seed and mix with the butter. Cream the butter, oil, honey, egg, water, and vanilla together. Sift the flour, salt, and soda together, and add to the creamed mixture. Blend this mixture well and stir in the oats. Drop by tablespoonfuls onto a greased cookie sheet. Lightly press a teaspoon of jam into the center of each cookie and bake for 12 to 15 minutes. Makes about 2½ dozen.

2 t. anise seed
1 cube butter, softened
½ c. oil
¾ c. honey
1 egg
¼ c. water
1 t. vanilla
1 c. whole wheat pastry flour,
    sifted
1 t. salt
½ t. baking soda
3 c. rolled oats
2 c. favorite fruit jam

COSMIC COOKIES ❧

An excellent rainy-day project to do with children. They will love the mixing, cutting, and decorating. Make vanilla icing to put on the tops of the baked cookies and then decorate them with nuts and seeds.

Preheat oven to 350° F. In a bowl, cream the butter, honey, and eggs together. Next, mix in the wheat germ, vanilla, lemon rind, and milk. In another bowl, sift together the baking powder, salt, and flour. Mix dry and wet ingredients, adding more flour, if necessary, to make a firm dough for rolling. Roll the dough out and cut into shapes with cookie cutters. Decorate with raisins, nuts, seeds, carob chips, or cinnamon. Bake for about 8 minutes. Makes 3 dozen cookies.

1 cube butter
¾ c. honey
2 eggs, beaten
½ c. wheat germ
2 t. vanilla
1 t. lemon rind
3 T. low-fat milk
2 t. baking powder
½ t. salt
½ t. ground cardamom
½ c. skim milk powder
1½ c. whole wheat pastry flour
½ c. barley flour

OATMEAL GEMS ❧

An old-time recipe full of tasty delights.

Preheat oven to 350° F. Cream the eggs, honey, and sour cream together. Sift the dry ingredients (except the oats), and add them and the oats to the egg mixture. Stir in the nuts and raisins and drop by teaspoonfuls onto an oiled cookie sheet. Bake for about 10 minutes or until golden.

2 eggs, beaten
1 c. honey
1 c. sour cream
2 c. rolled oats
2 c. barley or whole wheat pastry flour or 1 c. each
1 t. soda
1 T. grated chocolate or carob powder
½ t. cinnamon
½ t. cloves
½ t. nutmeg
½ t. salt
1 c. chopped raisins
½ c. chopped nuts

AVA LEE'S OATMEAL COOKIES ✌

As you can see from all the ingredients, this is not your average oatmeal cookie recipe. But it is a wonderful way to use up odds and ends in the pantry to create a nutritious snack. Thanks to Ava Lee, these cookies have a wonderful light texture and flavor.

Preheat oven to 350° F. Using a wire whisk, blend all the wet ingredients together in a bowl. Sift the dry ingredients one at a time into the bowl, and mix well. Chill the dough for 15 minutes. Take a tablespoon of dough and roll out between your palms. Next, flatten the dough with your palm onto an oiled cookie sheet and bake for 12 to 15 minutes. Makes 5 dozen cookies.

Wet Ingredients:

½ c. oil
¼ c. molasses
½ c. honey
¾ t. vanilla
½ t. salt
½ c. low-fat milk

Dry Ingredients:

2 c. whole wheat pastry flour
1 c. quick-cooking rolled oats
⅛ c. soy milk powder
⅓ c. bran
2½ t. soda
½ t. cinnamon
¼ t. allspice
¼ t. coriander
¾ c. coconut
½ c. raisins, softened in hot water
½ c. chopped nuts

ALMOND FRUIT KISSES ✤

If cherries are not in season, don't let that stop you. Try peaches, oranges, or figs chopped into small pieces.

In a saucepan, combine the fruit and honey and cook over medium heat. With a large wooden spoon, mash down the cherries to expel the liquid. Stir in the coconut flakes and almonds and continue cooking until the liquid is cooked out. Cool, drop from a teaspoon and roll in coconut. Arrange the candies on a tray lined with wax paper and chill in the refrigerator. You may also freeze the candies until chewy. Makes about 4 dozen, depending on the size ball you make.

UNSWEETENED VARIATION: Replace the honey with an equal measure of frozen apple juice concentrate.

2 c. cherries, pitted
¾ c. honey
1 c. coconut flakes
1 c. finely chopped almonds
Coconut for rolling

LEMON DROPS ✤

This candy has a natural sweet and sour flavor and is packed with nutrients too.

Peel both lemons, cut the lemon peels into thin strips and chop into small pieces. Mix the lemon juice, peel, water, honey, and date sugar together in a saucepan and bring to a boil. Simmer gently for about 30 minutes to allow the mixture to cook down to its essence. Use a ½ teaspoon measure and drop the candy onto an oiled plate to cool. Wrap the candies in wax paper and twist the ends to keep in place. Place the candies in the freezer to make them hard. Makes about 24 small candies.

2 medium lemons, juiced
Lemon peels from the 2 lemons
1 c. water
2–4 T. honey
2 T. date sugar
1 T. butter

RASPBERRY ORANGE KISSES ✌

Try this recipe with strawberries or fresh figs.

In a saucepan, combine the raspberries, grated rind, and honey and cook over medium heat. Add ¾ cup coconut flakes and cook until all liquid has been cooked off and the candy mix is stiff, about 30 minutes. Cool mix enough to handle, then drop by ½ teaspoonfuls onto wax paper covered with the remaining coconut. Shape into balls, using more coconut to thicken if necessary. Makes about 3 dozen small candies.

1 c. fresh raspberries
Grated rind of 1 orange
¾ c. honey
1 c. coconut flakes

UNSWEETENED VARIATION: Replace the honey with an equal measure of frozen orange juice concentrate.

PINEAPPLE DATE KISSES ✌

These candies will remain chewy and somewhat sticky if left in the refrigerator. However, freezing them semihard eliminates the stickiness and makes an easy-to-serve candy.

In a saucepan, combine the pineapple, honey, and dates and cook over medium heat. Add the coconut flakes and cook until the liquid has evaporated and candy mix is stiff. Stir frequently to prevent sticking or scorching. Cool mixture enough to handle. Drop by teaspoonfuls onto wax paper covered with coconut and roll into balls. Makes about 30 candies.

1 c. fresh or canned crushed
pineapple, drained
½ c. honey
½ c. dates, finely chopped
1 c. coconut flakes
Coconut for rolling

UNSWEETENED VARIATION: Replace the honey with an equal measure of frozen apple juice concentrate.

CAROB FUDGE ✌

This uncooked confection is quite rich and nutritious, so a little goes a long way. It may also be frozen to a semihard candy bar.

Line a 9 x 13-inch baking pan with wax paper. Using a wire whisk, beat the honey and molasses together until blended. Mix together the carob powder and skim milk powder and add them to the honey mixture. Use a spoon to mix in the peanut butter and peanuts. Finally, mix in the coconut and sesame meal.

Since the mixture is very stiff and sticky, I have found it easiest to mix the fudge with my hands, so that all the coconut and sesame meal are thoroughly mixed in.

Spread the candy mix onto the wax papered pan and flatten with the palm of your hand until the fudge is packed down evenly. Cover with plastic wrap and refrigerate for 2 hours or more. Cut into small squares and serve.

UNSWEETENED VARIATION: Replace the honey and molasses with 2 cups pitted dates blended in a food processor with ½ cup water added.

1¼ c. honey
¾ c. molasses
1½ c. carob powder
¾ c. skim milk powder
1½ c. chunky peanut butter
1 c. roasted peanuts
5 c. coconut
4 c. sesame meal

FUDGE CHEWS ✕

This semisoft candy can be frozen for an hour or more to make a harder confection.

Mix all the ingredients except the last two in a saucepan and slowly bring to a full rolling boil, stirring constantly. Boil for about 1 minute, then add the vanilla. Beat the mixture until thick and add the nuts. Pour the mix into a pan lined with lightly oiled wax paper. Refrigerate 2 or more hours before cutting.

6 T. carob powder
1 c. honey or date sugar
⅔ c. low-fat milk
1 cube butter
¼ t. salt
1 t. vanilla
½ c. chopped nuts

PEANUT BRITTLE ✕

This one is fantastic!

Measure the molasses, honey, vinegar, and salt into a heavy saucepan and attach a candy thermometer to the inside. Bring mixture to a boil and continue boiling at 270° F until a drop of the mixture turns brittle in a cup of cold water. Add the butter and pour the peanuts into the pot. Stir thoroughly and then pour the peanut brittle into a baking pan or cookie sheet lined with wax paper. Allow the brittle to cool, then remove from pan and break into pieces.

1 c. molasses
½ c. honey
1 T. vinegar
⅛ t. salt
1 T. butter
1 c. peanuts

PARTY POPCORN BALLS: Pour the hot peanut brittle into a bowl of approximately 4 cups fresh popcorn. Mix thoroughly and form into balls. Wrap in wax paper and store on a tray to cool. Makes 8 balls.

WALNUT CAROB CREAM ROLL ❧

Definitely the Rolls-Royce of natural confections! This recipe requires a little time to assemble, but its flavor and texture are outstanding.

Put the walnuts through a food mill or meat grinder and set aside. Next, put the raisins through the mill and knead or press them into a ball. Dust the ball with a little of the ground walnuts to keep it from sticking to your hands.

Roll out the ball between two pieces of wax paper to a rectangle of about 11 x 17 inches and a thickness of ⅛ inch. Remove the top paper and evenly spread the ground walnuts on top. Use a rolling pin to press the walnuts into the raisin mix. Put the paper back on and turn the raisin mix over. Carefully peel off the top paper.

In a bowl, cream the butter, honey, and vanilla together with a fork. Sift in the skim milk and carob powders and beat until creamy. Mix in the chopped walnuts and pile up the filling along the center of the length of the raisin mix. Roll the raisin mix over once lengthwise to overlap about ¼ inch, or until the roll and filling fit snugly. Press to join the seam and roll up in the wax paper. Freeze for 2 hours. Cut into ½-inch slices and serve with tea. These slices should be wrapped and kept in the freezer until ready to use again. They will not freeze hard, but will be firm, cool, and easy to handle. Makes about 24 slices.

Roll Mix:

½ c. walnuts
2 c. raisins

Cream Filling:

1 cube butter, softened
½ c. honey
1 t. vanilla
½ c. skim milk powder, sifted
1 T. carob powder, sifted
½ c. coarsely chopped walnuts

APRICOT DIVINITY ROLL ✌

An inexpressibly delicious cream roll with a tantalizing array of colors and textures and a gourmet taste.

Using a food mill or meat grinder, grind, measure, and set aside the cashews. Next, grind the apricots and press and knead them into a ball that holds together. Roll out the ball between two pieces of wax paper until a rectangle roll is formed. The rectangle should be about ⅛ inch thick. Mend any cracks that form as you roll.

Remove the top paper and spread the ground cashews evenly over the rectangle. Use a rolling pin to press the cashews into the apricot roll. Cover with the paper again and turn over, removing the top paper.

To make the cream filling, cream the butter, honey, and vanilla together with a fork until blended. Sift in the milk powder and beat until creamy. Stir in the pumpkin seeds. Pile cream filling down the center of the full length of the apricot roll. Carefully roll over one time lengthwise making a ¼ inch overlap. Press to join the seam and wrap in wax paper. Freeze for at least 2 hours until the filling is firm. Cut with a sharp knife into ½ inch pieces and freeze until ready to use. Makes about 24 slices.

Roll Mix:

¼ c. cashews, ground
2 c. dried apricots, ground

Cream Filling:

1 cube butter, softened
½ c. honey
½ c. skim milk powder, sifted
½ c. pumpkin seeds

Cakes & Breads

THE LIGHTEST CAKES AND BREADS are made with whole wheat pastry flour. If it is unavailable in your area, whole wheat flour works just fine. After you have become familiar with these recipes, try adding small amounts of other flours—such as millet, barley, graham, oat, and cornmeal—for variety in flavor and texture. There is more detailed information about their use and nutritional benefits in Part One, *Whole Grain Flours*, and Part Two, *The Natural Pantry*, where you will find them listed alphabetically.

All these cake recipes use honey, which means the cakes brown faster in the oven than sugar cakes. So set your timer for 5 or 10 minutes less than the suggested baking time in case your oven temperature is off. For baking purposes, I recommend using the mild-flavored unrefined oils such as safflower, sunflower, and sesame oils.

In most cases I recommend using butter to grease the cake pans, since it withstands oven temperatures better than vegetable oils. (However, you may use oil if you prefer. Do not use the spray no-stick oils; these are unhealthy.) I use a hard stick of butter to apply a light coating to the pan.

When dusting the cake pans with flour is indicated, put 1 or 2 tablespoons of whole wheat pastry flour or barley flour in each pan and turn and pat the pans to coat them evenly. Shake out the excess flour.

To check a cake for doneness, the toothpick test is usually the best indication. Insert a big, clean toothpick in the center of the cake. If it comes out clean, the cake is done. Another check is just to look at the top of the cake. When the cake pulls away from the sides of the pan, or begins cracking around the center and top, it is usually done.

Substituting Honey for Sugar. If you wish to use honey in old recipes that call for sugar, reduce the amount of sweetener to be used by one-half (1 cup of sugar becomes ½ cup of honey). After trying this formula, you may decide to add more or less honey to suit your taste. Honey adds moisture, so the original amount of liquid must be reduced by ⅛ cup. If the recipe doesn't contain liquid, add 3 tablespoons of additional flour for each ½ cup of honey used.

Other Sweet Substitutions. Replace 1 cup of firmly packed brown sugar with 1 cup of firmly packed date sugar.

Replace 1 cup of white sugar with 1 cup of sorghum syrup, or 1¼ to 1½ cups of maple syrup or malt syrup.

Flour Substitutions. If you wish to convert your recipes using white flour to more nutritious alternatives, here are some substitutions to try: 1 cup of white flour or enriched white flour can be replaced by ¾ cup of coarsely ground whole wheat flour, or ⅞ cup of whole wheat pastry flour, or ¾ to 1 cup of finely ground general-purpose whole wheat flour.

RASPBERRY BUCKWHEAT CAKES ❧

Who said pancakes are only for breakfast? I remember being thrilled as a child whenever my mother would serve pancakes for dinner. It was a special departure from the usual dinner fare.

Beat the egg yolks, oil, honey, and milk together in a bowl. Stir in the dry ingredients, mixing thoroughly with the wet ingredients. In another bowl, beat the egg whites until soft wet peaks form. Gently fold the beaten whites into the batter. Thin with more milk if necessary. Spoon onto a heated, oiled griddle, and cook as for pancakes. Serve with maple syrup or fruit syrup.

3 eggs, separated
1 T. oil
1 T. honey, optional
2 c. low-fat milk
1 c. whole wheat flour
1 c. buckwheat flour
1 t. baking soda
2 t. baking powder
2 c. ripe raspberries (or 2 ripe bananas)

BANANA CORN CAKES ❧

A delicious, filling pancake for Sunday brunch or special dinners, this is a wonderful way to use overripe bananas.

Mix the dry ingredients together in a bowl. In another bowl, mash the bananas and add the yogurt and milk. Combine the wet and dry ingredients, adding more liquid if necessary to make a pourable batter. Ladle the batter onto an oiled heated grill and cook as for pancakes. Makes 12 to 15 large pancakes.

2 c. cornmeal
1 c. whole wheat flour
1 c. buckwheat flour
2 t. baking soda
½ c. low-fat yogurt
2 c. low-fat milk
3 ripe bananas

STRAWBERRY YOGURT SHORTCAKE ❧

A natural alternative to a summertime favorite.

Preheat oven to 425° F. Mix together the flour, baking powder, and salt. Cut in butter until mixture looks like coarse crumbs. Stir in the oats. Combine the beaten egg, milk, and honey in another bowl and add to the dry mixture, stirring until moistened.

Use a serving spoon to drop batter onto an oiled baking sheet, forming 6 large shortcakes. Bake for 12 to 15 minutes. Slice the shortcakes in half, cover with strawberries and top with yogurt. Drizzle a little honey over the top if you like your yogurt on the sweeter side. Serves 6.

1 c. whole wheat pastry flour
½ t. baking powder
½ t. ground coriander
¼ t. salt
3 T. soft butter
1 c. rolled oats
1 beaten egg
½ c. low-fat milk
3 T. honey or date sugar
4 c. fresh strawberries, destemmed
    and halved
2 c. yogurt

HONEY DONUTS ❧

The honey in this recipe makes the donuts a delicious brown, and also keeps them moist for a long time.

Cream the honey and butter together and add the egg. Beat well, then add the remaining ingredients, enough flour to roll out and cut easily. Roll the dough out and cut with a donut cutter. Fry in oil.

1 egg
1 c. milk
1 c. honey
2 T. butter
1 t. cream of tartar
1 t. soda
Whole wheat pastry flour
Pinch of salt

APPLE RAISIN NUT CAKE ❧

A very tasty basic fruit-nut cake. You can substitute fresh apricots, pineapple, or any assortment of dried fruits.

Preheat oven to 350° F. Measure the oil, honey, molasses, and apple juice (or milk) into a bowl and whisk together until blended. Add the grated apples and mix.

In another bowl, measure the flours, salt, soda, and spices. Sift these gradually into the wet ingredients, mixing as you go. Fold in raisins and chopped nuts.

Pour the batter into an oiled 8 x 8-inch baking pan or bread pan, spreading batter evenly into the corners. Bake for 1 hour or until a toothpick inserted in the center comes out clean. Delicious served with butter, or topped with *Lemon Icing* (see p. 297).

UNSWEETENED VARIATION: Replace the honey and molasses with ½ cup date sugar mixed in ½ cup frozen apple juice concentrate.

¼ c. oil
½ c. honey
½ c. molasses
2 c. apple juice or low-fat milk
4 apples, grated
3 c. whole wheat pastry flour
2 T. soy flour
¾ t. salt
1½ t. baking soda
¾ t. cloves
¾ t. allspice
¾ c. raisins
¼ c. chopped nuts

CHERRY COBBLER ❧

This cobbler combines all the flavor of old-fashioned baked cherry pie with an incredibly simple-to-make batter.

Preheat oven to 375° F. Cream the butter, honey, and salt together with a fork. Add the milk and blend well. Sift the flour, measure, and add the dry ingredients. Pour batter into a buttered, deep baking dish. Gently pour the cherries on top of the batter to cover, and follow with the juice. Bake uncovered for 45 minutes. Serve warm with a scoop of ice cream. Serves 6.

UNSWEETENED VARIATION: Replace the honey with ½ cup date sugar and increase cherry juice to 1½ cups.

4 T. butter, softened
½ c. honey
½ t. salt
½ c. low-fat milk
1 c. sifted graham, whole wheat
    pastry flour, or oat flour
2 t. baking powder
1 c. unsweetened black cherry
    juice
3 c. Bing cherries, pitted

CAROB CHIP CAKE ❧

A rich cake with an unusual crunchy texture. This one needs no icing, thanks to the carob chips. For a nice change, try: 1½ c. whole wheat flour and ¼ c. oat flour.

Preheat oven to 350° F. Cream the honey, oil, eggs, and vanilla together. Sift the flour, soda, and salt together and add to wet ingredients, alternating with the hot water. Add the nuts and ½ the carob chips. Spread evenly in a buttered 9 x 13-inch cake pan and sprinkle the last half of the chips over the top. Bake for about 35 to 40 minutes. Cut into squares.

½ c. honey
¼ c. oil
2 eggs
1 t. vanilla
1¾ c. sifted whole wheat flour
1 t. baking soda
½ t. ground cardamom
½ t. salt
1¼ c. coffee or coffee substitute
1 c. chopped walnuts
2 T. carob powder
6 oz. carob chips

GERMAN CAROB CAKE ❧

A very moist carob cake. When topped with Coconut Caramel Topping, it is reminiscent of a "real" German Chocolate Cake.

Preheat oven to 350° F. Beat the eggs and then add the milk, honey, and salt. In another bowl, sift the carob powder, flour, and baking powder. Add dry to wet ingredients and beat well until very smooth. The batter will be thin. Add the chopped walnuts, stir well, and pour into a buttered 8 x 8-inch baking pan. Bake for 45 minutes, or until a toothpick comes out clean. Top with *Coconut Caramel Topping* or *Carob* or *Vanilla Frosting* (see *Toppings and Fillings,* pp. 295–296) and cut into squares.

UNSWEETENED VARIATION: Replace honey with ¼ cup date sugar mixed in ¼ cup frozen apple juice concentrate.

2 large eggs, beaten
1 c. low-fat milk
½ c. honey
½ t. salt
½ c. carob powder
1½ c. whole wheat pastry flour
1 t. baking powder
½ c. chopped walnuts

MOLASSES WALNUT SQUARES ❧

This cake stores well for weeks when wrapped in foil, and makes an excellent holiday gift for family and friends.

Preheat oven to 350° F. In a bowl, whisk together the oil, molasses, honey, milk, vanilla, and salt. Stir in the chopped walnuts. Measure all the dry ingredients into another bowl, and mix well. Then sift gradually into the wet ingredients, mixing as you go. Pour batter into a buttered 8 x 8-inch baking pan and bake for 40 minutes. When done, the cake should be golden brown and moist. Cool and cut into squares.

¼ c. oil
¾ c. molasses
¾ c. honey
¼ c. low-fat milk
1½ t. vanilla
¼ t. salt
1½ c. chopped walnuts
2½ c. whole wheat pastry flour
¼ c. soy milk powder
1 t. soda

PINEAPPLE UPSIDE-DOWN CAKE ❧

Every bit as good as mom used to make. The maraschino cherries are omitted due to the red dye, but you can use fresh cherries, dates, or raisins to decorate centers of the pineapple rings.

Preheat oven to 375°F. In a small saucepan, melt the butter and add the honey, molasses, and pineapple juice. Dissolve the cornstarch in water and add it to the juice mixture. Stir until mixture thickens and remove from heat. Arrange the pineapple rings on the bottom of an 8x8-inch baking pan and pour the sauce evenly on top.

In a bowl, cream the eggs, salt, honey, milk, oil, and vanilla. Add the flour and baking powder and blend well. Gently pour the cake batter over the pineapple rings and bake for 20 to 30 minutes, or until the cake is golden brown. Turn upside down on a decorative plate and cool.

Topping:

2 T. butter, melted
2 T. honey
2 T. molasses
1 T. cornstarch
¼ c. cold water
½ c. unsweetened pineapple from
     1 8-oz. can pineapple rings

Batter:

3 eggs, beaten
¼ t. salt
½ c. honey
¾ c. low-fat milk
1 T. oil
1 t. vanilla
½ t. ground ginger
1½ c. whole wheat pastry flour
1½ t. baking powder

ANISE ZUCCHINI CAKE

An excellent cake to make in a large batch and freeze. Instead of vanilla flavoring, try lemon, almond, or anise extract for variety.

Preheat oven to 350° F. In a large bowl, mix together the milk, oil, and honey using a wire whisk to blend thoroughly. Next, add the vanilla and zucchini. In another bowl, combine the remaining ingredients and add them to the honey and oil mixture. Spoon into an oiled 8 x 8-inch baking pan and bake for 40 minutes.

1 c. low-fat milk
½ c. oil
1 c. honey
1 T. vanilla
2 c. grated zucchini
3 c. whole wheat flour
½ t. salt
½ t. baking powder
1 T. anise seeds
½ c. chopped walnuts
½ c. raisins, optional

TAHINI SPICE CAKE

A somewhat dense cake, not too sweet.

Preheat oven to 350° F. Cream together the tahini, eggs, vanilla, date sugar, and juice. In another bowl, mix together the spices, flours, soda, and powder. Mix the dry ingredients into the wet, blend well, and pour into a greased and floured 8 x 8-inch baking pan. Sprinkle the sesame seeds evenly over the top of cake and bake about 1 hour or until done. Serve with a fruit sauce of your choice. Makes 12 servings.

¼ c. sesame tahini
2 eggs, beaten
1 t. vanilla
1¼ c. apple juice
4 T. date sugar
1 t. cinnamon
½ t. nutmeg
¼ t. cloves
¼ t. allspice
¼ t. ginger
2 c. whole wheat flour
¼ c. brown rice flour
1 t. baking soda
1 t. baking powder
¼ c. sesame seeds

LEMON FENNEL CAKE ❧

Although made in a mold or Bundt pan, this cake is moist without being heavy. Lemon Icing is a must on this dessert.

Preheat oven to 325° F. Place the dates in a bowl, pour the boiling water over them, and let them stand until cool. Cream the oil, honey, and eggs together until well blended. Beat in the lemon juice and rind, and then beat in the yogurt. Stir in the four dry ingredients and mix well. Add the date and water mixture, blend well, and pour into a buttered and floured Bundt pan. Bake for 50 to 60 minutes. Cool a few minutes, unmold, and cool completely on a platter before icing with *Lemon Icing* (see p. 297).

UNSWEETENED VARIATION: Replace the honey with ½ cup date sugar and ½ cup frozen apple juice.

2 c. dates, pitted and halved
1 c. boiling water
½ c. oil
1 c. honey
2 eggs
½ c. lemon juice and grated rind
    of the lemons
½ c. low-fat yogurt
½ t. salt
1 T. fennel seeds, ground
2 t. baking soda

CHAMPION CARROT CAKE ❧

This recipe utilizes the pulp leftover when carrot juice is made in a vegetable juicer. The pulp is best made into a cake right away, when fresh, but stores well in plastic bags in the refrigerator for about a week.

Preheat oven to 350° F. Combine the eggs, oil, and honey and beat with a wire whisk until well blended. Add the remaining ingredients in the order given. Turn into an oiled and floured 8 x 8-inch cake pan. Then bake for 30 minutes.

UNSWEETENED VARIATION: Replace honey with ½ cup date sugar and add ½ cup frozen orange juice concentrate.

2 eggs
½ c. oil
1 c. honey
½ c. low-fat yogurt or milk
2 c. whole wheat flour
¼ t. salt
1 t. baking soda
2 t. cinnamon
1 t. ginger
1 t. allspice or cloves
2 c. carrot pulp (pressed firmly)

PUMPKIN TEA RING ❧

Another harvest-time recipe useful in recycling pumpkins. Make up several batches and freeze for later. A lovely dessert to serve warm with an evening tea.

Preheat oven to 350° F. Mix together the eggs, honey, oil, lemon rind, vanilla, and pumpkin until creamy. Sift in all the dry ingredients, blend well, and pour into a well-buttered ring mold. Bake for 40 to 45 minutes. Loosen from mold and serve warm.

UNSWEETENED VARIATION: Replace the honey with ¼ cup frozen apple juice concentrate.

2 eggs, beaten
¼ c. honey
½ c. oil
1 T. grated lemon or orange rind
½ t. vanilla
2 c. grated raw pumpkin
1¼ c. whole wheat pastry flour
1 t. baking powder
½ t. salt
½ t. cinnamon
½ t. nutmeg
½ t. ground cloves
½ t. baking soda in 1 T. water

PEANUT BUTTER BUNDT CAKE ❧

For peanut butter lovers only! As a girl, one of my favorites was a peanut butter cake made from a box. These ingredients from scratch are just as tasty and healthier too. Try the Peanut Butter Honey Glaze for a topping.

Preheat oven to 350° F. Cream the eggs, honey, oil, peanut butter, milk, vanilla, and salt together. Sift the flour and baking powder into the wet ingredients and beat until creamy. Butter and lightly flour the Bundt cake pan. Pour batter into the pan and bake for 35 to 40 minutes. Be careful not to overbake. (Use toothpick to test for doneness.) Cool for 10 minutes and then turn out onto a platter to complete the cooling. Top with *Peaunt Butter Honey Glaze, Vanilla Honey Glaze,* or *Mocha Caramel Glaze* (see *Toppings and Fillings,* pp. 295–298).

3 eggs
1 c. honey
½ c. oil
1 c. peanut butter
1¼ c. low-fat milk
1 t. vanilla
½ t. salt
2 c. whole wheat pastry flour
½ c. rice polishings
2 t. baking powder

BRANDY PEAR CAKE ✋

Served warm with brandy topping, this cake is a lovely addition to tea, coffee, and friends.

Preheat oven to 350° F. Mix until smooth 1½ cups of the pears and the honey, butter, brandy, and lemon juice and rind. Pour into a bowl and add the salt, spices, soda, and flour. Mix well and pour into an 8 x 8-inch buttered and floured baking pan. Decorate the top with the remaining pear slices and bake about 40 to 45 minutes.

Combine all ingredients for the topping in a small saucepan and cook until thickened. Makes about ½ cup. Spread evenly over the top of the warm cake.

UNSWEETENED VARIATION: Replace the honey in the batter and topping with equal amounts of frozen apple juice concentrate.

Batter:

*3 large pears, pared, peeled, and
   sliced*
½ c. honey
1 cube butter, softened
½ c. brandy
Juice and grated rind of 1 lemon
1 t. salt
½ t. allspice
½ t. mace
1 t. baking soda
*2 c. sifted whole wheat pastry
   flour*

Topping:

1 large pear, blended in the brandy
2 T. butter
¼ c. honey
¼ c. brandy
¼ t. allspice

DARK FRUIT CAKE ～

I like to send fruit cakes to family and friends at holiday time, so the proportions for this cake can be cut down if you only want one or two loaves.

Heat the first 6 ingredients (the dried fruit and juice) in a large stainless steel pot for about 5 minutes, then soak them for 12 to 15 hours, with the lid on.

Preheat the oven to 350° F. Sift the whole wheat pastry flour, then sift again with the remaining dry ingredients (except nuts). In a large bowl, cream together the honey, butter, eggs, and vanilla. Stir in the flour mixture, then the fruit mixture, and finally the nuts. Spoon the batter into 3 loaf pans that have been oiled and wax papered and 2 oiled cake pans. Bake for 3–3½ hours or until done. Cool, wrap in foil, and store. These cakes can also be frozen. Makes 5 holiday fruit cakes.

1½ c. white grape juice, unsweetened (or apple juice)
2½ c. seedless white raisins
2½ c. seedless raisins
1 c. pitted, chopped dates
2 c. dried, chopped pineapple
2 c. dried, chopped apricots
6 c. whole wheat pastry flour
2 t. salt
½ t. baking soda
2 t. cinnamon
1 t. each allspice and nutmeg
½ t. ground cloves
¼ t. ground cardamom
2 c. butter
1⅓ c. honey
10 eggs
2 T. vanilla
2 c. shelled pecans, coarsely chopped
1 c. shelled walnuts, coarsely chopped

BANANA ALMOND TORTE ✒

A very filling rich cake, layered with a creamy butter frosting. If oat flour is unavailable, use all pastry flour instead. However, oat flour adds extra lightness!

Preheat oven to 350° F. Cream the butter or oil, honey, and eggs together until well blended. Beat in the yogurt, almond extract, and mashed bananas until well blended.

In another bowl, mix the flours together with the spices, salt, and soda. Sift dry ingredients into wet ingredients and add the almonds. Mix well so that everything is blended. Pour into two buttered and floured 8 x 8-inch cake pans and bake for 30 to 45 minutes. Remove and cool completely. Carefully slice each cake evenly in half, using a sharp serrated bread knife. Frost the layers with *Almond Butter Frosting* (see p. 303).

1 cube butter or ½ c. oil
1 c. honey
3 eggs
1 c. plain low-fat yogurt
½ t. almond extract
1 t. ground cloves
1½ t. cinnamon
2 t. baking soda
½ t. salt
½ c. roasted almond slivers
1½ c. whole wheat pastry flour
½ c. oat flour
2 ripe bananas, mashed

APRICOT DATE FRUIT CAKE ✒

The honey in this light fruit cake acts as a preserving agent, and keeps the cake moist if the cake is wrapped in tin foil and stored in a cool, dry place. For this reason, it is an excellent holiday gift. You can send it through the mail without worry of spoilage.

Preheat oven to 350° F. Mix the dry ingredients together, along with the nuts and dried fruits, so they are well-floured. In another bowl, cream the butter, honey, eggs, and vanilla. Combine the two mixtures and mix well. Spoon the batter into two 4 x 8½-inch bread pans that have been oiled and lined with wax paper. Bake for 1 hour. Makes 2 loaves.

1⅓ c. dates, pitted and chopped
1⅓ c. chopped dried apricots
1 c. pecans, chopped coarsely
⅓ c. walnuts, chopped coarsely
4½ c. whole wheat pastry flour
1 t. double-acting baking powder
½ t. salt
¾ c. butter
1⅓ c. honey
5 eggs
1 t. vanilla

HOLIDAY FRUIT CAKE ❧

Makes a nice gift for family and friends. Wrapped in tin foil, this cake will last for weeks.

Preheat oven to 300° F. Cream the oil, honey, molasses, eggs, and vanilla until well blended. Stir in the dry ingredients. Fold in the dates, nuts, and apricots. Pour into two small, well-buttered and floured loaf pans and bake for 1½ hours. Cool completely before slicing.

UNSWEETENED VARIATION: Replace the honey and molasses with ¾ cup date sugar and add ¼ cup frozen orange juice concentrate.

¼ c. oil
½ c. honey
¼ c. molasses
2 eggs
1 t. vanilla
¾ c. whole wheat pastry flour
½ t. baking powder
½ t. salt
1 t. ground cardamom
1 c. Bahri dates or other soft dates, pitted
1 c. Brazil nuts, thinly sliced
1 c. pecan halves
1 c. dried apricots, soaked in boiling or hot water

SOUR CREAM CAROB CAKE ❧

My children also ask for this one on birthdays. It can be doubled to make a large sheet cake or a two-layer cake and iced with vanilla or carob frosting.

Preheat oven to 350° F. Cream the butter, honey, eggs, and vanilla. Add the carob powder and blend well. Next beat in the sour cream. Add the dry ingredients, mix well, and then stir in the hot coffee. The batter should be thin. Pour into a buttered and floured 8 x 8-inch baking pan and bake for 50 minutes. Cool and loosen from pan. Ice with *Basic Butter Frosting* (see p. 30), or *Carob Cream Frosting* (see p. 302).

UNSWEETENED VARIATION: Replace the honey with ½ cup frozen apple juice concentrate.

6 T. butter
½ c. honey
1 egg
½ t. vanilla
3 T. carob powder
½ c. sour cream
1 c. whole wheat pastry flour
1 t. baking soda
¼ t. salt
½ c. strong hot coffee or coffee substitute

"SUGAR" PLUM COFFEE CAKE ❧

A wonderful dinner dessert or Sunday brunch coffee cake when plums are in season. Other suitable fruits: cherries, peaches, apples, and pineapple.

To make cake dough, cream the oil and honey and beat in the eggs and vanilla. In another bowl, sift the flours with baking powder and salt and add to the cream mixture. Alternate the dry ingredients with the orange juice. Stir in the grated orange rind. Refrigerate dough several hours or preferably overnight.

Slice the plums into a bowl, toss with the cinnamon and honey, and spread evenly over the dough. To make the topping, mix the remaining dough with the granola and flour and spread over the plums. Dot with butter and bake for 45 minutes or longer. Do not underbake.

UNSWEETENED VARIATION: Replace the honey in the dough with ½ cup frozen apple juice concentrate. For the filling, use fruit juice or water instead of honey to add a little moisture to the plums.

Dough:

1 c. oil
½ c. honey
2 eggs
½ t. vanilla
1 c. oat flour
2 c. whole wheat pastry flour
2¼ t. baking powder
1 t. salt
¾ c. orange juice and grated rind
    of 1 orange

Filling:

24 plums (Italian plums,
    preferably)
½ t. cinnamon
2 T. honey or juice

Topping:

½ c. nut granola
⅓ c. whole wheat pastry flour
butter

CARROT CAKE SUPREME ✖

A great cake to serve for birthdays. Oat flour is a nice addition: try 1½ cups whole wheat pastry flour and ½ cup oat flour.

Preheat oven to 350°F. Beat eggs in a large bowl. Add the oil, honey, and yogurt and mix well. Add flour and mix well. Next, mix in the salt, soda, cinnamon, and ginger. Finally, stir in the grated carrots and orange rind.

Butter and flour a 9-inch mold and pour in the batter. Bake for 30 minutes. When the cake is done, reverse mold onto a platter and gently tap the bottom until cake loosens. To make a sheet cake, double the recipe and use a 9 x 13-inch baking pan. Watch cooking time carefully. Cool and frost with *Lemon Icing* (see p. 297).

2 large eggs
½ c. oil
1 c. honey
½ c. low-fat yogurt
2 c. whole wheat pastry flour
¼ t. salt
1 t. baking soda
1½ t. cinnamon
1 t. ground ginger
2 c. grated carrot
Grated rind of 1 orange, using
    large-holed side of the grater

CHERRY COCONUT SQUARES ✖

Very easy to make. A great dessert for potlucks.

Preheat oven to 350°F. In a bowl, mix together the wheat germ and flour. Add the oil and blend well. Pour mix into a buttered 8 x 8-inch baking pan and bake for 12 minutes.

Cream together the honey and eggs, then sift in the flour, baking powder, and salt. Add the coconut, the cherries, and finally the walnuts. Stir the mixture well and pour it over the top of the wheat germ bottom crust. Spread evenly and return to the oven to bake for 25 minutes. Cool and cut into squares.

UNSWEETENED VARIATION: Replace honey with ½ cup date sugar mixed with ½ cup more juice.

Crust:

½ c. wheat germ
½ c. whole wheat pastry flour
½ c. oil

Filling:

½ c. honey
1 c. cherry cider, unsweetened
2 eggs, beaten
1 T. whole wheat pastry flour
½ t. baking powder
⅛ t. salt
¾ c. coconut
2 c. Bing cherries, pitted and
    halved
½ c. chopped walnuts

PEACH BUNDT CAKE ❧

Other moist fruits would work well here, such as pineapple, blackberries, raspberries, or plums.

Preheat oven to 350° F. Cream eggs, honey, oil, milk, yogurt, vanilla, and salt together. Sift the flour and baking soda into the wet ingredients and beat until creamy. Quickly whiz batter in blender to take care of any remaining lumps, and stir in the peaches.

Butter a Bundt cake pan and flour lightly. Pour the cake batter into the pan and bake for 50 minutes. Cool for 10 to 15 minutes and turn out onto a platter to complete cooling. Suggested toppings: *Vanilla Honey Glaze, Coconut Cream Glaze,* or *Brandy Cream Topping* (see *Toppings and Fillings,* pp. 294–298).

UNSWEETENED VARIATION: Replace the honey with 1 cup date sugar mixed in ½ cup frozen apple juice concentrate.

3 eggs
¾ c. honey
¾ c. oil
½ c. low-fat milk
¼ c. plain low-fat yogurt
1 t. vanilla
1 t. ground ginger
½ t. salt
3 c. whole wheat pastry flour, sifted
2½ t. baking soda
2 c. peaches, peeled and chopped

RAISIN WHOLE WHEAT SOY BREAD ❧

This bread is a semisweet flavored bread. You can make it sweeter by adding another ¼ cup of honey.

Preheat oven to 350° F. Mix all the dry ingredients together in a bowl. In another bowl, blend all the wet ingredients well, and add the dry ingredients to them. Pour the batter into an oiled loaf pan and bake immediately. Bake about 1 hour.

2 T. oil
2 c. buttermilk, sour milk, or 1¾ c. milk with ¼ c. cider vinegar added
¼ c. honey
2½ c. whole wheat flour
½ c. plus 2 t. soy milk powder
2 t. baking soda
½ t. salt

WHOLE WHEAT SPICE BREAD ❧

Serve with butter, jam, and cream cheese.

Preheat oven to 350° F. In a bowl, blend together the two flours, salt, spices, and soda. In another bowl, beat together the molasses, yogurt, and milk. Stir in the raisins, and add the wet ingredients to the dry. Mix well and pour into an oiled 2-pound bread pan. Bake 50 to 60 minutes.

2½ c. whole wheat pastry flour
½ c. millet flour
1 t. salt
1 t. allspice
1 t. nutmeg
1 t. cinnamon
1½ t. baking soda
½ c. molasses
½ c. low-fat yogurt
1⅓ c. low-fat milk
½ c. raisins, soaked

GOLDIE'S MANDEL BREAD ❧

My husband's grandmother is an ethnic cook par excellence. This recipe has been in her family for years, and she passed it on to me. I have made a few substitutions with honey and flour, but it retains its distinctive nutty taste.

Preheat oven to 350°–375° F. In a bowl, beat together the eggs, date sugar, oil, and vanilla. Sift the flours and add all the dry ingredients to the wet ingredients and mix well. Flour a bread board and divide the mixture into four parts. Knead each into a roll, adding more flour to the board as needed. Bake the rolls for 20 to 25 minutes.

Brush the tops of the rolls with a mixture of egg yolk and a little cold water. Slice the rolls immediately, sprinkle with more date sugar and cinnamon. Toast the slices in the oven for 10 to 12 minutes at 375° F.

3 eggs
1 c. date sugar, or ½ c. honey
¾ c. oil
1 t. vanilla
1 c. chopped almonds
2 t. baking powder
1 c. whole wheat pastry flour
1 c. barley flour
1 c. oat flour

PUMPKIN BREAD ❧

Friends rave about this recipe. If you think pumpkin is tasteless, you must give this a try!

Preheat oven to 350° F. Cream the eggs, honey, and oil together and mix in the pumpkin. Sift the flour, soda, salt, and spices into the wet ingredients. Mix well and stir in the raisins and nuts. Add the water or yogurt if necessary and pour into 2 oiled bread pans. Bake for 65 to 75 minutes.

2 eggs
1 c. honey
½ c. oil
1 c. grated pumpkin
2 c. whole wheat pastry flour
1 t. soda
½ t. each—salt, nutmeg, and cinnamon
¼ t. ginger
1 c. raisins
½ c. chopped nuts
½ c. water or low-fat yogurt, if needed

CRANBERRY BREAD ❧

A tasty addition to holiday meals. Instead of rice flour, you can try the same amount of rice polishings.

Preheat oven to 350° F. Cream the butter and honey together and then beat in the egg. Sift flours, baking powder, salt, and soda together into the creamed mixture, alternating with the orange juice. Next, add the rind, nuts, and cranberries. Pour into a loaf pan and bake for about 1 hour.

3 T. butter
½ c. honey
1 egg
1½ c. whole wheat flour, sifted
½ c. rice flour
1½ t. baking powder
½ t. salt
½ t. soda
⅔ c. orange juice and grated rind of 1 orange
1 c. chopped nuts
1 c. chopped, fresh cranberries

BANANA FANTASY BREAD ✺

A wild combination of colors, flavors, and textures. If cherries are not in season, substitute with one more banana. Serve as tea bread. If barley flour is unavailable, try rice flour or add more pastry flour.

Preheat oven to 350°F. Cream the oil and honey until light and fluffy. Beat in the eggs until well blended. In another bowl, sift together the flours, baking powder, salt, and soda. Stir in the fruit and nuts. Add the dry ingredients alternating with the mashed banana. Mix just enough after each addition to moisten the dry ingredients. Pour into a greased loaf pan and bake for 1 hour. Cool completely before slicing.

½ c. oil
½ c. honey
2 eggs
1½ c. whole wheat pastry flour, sifted
½ c. barley flour
2 t. baking powder
1 t. ground coriander
½ t. salt
½ t. baking soda
½ c. Bing cherries, pitted and halved
½ c. sliced Brazil nuts
1 c. mashed ripe bananas (2 to 3 bananas)

PECAN BREAD ✺

We love this toasted and served with butter and a pot of tea.

Preheat oven to 350°F. Sift dry ingredients three times. Stir in the nuts. In a separate bowl, blend together the honey, egg, and milk. Then pour this mixture into the dry ingredients. Mix to form a dough. Pour into a well-greased bread pan and bake about 45 minutes. Serve with butter.

2 c. whole wheat pastry flour
⅔ c. barley flour
3 t. baking powder
½ c. chopped pecans
½ c. honey
1 egg
1 c. low-fat milk

ORANGE DATE NUT BREAD ❧

This dessert bread is sweet and hearty. Delicious with cream cheese too.

Preheat oven to 350° F. Cream the butter or oil with the honey, and beat in the eggs and vanilla. Add the orange juice. Sift the flour, baking powder, and salt together, and stir into the wet ingredients. To soften the dates, cover with 1 cup boiling water. Use a slotted spoon to remove dates from the pan. (You can save the sweetened water for another use.) Stir in the dates and walnuts and pour into an oiled loaf pan. Bake for 1 hour.

⅓ c. butter or oil
½ c. honey
2 eggs
1 t. vanilla
1 c. orange juice and grated rind
    of 1 orange
1½ c. whole wheat pastry flour,
    sifted
1 t. baking powder
1 t. salt
½ c. bran
1 c. chopped dates, softened
1 c. chopped walnuts

ZUCCHINI NUT BREAD ❧

Summer is zucchini time. Make up several loaves and freeze for winter. For a different texture and flavor, add ½ cup of yellow cornmeal and leave out ½ cup of the wheat flour.

Preheat oven to 300° F. Combine the flours, cinnamon, baking soda, and salt in a bowl and mix well with a whisk. In another bowl, mix the honey, molasses, oil, eggs, and vanilla and beat until smooth. Add the dry ingredients to the wet and blend until creamy. Add the nuts and grated zucchini. Pour the batter into an oiled 9x9-inch baking pan and bake for 1 hour.

2 c. whole wheat flour
½ c. soy flour
¼ c. molasses
2 t. cinnamon
2 t. baking soda
½ t. salt
½ c. honey
½ c. chopped nuts
2 c. grated zucchini
1 c. oil
2 eggs
2 t. vanilla

CINNAMON PLUM BREAD ❧

Serve with coffee or Rostaroma tea for satisfying conclusion to a light meal.

Preheat oven to 350° F. In a bowl, blend together the flours, salt, baking powder, and cinnamon. In another bowl, beat the egg and stir in the molasses and milk. Toss the dates and plums in a little of the flour mixture and then stir into the wet ingredients. Add the dry ingredients to the wet, mix well, and pour into an oiled bread pan. Sprinkle the date sugar and cinnamon evenly over the top of the bread. Bake for 50 to 60 minutes.

Dough:

1¾ c. whole wheat pastry flour
¾ c. rye flour
1 t. salt
4 t. baking powder
2 t. cinnamon
1 egg
⅓ c. molasses
1½ c. low-fat milk
¼ c. soft dates
½ c. chopped plums

Topping:

1 T. date sugar
¼ t. cinnamon

Toppings & Fillings

THERE ARE SO MANY USES FOR TOPPINGS AND FILLINGS. Some of these recipes are best suited for drizzling over cakes and ice cream. Others are thick and spreadable and excellent for cake frostings. They all add the finishing delicious touch to cakes, pies, and ice cream by offering contrasting flavors, textures, and colors. Some are good enough to serve as they are in a dessert bowl.

Fillings are similar to toppings. As a matter of fact, the thick toppings and frostings can also be used as fillings. The difference lies with the function. Fillings are used inside cakes, breads, cookies, and pastries. For layer cakes or tortes, the inside layer is spread with the filling while the top and sides are iced with the frosting. This really dresses up an ordinary cake.

Cookies can accommodate fillings; just make a depression in the center and add a spoonful of filling. Breads can be rolled out, spread with a filling, and then rolled up into a loaf and baked. Any way you look at it, toppings and fillings can make a difference!

Included in this section are some special recipes worth mentioning. Homemade yogurt and yogurt cheese are simple and economical to make. These low-fat foods are the foundation of the "mock" recipes in this section. For the fat-restricted diet, *Mock Sour Cream*, *Mock Whipping Cream*, and *Mock Cream Cheese* are presented as low-fat substitutes. These recipes offer much more nutrition than their rich counterparts, and I think you will enjoy using them.

I put a homemade granola recipe in this section because it makes a wonderful topping for ice cream and pies. Homemade date sugar is easy to make, and if you are in an area where you can't find it in your stores, this recipe is for you.

HOMEMADE YOGURT

Put the milk in a heavy pot with an asbestos pad underneath to prevent the milk from scorching. Use a candy thermometer to measure the rising temperature. When the milk reaches about 180° F, remove from heat and allow it to cool. If you don't have a candy thermometer, bring the milk to a boil and immediately reduce the heat so the milk simmers for another minute or so. Then remove from the heat to cool.

Cool the milk to about 125° F or until it is warm to the touch. A skin may have formed over the yogurt. This can be skimmed off or stirred back into the yogurt. Slowly add the skim milk powder, using a wire whisk to stir into the milk. Now pour the milk through a strainer into a nonmetallic bowl or ceramic crock.

Add the plain yogurt and stir it in gently, stirring in one direction until it is blended into the milk. Cover the yogurt with a lid or plastic wrap, then wrap the whole container in heavy towels and place in a warm, draft-free place for about 8 hours. If your oven has a pilot light, you can speed up the process by putting the wrapped container on the shelf in the oven for about 6 to 7 hours.

Refrigerate after the yogurt has set. The yogurt will last a week. Save a little from this batch to make your next quart of yogurt. The skim milk powder adds extra protein and helps thicken it a bit, but is not necessary to make the yogurt, so if you wish, it can be omitted. Makes one quart.

1 qt. milk
½ c. noninstant skim milk powder
2 T. plain yogurt

HONEY SPICED YOGURT ✍

Prepare the yogurt as directed in *Homemade Yogurt* in the previous recipe. After the skim milk powder and plain yogurt have been added, stir in the honey and spice. Proceed with the remaining directions, and incubate for 8 hours. Refrigerate when set.

VARIATION: Try other spices: cinnamon, coriander, allspice, instead of cardamom. Use the same measure as for the cardamom.

1 qt. milk
½ c. noninstant skim milk powder
2 T. plain yogurt
¼ c. honey
1 t. ground cardamom

YOGURT CHEESE ✍

A very good substitute for cream cheese. It has a thick, creamy consistency, but many fewer calories. Its tartness can be cut by adding spices and honey. Add to frostings, gelatins, and bread.

Whole milk yogurt makes a creamier cheese, but the skim milk or low-fat variety makes a good soft cheese too. Fold cotton cheesecloth into 2 or 3 layers and place in a bowl. Spoon the yogurt into the center, fold the sides into a sack. Tie up the neck of the sack and suspend it from the kitchen faucet. Allow the yogurt to drain for at least 3 hours for a soft cheese, or overnight for a thick creamy cheese. I like to mash the cheese with a fork until it is smooth and creamy before I refrigerate it. This is the time to add any sweetener or spices. Refrigerate in a container with a tight-fitting lid. Makes about 1 cup.

1 lb. whole milk yogurt (or 2 c. homemade)

MOCK WHIPPED CREAM ❧

A tasty alternative for those who wish to reduce the fats in their diet.

Mix all the ingredients together in a bowl, using a wire whisk to blend in the honey thoroughly. The whisking action will also loosen the yogurt making it thinner in consistency. Refrigerate the mixture and use it as a topping instead of whipped cream.

1 c. plain low-fat yogurt
1 t. vanilla
1 t. honey

MOCK SOUR CREAM ❧

Another alternative for those watching their fat intake.

Place all the ingredients in a blender and whir until creamy. Spoon into a container, cover tightly, and refrigerate. Use in place of sour cream.

1 c. low-fat cottage cheese, or part-skim ricotta cheese
1 c. plain low-fat yogurt

HOMEMADE GRANOLA ❧

Make this ahead of time and store in an air-tight container so it will be on hand to use as a topping for ice cream, yogurt, or pies.

Preheat oven to 300°F. Melt the sauce ingredients in a small saucepan, then add to the dry ingredients. Mix them thoroughly, and spread on a baking sheet. Bake in the oven until brown. Makes about 8 cups of granola.

1 c. wheat germ
5 c. rolled oats
1 c. dried coconut shreds
¼ c. sesame seeds
¼ c. sunflower seeds
½ c. chopped nuts

Sauce:

1 c. butter or oil
½ c. honey or molasses
1 T. milk, optional

HOMEMADE DATE SUGAR ❧

Naturally, it is much easier to buy date sugar at the health food store, but in case you don't have one in your area, this is easy to make. Date sugar adds an interesting flavor, and is an unrefined carbohydrate with vitamins and minerals.

Preheat oven to 250° F. Arrange the dates on an ungreased baking sheet, making sure they don't overlap. Put them in the heated oven for 12 to 15 hours, or until they are completely dried and hard. The moisture content will vary, so the cooking time is only approximated. Be careful the dates don't burn.

32 dates, pitted and sliced

When done cooking, turn off the heat, leave the oven door ajar, and allow the dates to cool completely. If you have a food processor, use the chopping blade. Add a couple of dates at a time, and grind them into a fine, sugarlike powder. Continue adding the dates, a few at a time, until they are all ground. If you use a blender, add a couple of dates at a time. When the blender is about ¼ full, or less, remove the date sugar, and continue adding the dates, a couple at a time, until they are all ground. Store in an air-tight container in a cool, dry place. Two dates make a tablespoon of date sugar. Makes 1 cup of date sugar.

COCONUT CREAM GLAZE ❧

Excellent with German Carob Cake (see p. 272), Peach Bundt Cake (see p. 283), or Apple Raisin Nut Cake (see p. 270).

Mix all the ingredients together in an oven-proof pan and place under the broiler for 8 to 10 minutes or until golden brown. Drizzle the glaze over cake or ice cream. Makes about 1½ cups.

6 T. butter, melted
¼ c. honey or sorghum
¼ c. cream
1 t. vanilla
1 c. coconut

APPLE DATE TOPPING ✀

This uncooked topping is delicious when spread on bread, muffins, cupcakes, or cakes.

Combine all the ingredients in a blender, or run through a food mill. Blend until smooth, thick, and creamy. Spoon into a jar and cap with a tight-fitting lid. Refrigerate until ready to use. Makes about 3 cups.

5 apples, cored and quartered
1 c. soft dates, pitted and chopped
1 T. lemon juice or water

VANILLA HONEY GLAZE ✀

A versatile topping that goes well with any Bundt or fruit cake.

Melt butter in a saucepan, add the honey, and stir until dissolved. Remove from heat and add vanilla. Sift in the skim milk powder and beat until creamy. Cool for 10 to 20 minutes to allow glaze to set up before drizzling over the top of cake or ice cream. Makes 1½ cups.

1 cube butter, melted
4 T. honey
1 T. vanilla
6 T. skim milk powder, sifted

WHIPPED CREAM TOPPING ✀

The honey and vanilla perk up the blandness of the cream.

Mix all ingredients in a bowl. Using a wire whisk or electric beater, beat the mixture until stiff enough to form peaks. Decorate the tops of cakes, cream pies, pumpkin pie, or puddings.

½ pt. whipping cream
1 t. honey, optional
1 t. vanilla

COCONUT CARAMEL TOPPING ✖

This topping is delicious in combination with German Carob Cake (see p. 272), and as a sauce for vanilla ice cream.

Melt the butter in a saucepan. Add the honey and stir well. Next, add the coconut and walnuts and cook for about 10 minutes, stirring frequently to keep the sauce from sticking. When the sauce has thickened and caramelized, spread it evenly over the top of the cake. Allow icing to cool before cutting and serving. Makes 1½ cups.

1 cube butter, melted
1 T. honey or malt syrup
½ c. dried coconut
½ c. chopped walnuts

JIFFY CAROB SAUCE ✖

Not only delicious with ice cream, but also can be used to flavor milkshakes and blended drinks.

Combine all ingredients, except the oil, in a blender and whip until smooth and creamy. Slowly add the oil, a little at a time, and continue blending for a few minutes. Pour into an airtight jar and refrigerate. The mixture will become much thicker and more flavorful with refrigeration. Makes about 3½ cups.

CAROB FONDUE: Put the sauce in a decorative bowl and serve it with bits of pineapple, strawberries, peaches, or cream cheese cubes speared on toothpicks for dipping.

½ c. skim milk powder
½ c. soy milk powder
½ c. carob powder
¼ c. strong coffee or coffee substitute
½ c. milk
½ c. honey
¼ c. oil

MOCHA CARAMEL GLAZE ✌

The molasses gives this a slightly caramel flavor. Try it on Peanut Butter Bundt Cake (see p. 276), vanilla, coffee, or carob ice cream.

Melt butter in a small pan, add the honey and stir until dissolved. Remove from heat and add the coffee. Sift the carob powder and skim milk powder together and beat into the wet ingredients. When the glaze becomes smooth and creamy, allow it to cool for 10 to 20 minutes and then drizzle it over cake or ice cream. Makes about 2½ cups.

1 cube butter, melted
3 T. honey
4 T. molasses
4 T. strong coffee or coffee
  substitute
3 T. carob powder, sifted
7 T. skim milk powder, sifted

LEMON ICING ✌

For a more lemony flavor, add a few drops of lemon extract.

Cream the butter, honey, and vanilla together in a bowl until blended. Sift in the skim milk powder a bit at a time, stirring well after each addition. Alternate with the lemon juice until both ingredients are added. Stir in lemon rind and beat the icing until it is very smooth and creamy. If necessary, add more juice or milk to thin. Makes 1½ to 2 cups icing. Double the recipe for a two-layer cake.

UNSWEETENED VARIATION: Replace the honey with ¼ cup frozen apple juice concentrate.

1 cube butter, softened
¼ c. honey
1 t. vanilla
¾ c. skim milk powder, sifted
¼ c. lemon juice and grated rind
  of 1 lemon

PEANUT BUTTER HONEY GLAZE ❧

Gives a golden glow to Peanut Butter Bundt Cake (see p. 276), and Carob Chip Ice Cream (see p. 244).

Melt butter in a saucepan and add the honey, peanut butter, and vanilla. Stir over low heat until dissolved. Mix the cornstarch into the milk and pour into the glaze. Stir until the mixture thickens a bit. Remove from heat and cool 10 to 20 minutes before drizzling glaze over the top of cake or ice cream. Makes about 2½ cups.

1 cube butter, melted
4 T. honey or molasses
1 T. creamy peanut butter
1 T. vanilla
1 t. cornstarch
5 T. low-fat milk

BRANDY CREAM TOPPING ❧

Makes a good substitute for hard sauce, which is traditionally used on Christmas plum pudding. Delicious on top of our Steamed Holiday Pudding (see p. 237) or other Bundt cakes.

Mash the cream cheese, vanilla, and milk until smooth and creamy. Add the brandy, one tablespoon at a time. For cakes and baked puddings, a fairly thick sauce is desirable. Ice the top of your pudding or cake thickly, allowing any extra to run down the sides. Sprinkle the top with nutmeg.

8 oz. cream cheese, softened
1 T. low-fat milk
Brandy to taste
½ t. vanilla
Pinch of nutmeg

POPPY SEED GLAZE ❧

The crunchy texture contrasts well with soft fruit cakes such as Peach Bundt Cake (see p. 283), and Pumpkin Tea Ring (see p. 276).

In a small saucepan, melt butter and stir in the honey and vanilla until dissolved. Sift in the skim milk powder and beat until creamy. Add the poppy seeds and mix well. Makes about 1 cup.

4 T. butter, melted
3 T. honey or maple syrup
1 T. vanilla
2 T. skim milk powder, sifted
1 T. poppy seeds

HONEY SYRUP FOR CREPES ❧

Although this syrup is especially made for dessert crepes, it is also great for breakfast pancakes. You can make it in advance and store in air-tight jars in the refrigerator.

Combine the first three ingredients in a saucepan and cook for 15 minutes over medium-low heat while the crepes or pancakes are cooking. Dissolve cornstarch in the water and add to the syrup, stirring until it thickens to the desired consistency. Makes about 2 cups.

¾ c. honey
¼ c. molasses
1 c. fruit juice or water
1 T. cornstarch
¼ c. water

FRUIT JUICE SYRUP ❧

This syrup is excellent for people who cannot use any sweeteners in their food. It is a delicious topping for pancakes, crepes, or Bundt cakes.

Heat the juice in a saucepan until it is simmering gently. Mix 1 tablespoon of cornstarch with 2 tablespoons of water and stir into the juice. Continue stirring until the sauce is thickened. Add more thickener if necessary.

2 c. orange, apple, or other fruit
   juice of your choice
1 to 2 T. cornstarch

BRANDIED FRUIT SAUCE ❧

Added to cakes, ice cream, or yogurt, this is a light and elegant dessert that makes a gracious ending to a candlelight dinner.

Combine all the ingredients in a saucepan and cook over medium heat until fruit is very tender and the sauce is thickened. Makes 2½ cups.

UNSWEETENED VARIATION: Replace the honey with ½ cup water or juice and increase the allspice to 1 teaspoon.

2 c. sliced pears, peaches, plums,
   or cherries
4 T. butter
½ c. honey
½ c. brandy
½ t. allspice

PEACH SAUCE ✌

A nice sauce for cakes and pancakes.

Drain off the juice from the peaches into a small saucepan. Dissolve the arrowroot powder into the juice and cook over medium heat until it begins to thicken. Stir to prevent lumping. As it thickens, add the remaining ingredients except the peaches. Slice the peaches into the sauce 5 minutes before serving time. Serve over *Tahini Spice Cake* (see p. 274). Pour the sauce over the entire cake and poke holes in the top of the cake with a toothpick, to allow the sauce to soak into the cake.

1 can unsweetened peach halves
  (in white grape and pear
  juice) or 2 c. fresh sliced
  peaches
1 T. arrowroot powder
2 t. date sugar
½ c. apple juice
1 t. cinnamon

FRUIT TOPPING ✌

A thick, rich addition to vanilla ice cream.

Combine dates, figs, honey, and water in a small saucepan. Cook and stir over low heat until the mixture thickens, about 15 to 20 minutes. Remove from heat and stir in the nuts. Serve warm or cool over ice cream or yogurt. Makes 1½ cups thick sauce.

UNSWEETENED VARIATION: Replace the honey with water or juice.

1 c. finely chopped dates
½ c. finely chopped figs
4 T. light honey
1½ c. water
4 T. roasted peanuts, walnuts, or
  pecans, coarsely chopped

ORANGE BUTTER FROSTING ✌

The rich tangy flavor is a superb addition to cakes.

Cream the butter and honey until well blended. Stir in the grated orange rind. Sift in the skim milk powder, alternating with the orange juice. Mix well after each addition. Beat until smooth and creamy and gradually add more milk powder if you want thicker frosting. Recipe makes enough icing to frost a single-layer 8 x 8-inch or 9 x 13-inch cake. Makes about 1½ cups.

UNSWEETENED VARIATION: Replace the honey with ¼ cup frozen orange juice concentrate.

4 T. butter, softened
¼ c. honey
1 T. grated orange rind
¾ c. skim milk powder, sifted
¼ c. orange juice

CAROB FROSTING ✌

Carob has a richness that blends well with coffee and picks up the flavor of any cake.

Cream the butter, honey, and vanilla until well blended. Sift the skim milk and carob powders into the cream mixture, alternating with the coffee. Mix well after each addition and beat until smooth and creamy. A blender will remove any remaining lumps. Makes 1½ cups.

UNSWEETENED VARIATION: Replace the honey with ¼ cup frozen apple juice concentrate.

1 cube butter, softened
¼ c. honey
½ t. vanilla
¾ c. skim milk powder
1 T. carob powder
2 T. strong coffee or coffee
    substitute

CREAM CHEESE FROSTING ❧

A cup of chopped, dried fruits, such as apricots, dates, or peaches, can be cooked in a little water until softened and added to this frosting for a festive and tasty touch.

Sift the skim milk powder and set aside. In another bowl, whip up the butter until smooth. Add the honey, milk, vanilla, and skim milk powder one at a time. Add the cream cheese and whip until smooth. Thin with more vanilla or milk if necessary. Frost the cake and sprinkle walnuts on the sides and top. This recipe will frost a two-layer cake. Makes about 3 cups.

UNSWEETENED VARIATION: Replace the honey with ¼–½ cup frozen apple juice concentrate. Add more concentrate if necessary to adjust the consistency. Orange juice concentrate would also be nice.

1½ c. skim milk powder, sifted
1 cube butter, softened
½ c. honey
¼ c. low-fat milk
1½ t. vanilla
8 oz. cream cheese
1 c. chopped walnuts

CAROB CREAM FROSTING ❧

This deliciously creamy icing with a light color makes an excellent topping for carob cakes, brownies, and cupcakes.

In a mixing bowl, cream the butter, honey, cream cheese, and vanilla together with a fork. Sift the skim milk and carob powders directly into the bowl and beat until creamy. Makes about 2 cups.

1 cube butter, softened
½ c. honey
3 oz. cream cheese
1 t. vanilla
½ c. skim milk powder, sifted
2 T. carob powder, sifted

BASIC BUTTER FROSTING ✌

A basic frosting to which you can add lemon, peppermint, maple, almond, or anise extracts for a variety of flavor possibilities.

Cream the butter, honey, and vanilla together until well blended. Sift in the skim milk powder and mix in well. Add the milk and beat until very smooth and creamy. There is enough here to frost an 8 x 8-inch cake. Makes about 1½ cups.

UNSWEETENED VARIATION: Replace the honey with ¼ cup frozen apple juice concentrate.

1 cube butter, softened
¼ c. honey
1 t. vanilla
3 c. low-fat milk
½ c. skim milk powder, sifted
6 oz. cream cheese

ALMOND BUTTER FROSTING ✌

A perfect icing for Banana Almond Torte (see p. 279). Also suitable for Bundt cakes.

Cream the butter, honey, and almond extract until well blended. Sift in the skim milk powder, alternating it with the milk. Stir well after each addition. Beat until smooth and creamy and stir in the roasted almonds. This recipe will ice a double layer cake. Makes 3 cups.

UNSWEETENED VARIATION: Replace the honey with ½ cup frozen apple juice concentrate.

1 cube butter, softened
½ c. honey
1 t. almond extract
1¼ c. skim milk powder, sifted
¼ c. low-fat milk
½ c. roasted chopped almonds

FUDGE NUT FROSTING ✍

A very rich, thick frosting that can also be frozen and cut into bars.

In a bowl, cream together the honey and carob powder until the carob powder is completely absorbed. Next add the peanut butter and blend well with a fork or wooden spoon. Add water or milk a little at a time, until you get a creamy texture and the desired consistency. Makes approximately 2 cups.

⅔ c. honey
½ c. carob powder
½ c. crunchy peanut butter
Water or milk for thinning

FROZEN FUDGE BARS: Add water or milk to thin a little, spread the fudge frosting mix into a small pan and freeze for several hours. Cut into bars and take along to the movies for a treat.

UNSWEETENED VARIATION: Replace the honey with 1 cup pitted dates. Blend them with enough water to make a thick creamy paste. Add the remaining ingredients.

Pies & Pastries

PROBABLY THE MOST ESSENTIAL INGREDIENT to a successful pie or pastry is the crust. At the end of this chapter you will find crust recipes using a variety of different flours. The "Basic Whole Wheat Crust" uses whole wheat pastry flour and produces a light, tasty, and flaky crust you will be proud to serve. Barley and graham flours are also excellent for making light crusts.

Here are some tips for mixing and rolling out the crust: To mix, use a fork or pastry knife to distribute the shortening uniformly throughout the dry ingredients. Add ice water, using the fork or knife to mix it in well until the dough holds together when pressed between two fingers.

Press the dough into a ball and dust it with flour if sticky to the touch. At this point it helps to "rest" the dough in the refrigerator before rolling out. You may also freeze the dough at this stage and store for weeks. Flatten out the ball on a piece of wax paper, by pressing down gently with the palm of your hand. Cover the dough with another piece of wax paper. Start rolling in the center of the pastry and roll outward in all directions, using an even pressure, until you have made a circle about one inch larger than the pie pan. You can mend cracks by moistening with water, then gently pressing together. Avoid handling the crust too much: this makes the pastry tough.

Place the pie pan, inverted, over the pastry and flip the crust into the pan. Peel the paper off carefully. Tuck in the excess dough and flute the edges by pressing the crust between the index fingers. Before baking, prick the crust several times with a fork. If you are prebaking a pie shell, pie weights or a piece of bread placed in the bottom will prevent the single crust from buckling. For a top crust, do not flute the edges until the top crust has been adjusted and the excess dough trimmed away or tucked under. Cut four or five slits with a knife to allow steam to escape through the top crust during baking.

BANANA CREAM PIE ⮑

This pie can be made without the eggs. It sets up well and has a rich flavor.

Prepare and bake the pastry shell. Follow recipe for the pudding. Blend the banana and eggs together and add them to the pudding at the end of cooking time. Continue cooking 5 more minutes and remove from heat. Decorate bottom of the crust with the sliced banana. Pour filling into the pie shell and refrigerate until set.

1 Wheat Germ Crust, prebaked (see p. 324)
Vanilla Coconut Pudding (see p. 235)
1 banana, blended
2 eggs
1 banana, sliced in rounds or strips

PEAR CRUMB PIE ⮑

A delicate and lightly spicy flavor.

Preheat oven to 400° F. Prepare the piecrust and line a 9-inch pie pan, pricking it several times with a fork. In a bowl, mix together the pear slices, lemon juice, honey, flour, lemon peel, and allspice. Spoon fruit mixture into the pastry shell.

In another bowl, mix together the flour and spices and cut in the butter with a pastry knife. Mix in the date sugar, until the topping has a uniform crumb texture. Spread crumb mixture evenly over the top of the pears and bake for about 45 minutes or until the pears are tender. Serve warm or cool.

UNSWEETENED VARIATION: Replace the honey in the filling with ¼ cup date sugar mixed in ¼ cup apple juice. You may also use ½ cup juice.

1 Basic Whole Wheat Crust (see p. 323)

Filling:

6 medium Bartlett pears, peeled, cored, and sliced
3 T. lemon juice
½ c. honey
2 T. whole wheat pastry flour
1 t. grated lemon rind
1 t. allspice

Crumb Topping:

½ c. whole wheat pastry flour
4 T. butter, softened
½ t. ginger
½ t. cinnamon
¼ t. mace
½ c. date sugar

CAROB CREAM PIE ❧

You can omit the eggs here without losing texture or flavor. A pudding pie, delicious with whipped cream.

Prepare and bake the pie shell. Follow the recipe for Carob Pudding, and add the 2 beaten eggs toward the end of the cooking time. Continue cooking for 5 minutes, stirring frequently to prevent sticking. Pour filling into the baked pie shell and refrigerate for several hours. Serve with whipped cream.

1 Wheat Germ Crust, prebaked (see p. 324)
Carob Pudding (see p. 236)
2 eggs, beaten

BLACKBERRY PIE ❧

Blackberries are free for the picking along many roadsides. However, it is a good idea to check into the local spraying practices and wash the fruit well.

Preheat oven to 425° F. Prepare the crusts first. Mix all the remaining ingredients together in a bowl until well blended. Pour the fruit filling into the bottom crust and fit the top crust by turning the edges under and fluting. Make four slits on the top to allow steam to escape during baking. Bake for 40 minutes or until pastry is golden brown. Allow the pie to cool completely to set the filling.

JIFFY BLACKBERRY PIE: Prepare only a bottom crust and fill with the above filling. Bake and chill the pie, then spread whipped cream on top.

2 Basic Whole Wheat Crusts, unbaked (see p. 323)
4 c. ripe blackberries, washed and drained
½ c. honey
¼ c. cornstarch
Grated rind of 1 orange or lemon

FRESH CHERRY PIE ✖

My favorite as a child! Make a couple at a time, and freeze one for later.

Preheat oven to 425° F. Roll out bottom crust and line the pie pan, pricking it several times with a fork. In a bowl mix together the cherries, juice, honey, and cornstarch and pour this mixture into the pastry shell. Roll out top crust, tuck any extra crust under the bottom crust, and press and flute the edges. Slice top crust with a knife several times and bake for 35 to 40 minutes, or until the crust is a light golden brown. Cool completely before serving. Best when chilled.

2 Basic Whole Wheat Crusts (see p. 323)
5 c. Bing cherries, pitted
1 T. lemon or orange juice
⅔ c. honey
2 T. cornstarch

FRESH PEACH PIE ✖

There's nothing so flavorful as fresh peaches baked in a pie! But please let the pie cool in order for the filling to set.

Preheat oven to 425° F. Combine the peaches, orange juice, cinnamon, honey, salt, and cornstarch. Mix these ingredients together thoroughly and let them stand. Meanwhile, roll out the pastry and line a 9-inch pie pan.

Fill pie shell with the fruit mixture and dot with butter. Moisten the edge of the piecrust with water and fit top crust over the peaches. Seal the edge with a fork or flute with your fingers. Bake for 35 to 45 minutes or until the crust is golden brown. Serve warm with vanilla ice cream.

2 Basic Whole Wheat Crusts (see p. 323)
6 c. peaches, peeled, and sliced (10 to 12 medium peaches)
1 T. orange juice
½ t. cinnamon
⅔ c. honey
⅛ t. salt
1 T. cornstarch
1 T. butter

BLACK RASPBERRY PIE ❧

Our raspberry patch provides us with many pies and sauces. This is our favorite raspberry pie.

Preheat oven to 350° F. Mix the ingredients together in a bowl and let it sit for 15 minutes. Pour the filling into an unbaked pie shell and bake for 1 hour. Top with yogurt, sour cream, or whipped cream.

7 c. very ripe black raspberries
½–¾ c. honey (depending on ripeness of berries)
2 T. arrowroot
¼ c. water

APPLE CRUMBLE-NUT PIE ❧

A lazy cook's pie: you don't have to roll out a double crust, and the crumb top is made in a jiffy.

Preheat oven to 425° F. Roll out the pastry and line the pie pan, pricking the pastry shell with a fork. Toss the apples, honey, cinnamon, and cornstarch together and pour the mixture into the pastry shell.

To make the topping, mix the dry ingredients, then cut in the oil with a pastry knife. Mix in the water until the topping has a uniform crumb texture, and cover pie with the crumb topping. Bake for 35 minutes, and cool before serving.

UNSWEETENED VARIATION: Replace the honey with ½ cup date sugar mixed in ½ cup apple juice.

1 pastry shell, unbaked

Filling:

6 c. apples, peeled and sliced
½ c. honey
1 T. cinnamon

Crumb Topping:

½ c. rolled oats
½ c. whole wheat pastry flour
½ c. chopped walnuts
½ c. wheat germ
¼ c. shredded coconut
½ t. salt
⅔ c. oil
4 T. water

WALNUT PIE ✺

A special treat! Sorghum or malt syrup keeps this pie from being too sweet.

Preheat oven to 350° F. Prepare the pastry shell and line the pie pan. Prick the bottom with fork tines and then line the shell with the walnut halves. In a mixing bowl, beat the eggs until light and fluffy. Add the remaining ingredients and mix well. Pour the filling gently over the nuts and bake for about 40 minutes. Cool thoroughly to allow pie to set. Delicious served with whipped cream.

1 pastry shell, unbaked
1¼ c. walnut halves
3 eggs
1¼ c. sorghum or malt syrup
⅛ t. salt
1 t. vanilla
4 T. butter, melted

PUMPKIN PIE ✺

Recycle Jack o' Lanterns by freezing any edible portions: cut whole pumpkin into sections and bake at 350° F for 1 hour. Cool and remove skin. Cut into chunks and freeze in airtight bags until ready to use.

Preheat oven to 350° F. Line a pie pan with the pastry shell and prick the bottom several times. Mix together the strained pumpkin, milk, and eggs and beat well. Add the remaining ingredients, beat well and pour into the pastry shell. Bake for 40 to 45 minutes. The pie will be done when the top turns from shiny to dull, and when the cracks run into the center. Also, a knife inserted in the center should come out fairly clean. Allow the pie to cool, then chill before serving. Spread whipped cream on the top for an extra holiday touch.

1 pastry shell, unbaked
2 c. cooked and strained pumpkin
1 c. low-fat milk
2 eggs
½ c. honey
1 t. vanilla
1¼ t. cinnamon
¼ t. ground cloves
1¼ t. ground ginger
¼ t. ground nutmeg

RASPBERRY YOGURT PIE ✌

For this pie, try any berries in season. The soy milk powder replaces eggs and provides protein, making this a good choice for those on an eggless diet.

Preheat oven to 350° F. Prepare the piecrust and line a 9-inch pie pan. Mix the raspberries with the honey and spread the mixture evenly in the pie shell. In a bowl, blend the yogurt, honey, vanilla, and rind together with a wire whisk. Gradually add and blend in the salt, soy milk powder, and cornstarch. Pour filling over the berries and bake for 1 hour.

UNSWEETENED VARIATION: Replace the honey with an equal measure of frozen apple juice concentrate.

1 Wheat Germ Piecrust, unbaked
   (see p. 324)
2 c. fresh raspberries
1 T. honey
2 c. plain low-fat yogurt
1 c. honey
1 T. vanilla
1 t. grated orange rind
¼ t. salt
¼ c. soy milk powder
¼ c. cornstarch

NO-DAIRY PUMPKIN PIE ✌

A wonderful pie with a rich, creamy consistency.

Preheat oven to 425° F. Put all the above ingredients in a blender, or food processor (using the chopping blade), and blend until creamy. Pour into an unbaked pie shell and bake at 425° F for 15 minutes. Reduce the heat to 300° F, and continue baking for 1½ hours.

2¼ c. cooked, mashed pumpkin
1⅓ c. soy milk (⅓ c. soy milk
   powder plus 1 c. water,
   blended)
⅓ c. arrowroot (or ½ c.
   cornstarch)
½ c. honey
1 T. vanilla
½ t. nutmeg
½ t. allspice
½ t. ginger
½ t. cinnamon
¼ t. salt

NO-COOK CHEESECAKE WITH STRAWBERRIES ✌

This cheesecake is as quick and easy to make as turning on your blender!

Prepare and chill the crust. To make the filling, put the softened cream cheese and a little whipping cream into a blender. When the cream cheese is well blended, add the remaining whipping cream and blend for about 2 minutes. While mixture is blending, add the vanilla and the honey, a little at a time. Then add the lemon juice and grated rind.

Pour the mixture into the crust and chill at least 2 hours. Just before serving, clean and destem the fresh strawberries. Cut large berries in half, and arrange on top of the cheesecake.

1 Honey Graham Crust (see p. 322)
6 oz. soft cream cheese
½ pt. whipping cream
1 T. vanilla
3 T. honey
1 T. lemon juice and the grated rind
1 basket fresh strawberries

BAKED TROPICAL CHEESECAKE ✍

Very rich and creamy, this cheesecake has several layers, with the fruit on the bottom. If mangoes are unavailable, use any juicy fruit in season.

Preheat oven to 325° F. In a blender, combine the cream cheese, cottage cheese, honey, and vanilla. Blend until creamy. Add the grated orange rind, cornstarch, and eggs and blend thoroughly.

Line pie shell with the mango slices, then pour the cream filling evenly on top of the fruit. Bake for 25 minutes. Beat the sour cream and honey together and spread gently over the top of the pie. Return to the oven and bake for an additional 15 minutes. Serve chilled.

1 Graham-Sesame Crust (see p. 323)

Filling:

8 oz. cream cheese, softened or ricotta cheese
1 c. low-fat cottage cheese
½ c. honey
½ t. vanilla
1 t. grated orange or lemon rind
1 T. cornstarch
2 eggs
1 mango, peeled and sliced

Topping:

1 c. sour cream or mock sour cream
2 T. honey

JIFFY FRUIT CHEESECAKE ✌

You can cut cheesecake calories drastically by substituting the same amount of yogurt cheese for the cream cheese. To make your own yogurt cheese is quite simple. Follow the directions given on p. 292.

Prepare the pastry crust and refrigerate for 2 hours or freeze for 30 minutes. In a bowl, cream the cream cheese with a fork until thoroughly mashed and soft. Blend in the yogurt, honey, vanilla, and grated orange rind. Do not use a blender as this will break down the thick texture of the yogurt and as a result, the pie will not set up.

Line the bottom of the chilled piecrust with sliced fruit or berries and pour the cream cheese filling on top. Decorate the top with a little more sliced fruit if you like. Chill for several hours before serving.

UNSWEETENED VARIATION: Replace the honey with 1 tablespoon of frozen apple juice concentrate.

1 No-Bake Almond Crust (see p. 321)
1 c. plain low-fat yogurt
8 oz. cream cheese, softened
1 T. honey
1 T. vanilla
Grated rind of 1 orange
⅔ c. fresh fruit or berries in season

CRANBERRY PEAR PIE ✌

No baking—this is a quick autumn pie, perfect for a holiday dessert.

Prepare the crust and set aside. In a saucepan, add the berries, honey, and juice and cook for about 10 minutes. Add just enough water to the cornstarch to dissolve it, and add this mixture along with the pears to the cooking berries. Continue cooking until the mixture thickens. Then pour the fruit mixture into the prepared pie shell and chill for several hours. Top with the whipped cream before serving.

1 Graham-Sesame Crust (see p. 323)
2 c. cranberries, chopped in the blender
2 c. unfiltered apple juice
½ t. ground cardamom
1 c. honey
¼ c. cornstarch
1½ c. pears, peeled, cored, and sliced
½ pt. heavy cream, whipped

TOFU CHEESECAKE WITH BERRY GLAZE ✌

Tofu gives this cheesecake a smooth, thick texture, plus plenty of protein. For the fruit glaze, use any berries in season.

Prepare and chill the crust for 2 hours. To make the filling, blend the vanilla, lemon juice, tofu (a little at a time) and then the remaining ingredients. Pour filling into the chilled piecrust and refrigerate until ready to serve.

To make the topping, wash berries and heat them gently in a saucepan. When liquid forms, add the cornstarch and honey and stir until the sauce thickens. Remove from heat and cool. You may glaze the entire cheesecake before serving, or pour the glaze generously over each piece.

UNSWEETENED VARIATION: Replace the honey in the filling and glaze with the same measure of frozen apple juice concentrate.

1 Honey Graham Crust (see p. 322)

Filling:

1 T. vanilla
4 T. lemon juice
1½ boxes tofu, washed, drained, and cut into chunks
4 T. skim milk powder
1½ T. honey

Fruit Glaze:

2 c. blackberries
1 t. cornstarch, dissolved in 1 T. water
2 T. honey

PEACH COCONUT SQUARES ✨

Instead of peaches, try other fresh fruits in season, such as apples, cranberries, plums, or pineapple.

Preheat oven to 350°F. In a bowl, mix the oil, honey, spice, and flour and pour the resulting mixture into an oiled 8x8-inch baking pan. Bake for 10 minutes. Meanwhile, cream the honey and eggs, sift in the flour and baking powder, and mix well. Next, stir in the coconut and fruit. Pour topping over the pre-baked crust and bake for another 25 to 30 minutes, or until the top is golden brown. Cool and cut into squares.

UNSWEETENED VARIATION: Replace the honey in the crust and topping with the same measure of frozen apple juice concentrate.

Crust:

½ c. oil or 1 cube butter
1 c. whole wheat pastry flour
½ t. ground mace
2 T. honey

Topping:

⅓ c. honey
2 eggs
¼ c. whole wheat pastry flour
½ t. baking powder
½ c. coconut
1 c. sliced peaches
½ c. chopped nuts

LEMON MERANGO ✨

A pie for lemon lovers.

Preheat the oven to 350°F. Beat the egg yolks, then the honey. Beat in the flour, juice and grated rind of the lemon, and butter. Finally, add the milk. Pour into a pie-plate lined with a pastry shell pricked to prevent air blisters. Bake until set, about 45 minutes.

To make the meringue, beat the egg whites, honey, and lemon juice until stiff. Cover the pie with the meringue and brown the top lightly under the broiler.

1 Butter Barley Crust (see p. 322).

Filling:

3 eggs, separated
½ c. honey
1 T. barley flour
½ lemon
1 t. melted butter
1¼ c. half and half

Meringue topping:

3 egg whites
3 T. honey
Few drops lemon juice

APRI-CRUNCH SQUARES ✒

Instead of apricots, try fresh cranberries for a colorful, tasty change.

Preheat oven to 375° F. In a bowl, mix the granola and melted butter. Set aside ¼ of this mixture for the topping and press the remainder into an 8 x 8-inch baking pan. Mix the flour and nuts into the leftover granola topping.

In a bowl, toss the apples and apricots with the cinnamon and flour and pour into a saucepan. Next, add the apple juice. Cook for about 5 minutes, or until the juice begins to thicken and the apples begin to cook. Pour filling over the granola crust and sprinkle the topping on evenly. Bake for 40 to 45 minutes or until the apples are tender and topping is browned. Cool completely and cut into squares.

Crust and Topping:

2 c. natural granola
1 T. ground coriander
½ c. butter, melted
¼ c. whole wheat pastry flour
½ c. chopped walnuts

Filling:

6 c. firm apples, peeled and sliced
1 c. dried apricots, sliced
1¼ c. unfiltered apple juice
2 t. cinnamon
2 T. whole wheat pastry flour

BLUEBERRY CUSTARD PIE ✒

Other fruits also go well in this recipe: try fresh cherries, boysenberries, raspberries, or blackberries.

Preheat oven to 375° F. Prepare and roll out the crust to fit a 10-inch pie pan. If you only have a 9-inch pan, reduce amount of fruit to 3 cups.

In a bowl, mix together the berries, honey, salt, juice, and mace. Pour fruit mixture into the unbaked pastry shell and bake for 25 minutes. Meanwhile, mix together the remaining ingredients, except the cinnamon.

When the pie is finished cooking, pour the cream mixture over the blueberries and sprinkle the top with cinnamon. Lower the oven temperature to 325° F, and bake for 45 minutes. Chill before serving.

1 Butter Barley Crust, unbaked
   (see p. 322)
4 c. blueberries
2 T. honey
⅛ t. salt
1 T. lemon juice
1 t. mace
3 eggs
½ c. low-fat yogurt
1 c. sour cream
¼ c. honey
1 t. vanilla
½ t. grated lemon rind
Cinnamon

APRICOT POPPY SQUARES 🌿

For apricot lovers only!

Preheat oven to 350° F. Mix crust ingredients together until they form an even-textured crumb mixture. Press the crust into an oiled 8 x 8-inch baking pan. Bake for 10 minutes.

Next, boil the apricots in water for 3 minutes, and when done drain off the water. Blend the drained apricots with the honey and eggs. Pour the mixture into a bowl and mix in the baking powder and flour. Spread this filling evenly over the pastry and bake for 25 minutes. Meanwhile, prepare the topping. Heat the butter and honey together in a small saucepan until butter is melted. Remove from heat and stir in the remaining ingredients. Spread filling on the cooked pastry and refrigerate until the topping sets. Cut into small squares.

Crust:

2 T. honey
½ c. oil
1 t. anise seeds, crushed
2 T. poppy seeds
1 c. whole wheat pastry flour

Filling:

2 c. dried apricots
¼ c. honey
2 eggs
½ t. baking powder
¼ c. whole wheat pastry flour

Topping:

4 T. butter, melted
3 T. honey
2 T. skim milk powder, sifted
1 T. vanilla
2 T. poppy seeds

WALNUT FIG BARS ❧

A homemade Fig Newton!

Preheat oven to 350° F. In a medium saucepan, combine the figs, anise seed, grated peel, ⅛ teaspoon salt, and the water. Bring the mixture to a boil, cover, and cook for about 10 minutes. Remove and mash with a fork or put into a blender to make a fairly smooth mixture. Add the vanilla and honey, mix well, and set aside. In a bowl, mix together the remaining ingredients, plus ⅛ teaspoon salt.

Oil an 8 x 8-inch baking pan and spread ½ the crust mixture on the bottom, pressing it down with a fork. Spread the fig mixture over this and top with the remaining crust mixture. Bake for 40 to 45 minutes, or until the top is golden brown. Cool, then cut into 12 squares.

UNSWEETENED VARIATION: Replace the honey in the filling with ¼ cup frozen orange juice concentrate.

Filling:

3 c. dried figs, chopped
1 t. anise seed, crushed
1 T. grated orange or lemon rind
¼ t. salt
2 c. water
1 t. vanilla
¼ c. honey

Crust:

1 c. rolled oats
1 c. whole wheat pastry flour
1 c. chopped walnuts
¾ c. dried coconut
⅔ c. oil

GRANOLA CRUST ❧

Very simple to do, it is perfect for cream pies.

Mix all the ingredients and pat into a pie pan. Fill and bake or chill.

1 c. granola
½ c. wheat germ
¼ c. coconut
2 T. honey
1 cube butter, melted

OATMEAL CRANBERRY SQUARES ❧

Sandwiched between two crumb crusts—this filling has a pretty color and tart-sweet flavor.

Preheat oven to 400°F. Cream together the butter, oil, honey, soda, and salt. Mix in the oats and sifted flour and spoon half the mixture into a well-greased 8 x 8-inch baking pan. Press in firmly.

Mix together the cranberries, pineapple, honey, and vanilla and cook for 15 minutes. Dissolve the cornstarch into enough cold water to make a paste. Stir this into the fruit mixture and continue cooking until mixture thickens.

Then spread the fruit mixture evenly over the crumb mix and cover with the remaining crumbs, patting down lightly. Bake for 20 to 25 minutes. Let cool and then cut into squares.

Crust:

1 cube butter
½ c. oil
½ c. honey
½ t. baking soda
⅛ t. salt
½ t. allspice
1½ c. quick-cooking rolled oats
1½ c. whole wheat pastry flour, sifted

Filling:

2 c. cranberries, blended
1 c. drained, chopped, or crushed pineapple
½ c. honey
¼ t. vanilla
2 T. cornstarch

NO-BAKE ALMOND CRUST ❧

This is a deliciously sweet crust that goes well with creamy smooth fillings, such as the Raspberry Yogurt Pie (see p. 312).

Mix the first three ingredients together and run the resulting mixture through a food mill or blender. Stir in the butter and mix well. Press this mixture into a pie pan and refrigerate for 2 hours or freeze for 30 minutes.

1 c. rolled oats
1 c. almonds, chopped into small bits
½ c. dates, pitted and chopped
6 T. butter, melted

HONEY GRAHAM CRUST ✺

A basic crust for cheesecake or cream pies. Easy to make, no baking required.

Melt the butter and honey together, stirring until dissolved. Crush the crackers into fine crumbs. Put the crumbs in a pie pan and add the melted butter and honey mixture. Stir until the liquid is dispersed throughout all the crumbs. Pat the crumbs down firmly with your hand or a wooden spoon and shape the crust to the pie pan. Cover and refrigerate for 2 hours. Fill with cheesecake, cream fillings, or precooked fruit and chill until ready to serve.

UNSWEETENED VARIATION: Replace the honey with the same measure of frozen apple juice concentrate.

16 honey graham crackers, crushed
1 cube butter
2 T. honey

BUTTER BARLEY CRUST ✺

The lightest and best all around crust, it resembles the crusts made with white flour.

Preheat oven to 350° F. Mix the flour, butter, and salt together using a pastry knife or food processor (cutting blade). Add the ice water one tablespoon at a time unitl crust forms a ball. Roll out into a crust, fill, and bake.

2 c. barley
1 cube butter
½ t. salt
3–5 T. ice water

BASIC WHOLE WHEAT CRUST ✌

A flaky, flavorful crust. It may take some practice to perfect a whole wheat crust, since it is quite different to work with than white flour. Stick with it!

Preheat oven to 425° F. Mix the flour and salt together into a bowl. Cut in the butter with a pastry knife. Add the water one tablespoon at a time, adding only enough to moisten the dough so it can be formed into a ball.

Roll the ball out between two pieces of wax paper until it forms a circle about 3 inches larger around than the pie pan. Lay crust into the pan and fold under and flute edges. Prick the bottom several times with a fork. Bake at 425° F, or follow the instructions with the pie filling you are using.

1½ c. whole wheat pastry flour
¼ t. salt
1 cube butter, softened
3–5 T. ice water

GRAHAM–SESAME CRUST ✌

Graham crackers can be crushed with a rolling pin, food mill, or blender. This crust is made with little fuss and has a nice nutty flavor.

Melt the butter and honey in a small saucepan. In the pie pan, mix the graham cracker crumbs, sesame seeds, and wheat germ. Pour the butter-honey mixture into the pie pan and blend the liquid into the crumbs until it is thoroughly absorbed and well distributed. Pat the filling evenly into the pie pan and chill. Fill with cheesecake or pudding fillings.

UNSWEETENED VARIATION: Replace the honey with an equal measure of frozen apple juice concentrate.

1 cube butter
2 T. honey
8 whole wheat honey graham
    crackers, crushed
½ c. sesame seeds, toasted
¼ c. wheat germ

WHEAT GERM PIECRUST ✒

Nutritious, naturally sweet, and a bit chewy.

Preheat oven to 375° F. Put the flour in a bowl and add the rest of the ingredients one at a time, mixing well with a fork. When all ingredients are well blended, and the mixture has uniform crumb texture, press the mixture into a ball. Now lay the dough between two pieces of wax paper and roll to a 1/16-inch thickness. Lay the crust in a lightly oiled pie pan and trim off any excess dough from around the edges. To prevent buckling during baking, pierce the crust with a fork several times. Bake for about 12 minutes or until golden. Cool and fill with a fruit, pudding, or cheesecake filling.

1¼ c. whole wheat pastry flour
¼ c. wheat germ
⅓ c. oil
3–5 T. ice water

SWEET CASHEW CRUST ✒

If you're tired of the usual crust, try this one. The nuts give the crust a crunchy texture that is a nice contrast to creamy fillings.

Preheat oven to 375° F. Mix the cashews, flours, and cinnamon in a bowl. Melt butter in a small saucepan and add the honey. Stir this mixture into the dry ingredients, using a pastry knife to blend them well. Keep mixing and add the ice water a little at a time. When the texture is uniform, press the dough into a ball.

Roll out the dough between two pieces of wax paper, and transfer it to a 9-inch pie pan. Adjust the edges and flute. Prebake or follow baking instructions for the filling you wish to use.

½ c. finely chopped cashews
1 c. whole wheat pastry flour
½ c. barley flour
¾ t. cinnamon
6 T. butter, melted
2 T. honey, optional
3–5 T. ice water

~ *Index* ~

325